"The new attitude given to baptism and the Lord's Supper among evangelicals is a positive sign of the deepening of evangelical faith and worship. *Christ, Baptism and the Lord's Supper* is an important contribution to the current trend toward sacramental thinking because it is rooted in tradition and applied to the health of the present church. More than a study, it is a guide for thoughtful action."

ROBERT WEBBER, *Myers Professor of Ministry, Northern Seminary*

"Pastor Vander Zee invites evangelicals into a sacramental experience of the Savior they love. This engaging book unfolds biblical and theological teaching in ways that are both challenging and compelling."

M. CRAIG BARNES, *Meneilly Professor of Leadership and Ministry, Pittsburgh Theological Seminary*

"This insightful analysis from a pastor who practices what he preaches promises to deepen our view not only of baptism and the Lord's Supper but also of our Lord. Just as the eyes of Elisha's servant were opened to see the chariots of fire that encircled Elisha (2 Kings 6), so too the themes of this book can help us perceive the vibrant, nourishing ways that God works through worship. In an age tempted to treat worship merely as a means to other ends, this vision is one that will comfort, challenge and transform us."

JOHN D. WITVLIET, *Calvin Institute of Christian Worship, Calvin College and Calvin Theological Seminary*

CHRIST, BAPTISM
AND THE
LORD'S SUPPER

RECOVERING THE SACRAMENTS
FOR EVANGELICAL WORSHIP

LEONARD J. VANDER ZEE

InterVarsity Press
Downers Grove, Illinois

InterVarsity Press
P.O. Box 1400, Downers Grove, IL 60515-1426
World Wide Web: www.ivpress.com
E-mail: mail@ivpress.com

InterVarsity Press® is the book-publishing division of InterVarsity Christian Fellowship/USA®, a student movement active on campus at hundreds of universities, colleges and schools of nursing in the United States of America, and a member movement of the International Fellowship of Evangelical Students. For information about local and regional activities, write Public Relations Dept., InterVarsity Christian Fellowship/USA, 6400 Schroeder Rd., P.O. Box 7895, Madison, WI 53707-7895, or visit the IVCF website at <www.intervarsity.org>.

Scripture quotations, unless otherwise noted, are from the New Revised Standard Version of the Bible, *copyright 1989 by the Division of Christian Education of the National Council of the Churches of Christ in the USA. Used by permission. All rights reserved.*

Pages 136-39 adapted with permission from Leonard J. Vander Zee, "Hot Dogs and Holy Communion," Perspectives *(1996): 24.*

Design: Cindy Kiple

Images: Scala/Art Resource, NY

ISBN 0-8308-2786-2

Printed in the United States of America ∞

Library of Congress Cataloging-in-Publication Data

Vander Zee, Leonard J., 1945-
   Christ, baptism, and the Lord's Supper: recovering the sacraments
      p. cm.
   Includes bibliographical references and index.
   ISBN 0-8308-2786-2 (pbk.: alk. paper)
   1. Baptism. 2. Lord's Supper. 3. Sacraments. 4. Evangelicalism.
   I. Title.
   BV800.V36 2004
   265—dc22
                                                                    2004006653

P	20	19	18	17	16	15	14	13	12	11	10	9	8	7	6	5	4	3	2	1
Y	20	19	18	17	16	15	14	13	12	11	10	09	08	07	06	05	04			

To Jeanne Logan and in memory of Judith Vander Zee

CONTENTS

PREFACE

Since I grew up in the church, the sacraments were always a part of
my world, though decidedly in the background. In my younger years
my interest in them tended to focus on their immediate gratification in
sight, smell and sound rather than on their meaning. This all changed
when at Calvin Theological Seminary I was a member of a club called
Nisi Domino Frustra (which I translate "without the Lord, futility,"
seemingly a good motto for seminary education) under the wise and
kindly tutelage of the now-deceased Dr. Henry Stob. The club's purpose was a systematic study of Calvin's *Institutes of the Christian Religion*. The pattern was that for each meeting the group was assigned a
section of the *Institutes*, while one student was assigned to study it
more deeply and present an outline of it for the group. I was assigned,
much to my disappointment at the time, the chapters on the sacraments. But it was in those weeks of poring over Calvin on the sacraments that a deep and lasting appreciation of their theology and spiritual significance grew and continues to flourish in me. In Calvin's
theology of the sacraments I saw at the heart of his theology what Brian
Gerrish called "grace and gratitude."

Over the years in my reading and study as well as my preaching, my
interest in sacramental theology continued to deepen, but it wasn't until I enjoyed a sabbatical through a gracious grant from the Louisville
Foundation in 1998 that I was able to devote some significant time and
effort to sort out my thoughts on the subject. Naively, I decided to write

a book on the subject, having no real conception of the enormous undertaking it was going to be. As my three-month sabbatical came to an end with a ridiculously incomplete manuscript, I was left with snatching an evening here and there, or a week of study leave graciously offered by the congregation I have served through this entire project. And I cannot forget those refreshing two-day retreats I regularly took at the St. Gregory's Abbey, an Episcopal Benedictine monastery near Three Rivers, Michigan, where reflection on the sacraments blended in with the daily offices and Eucharist.

Why another book on the sacraments? Surveying the field, I find that while there are shelves of books devoted to the sacraments, they fall into several categories. There are the light and the heavy—those meant for spiritual growth and those seeking theological rigor. Some emphasize biblical thought, while others delve into historical and theological development. Most books on the sacraments are written by those who are deeply embedded in the traditionally sacramental churches—Roman Catholic, Anglican, Lutheran and a few Reformed. But there is a general absence of books from a more general evangelical Protestant perspective. Evangelicals apparently are not very interested in the sacraments, which seems to correspond to their lack of interest in ecclesiology in general. Sacraments do not count for very much in evangelical circles, as we shall discover, because evangelical theology offers them very little room. The emphasis is on personal faith in Christ through the proclamation of the gospel. The sacraments merely affirm, or for others, only give further personal testimony, to that faith.

I have come to believe that the reason evangelicals fail to appreciate the sacraments and to understand their biblical importance is that evangelicalism suffers from an inherent dualism—or worse, what Philip Lee calls Protestant gnosticism.[1] Evangelical theology tends toward a cleavage between the material and the spiritual, the earthly and the heavenly, which I find to be too insensitive to the world as God's creation and to the incarnation of Jesus Christ into our actual fallen humanity. In this essentially dualistic worldview the sacraments, which by their very nature function through material elements, cannot bear the weight of spiritual reality. Therefore, they are either suspect be-

---

[1]Philip Lee, *Against the Protestant Gnostics* (New York: Oxford University Press, 1987).

cause it seems heretical to think that water and bread and wine do actually unite us to Christ, or they are merely show-and-tell lessons, not worthy of any more study than a Sunday school flannelgraph.

My title, *Christ, Baptism and the Lord's Supper,* is meant to set out the thesis that the sacraments derive their meaning from Christ and that it is Christ who through them, by the Holy Spirit, unites us to himself. I hope to present an understanding of the sacraments here that is thoroughly biblical, Reformed and evangelical. That is, I strive for a theology of the sacraments that is grounded in the Bible, informed by the Reformation principles of *sola gratia, sola fidei, sola scriptura,* and harmonizes with the evangelical spirit of personal faith in Christ that has been so profoundly influential in the last century. Though I come at this study from a Reformed perspective by training and conviction, I also hope to be ecumenically sensitive since, unfortunately, the sacraments that should unite us still separate us.

The plan of the book is to begin with the concept of the world as a sacramental place by virtue of its creation by God and its ultimate re-creation through the incarnation of Jesus Christ. This will be followed by four chapters that set forth a general theology of the sacraments. Then I examine each of the "gospel sacraments" in turn, dealing first with their biblical background and then providing a contemporary analysis of their theology and practice.

I express my sincere gratitude to Rodney Clapp (now with Brazos Books), who first encouraged me to write this book; to the Louisville Foundation (with funding from the Lilly Foundation), which supplied the grant for the original sabbatical study time; and to Bruce Winter and the staff for their hospitality at Tyndale House in Cambridge, England, where we spent the three months. Thanks is due also to the patient editing staff at InterVarsity Press as they guided me through this process so new to me.

I am also grateful to my beloved and always-encouraging congregation, the South Bend Christian Reformed Church, for their enthusiastic support of my study. They endured years of my preoccupation with this work, not to mention the many sermons in which I tried out my still embryonic ideas (in a congregation with more than its share of philosophers and theologians, no less). I also thank a supportive and perceptive but anonymous reader of an earlier draft who also put me in touch again with the fine theology of T. F. Torrance.

The most faithful and perceptive reader of this work-in-progress was my wife, Jeanne M. Logan. Beginning on sabbatical in wonderful Cambridge, England, she patiently worked her way through ponderous drafts and informed me when it just didn't make sense to her highly literate but theologically untrained mind. She helped me shave away some of the jargon and lighten ponderous sentences. Whatever of either jargon or pretense remains is my own fault. But I'm grateful most of all that, for some reason, she loves me in ways that can make the impossible seem possible.

1

THE RESTORATION OF A SACRAMENTAL UNIVERSE IN THE SACRAMENT OF CHRIST

> For the little birds that sing, sing of God;
>
> the beasts call out for him;
>
> the elements fear him; the mountains echo him;
>
> the streams and fountains flash glances at him;
>
> and the grass and flowers laugh before him.
>
> JOHN CALVIN

One of my most vivid boyhood memories of church is of those quarterly Communion Sundays. In the then ethnically Dutch Christian Reformed Church, there were certain peculiarities to the celebration of this sacrament. For reasons I can only speculate upon, the noncommunicants, children and others who had not made Public Profession of Faith (which generally did not happen till sixteen or seventeen years old) sat separately from the communicants. This may have made it easier for the elders to police the table, for they did not want anyone to "eat and drink judgment unto themselves," as Paul warned and the liturgical form repeatedly emphasized. Nevertheless, as my brother and I sat in the balcony looking out over the unfolding drama, we always paid close attention, something that we did not often afford to the sermon that preceded it.

The whole service proceeded with a special decorum. The table, piled high with gleaming silver service, was always covered with a white linen cloth. When the Communion service was about to begin, a phalanx of a dozen or so elders would march solemnly to the front and take their place in the front row before the table. Two would then slowly remove the white covering, folding it with great ceremony. As soon as the cloth was removed, the most sensuous moment occurred, as the smells of bread and rich, sweet wine (Mogen David, of course) would fill the sanctuary, replacing the musty stale smell of old hymn-books or the sharp scent of ladies' Sunday perfume. A long, didactic form was read out of the back of the hymnal, but it was clear that the important moment came when the minister uttered the words of insti-tution, while breaking the bread and pouring the cup. Then the distri-bution, with the elders fanning out through the large congregation, passing the silver plates of cubed bread and containers of individual glass cups down the rows and returning, with military precision, in a double line down the center aisle. But the climax my brother and I were waiting for came just after everyone had tossed back their little cups of wine at the same moment. Then, with a giant unison clatter, the little cups were placed in their round wooden holders on the pew. After-ward ladies would politely cough, their throats presumably irritated by the sharp twang of alcohol—or at least, that's how it should appear.

I remember these things—these smells, these sounds and this strange ceremonial ballet by the elders and minister. After more than forty years, I can see it and smell it today in my mind's eye like it was yesterday.

That's not so strange, of course. Things—and the smells, sounds and sights attached to them—have the ability to speak to us in very inti-mate and powerful ways. I finger my wedding ring and remember the love and commitment it represents, and I remember last night. The smell of cigars brings to mind a picture of my grandfather, and the scent of incense, my visits to St. Gregory's monastery. I could go on and on. There is a powerful open channel of communication between what we see, taste, touch and smell, and our feelings, our imagination, our mind and our heart. This is true spiritually as well as in every other area of our lives. In our worship and practice as Christians, the place where the world of the spirit, mind and heart meets the world of the senses is in the sacraments. And yet, precisely at this point, many Protestants have deep suspicions.

There is a soliloquy in Walker Percy's *Love in the Ruins* that highlights the problem of the power of things in religious practice. Dr. Thomas More, Percy's Catholic protagonist, is having some conflict with his Protestant wife, Ellen, on matters of religious practice.

> What [Ellen] disapproves is not that I am doing public penance. No, what bothers her is an ancient Presbyterian mistrust of things, things getting mixed up with religion. The black sweater and the ashes scandalize her. . . . What have these things, articles, to do with doing right? For she mistrusts the Old Church's traffic in things, sacraments, articles, bread, wine, salt, oil, water, ashes. Watch out! You know what happened before when you Catholics mucked it up with all your things, medals, scapulars, candles, bloody statues![1]

Ellen's aversion to the things that "mucked up" her husband's Roman Catholic worship reminds me of the iconoclasm of the Reformation. The violent intensity of the smashing of images and the defacing of paintings and frescoes was brought home to me on visiting several cathedrals in England. Things in the church, especially things of great beauty, deeply offended the Protestant sensibility.

Remembering that at that time (and in some places today) images were adored, dressed, bowed to and paraded through the streets like gods, makes the Reformer's sentiments a little easier to understand. The impulse was not merely destructive, but solidly theological. It was done in obedience to their understanding of Scripture; and it was often (though not always, by any means) done, as Reformed Christians do all things, "decently and in good order." Here's one description:

> The committee as a body went into every church in Zurich. Once inside, they locked the doors behind them, and then, free from all disturbances from curious crowds without, began to dismantle the church. The work was done quietly and efficiently by the various experts who had been selected by the constable for that purpose, and as a result no unnecessary damage or useless destruction was reported. Every standing statue was

---

[1]Quoted in Lee, *Against the Protestant Gnostics*, p. 183.

removed from its niche or base, and together with the base, taken out of the church. It was then either broken up by masons, if made of stone or plaster, or burned, if made of wood. Every painting was taken down from the altar and burned outside. All murals were chipped away or scraped from the walls. The altars were stripped of all images and vessels, all votive lamps were let down and melted outside, and all crucifixes were removed. Even the carved choir stalls were taken up and burned. Then the walls were whitewashed so that no traces whatsoever of the old decoration and appointments might be seen.[2]

Along with the excesses of image "worship," the Reformers cited scriptures to back this destruction, most notably what is now widely recognized as a mistaken reading of John 4:24, "God is spirit, and those who worship him must worship in spirit and truth." Ulrich Zwingli of Zurich wrote that true belief must be of such an abiding intensity "that it cannot be diminished by any visible thing."[3] How Zwingli and many of his Puritan descendants loved that plain, purged, whitewashed church!

This uniquely Protestant impulse remains today. Vestments, incense and icons are seldom found among Protestant evangelicals. In many of the new auditorium-like church buildings with "seeker sensitive" services, the table and font are nowhere to be seen. And yet, having cleaned up their act and gotten rid of all those offensive and distracting "things," we now find that a significant number of evangelicals are migrating to Anglican/Episcopal or even Orthodox churches, the epitome of the "smells and bells" they were brought up to suspect and even ridicule.

At the heart of evangelical orthodoxy's mistrust of things and elevation of the spiritual lurks a way of viewing the world that owes more to deist rationalism and gnostic dualism than to Christianity.[4] Elaine Pagels is right when she declares that the "orthodox tradition implicitly affirms bodily experience as the central fact of human life. What one does physically—one eats and drinks, engages in sexual life or

---

[2]Charles Garside Jr., *Zwingli and the Arts* (New Haven: Yale University Press, 1966), p. 159.
[3]Ibid., p. 166.
[4]For a deeper consideration of the philosophical and theological relationship between Augustinian (not gnostic) dualism and modern Kantian rationalism, see T. F. Torrance, *Theology in Reconciliation* (Grand Rapids: Eerdmans, 1976).

avoids it, saves one's life or gives it up—all are vital elements in one's *religious* development."[5] In classic Christian orthodoxy, things matter because God created the world in Christ and is redeeming it in and through Christ. Creation matters because Christ is the one in whom and through whom all things were created and in whom "all things hold together" (Col 1:15-17). Creation matters because God in Christ entered creation in order to bring about its complete renewal. Evangelical orthodoxy has more and more discounted created things because it features a docetic Jesus whose divinity tends to overshadow his humanity and who only brushes against creation for a time to lift (or rapture) us to heavenly safety. If Christ is essentially unconnected with the created world except to come here and save some souls, then created things can never bring us in touch with divine reality. Or, more to the point of this study, sacraments can never be a means by which God unites us with Christ.

It has been commonplace in studies of the sacraments to base their meaning in the larger context of a sacramental world. Donald Baillie points out that nothing can be "in the special sense a sacrament unless everything were in a basic and general sense sacramental."[6] The only way in which particular sacraments can have meaning is if the universe is so created and structured that this can happen. Sacraments are material things that point beyond themselves to their Creator. They are windows into divine reality. "Things are more than just aggregates of matter lying around the universe," writes John Macquarrie. "They have the potentiality of lighting up for us the mystery of God himself. God is not a part of the world. . . . So we do not see him directly, but because he is universally present, there is, shall we say, a sacramental potentiality in virtually everything. This means that at some time, in some place, in some circumstances, for some person or persons, that thing may become a sacrament, that person's door to the sacred."[7]

That God reveals himself through created things, that God can speak through the things he created, is also a biblical given. To the Hebrew mind, the creation raises a cacophony of praise to the Creator.

---

[5]Quoted in Lee, *Against the Protestant Gnostics*, p. 130.
[6]Donald M. Baillie, *The Theology of the Sacraments* (London: Faber and Faber, 1957), p. 42.
[7]John Macquarrie, *A Guide to the Sacraments* (New York: Continuum, 1997), p. 8.

"Let the sea roar, and all that fills it; the world and those who live in it. Let the floods clap their hands; let the hills sing together for joy at the presence of the LORD, for he is coming to judge the earth. He will judge the world with righteousness, and the peoples with equity" (Ps 98:7-9). Only after this parade of creation's praise are human beings called upon to raise the shout of praise.

Created things, by their very being and nature, give praise to God. They do naturally and continually what we humans must decide to do. In fact, according to Paul, creation's pristine praise, and the revelation of God through it, condemns unbelieving and ungrateful people: "For what can be known about God is plain to them, because God has shown it to them. Ever since the creation of the world his eternal power and divine nature, invisible though they are, have been understood and seen through the things he has made. So they are without excuse" (Rom 1:19-20).

And there's the rub. As God's creation, the world may offer a sacramental window into transcendent reality, but sinful humans cannot or will not open their eyes. A sacramental world lies open before us, blazing with God's beauty, truth and power; but we walk through it blindly.

Alexander Schmemann, one of Orthodoxy's leading modern theologians, called the world a "sacrament of God" and therefore saw worship as belonging to the deepest aspect of human existence. "The term 'sacramental' means that for the world to be means of worship and means of grace is not accidental, but the revelation of its meaning, the restoration of its essence, the fulfillment of its destiny. It is the 'natural sacramentality' of the world that finds its expression in worship."[8] At its heart, worship is the world's "Eucharist," its profound thanksgiving to God, offering the world and humanity back to God in adoration and praise. Humanity was created as a priesthood that continually offers the eucharistic worship of the creation back to its Creator.

The secular worldview moves in precisely the opposite direction. Secular people see the world "as containing within itself its meaning and the principles of knowledge and action."[9] The secular vision re-

---

[8]Quoted in Nicholas Wolterstorff, *Until Justice and Peace Embrace* (Grand Rapids: Eerdmans, 1983), p. 196 n. 2.
[9]Ibid., p. 150.

fuses to see the world and its life as proceeding from "elsewhere." Therefore, in the secular mind worship only relates to a "sacred" that is outside of, and unrelated to, the world.

Because of the lostness and blindness caused by sin, the world cannot be a sacramental place apart from a new and redeeming sacramental act. Jesus Christ is that new and final sacrament. In Christ, God enters the world he made and transforms it into a new creation. Through the offering of himself in perfect obedience and love to God, Christ is the new human who clothes himself again in the priestly role to which God called humanity in the beginning. As Christians, we share in Christ's anointing to "present myself to him as a living sacrifice of thanks."[10]

That God created the world means that all material things reflect God's glory and power. The incarnation cements this connection. Christ's eternal and glorified new humanity means that human life is now enmeshed in the life of God. God's story and the creation's story come together in Christ, making things more than mere bits of matter, and opening our eyes to their ultimate transfiguration. Creation, incarnation and the ultimate re-creation of the cosmos reveal a God for whom matter matters, and material things open our eyes to the One who is above and beyond all things.

Jesus Christ, God incarnate; God as matter, stuff, body, flesh and blood, has forever bridged the divide of creation and creature. In Christ's incarnation, God now fully participates in the life of creation, and his creatures are represented before his throne with the ascended Lord. Christ is the primary and ultimate sacrament. By virtue of Christ's taking on flesh, God is no longer a distant creator, but now, in Christ, "This is my Father's world," and "he shines in all that's fair." Christ, the sacrament of God made flesh, can again make the whole creation a sacramental place.[11]

The recent renewal of interest in Celtic Christianity gives us a glimpse of a firm orthodox faith that is deeply trinitarian, Christ-centered and joyously earthy all at once. William Haley writes, "The

---

[10]Heidelberg Catechism, Q and A 32, *Psalter Hymnal* (Grand Rapids: CRC Publications, 1987).
[11]For a fuller treatment of Christ as the ultimate sacrament, see chapter four.

Western world is afflicted by the disease of compartmentalization in which the realm of God and the realm of the everyday real are too often separated. The primeval Celts knew no such dichotomy. For them every atom was suffused with the presence of God. Each drop of rain, each blade of grass . . . each chip of stone, everything from the minute to the grand was theophany."[12] The Celts viewed the world through the eyes of faith, seeing God present in and through everything, not because the world is God, but because in Christ this is God's world.

Nineteenth-century amateur anthropologist and folklorist Alexander Carmichael spent a lifetime collecting Celtic prayers and songs that could still be heard among the people of the Outer Hebrides in Scotland. He compiled them in an extensive anthology called *Carmina Gadelica*. Carmichael was impressed with the ways these deeply religious country folk would address the "great God of life, the Father of all living. They press upon him their needs and their desires fully and familiarly, but with all the awe and deference due to the great Chief whom they wish to approach." One Celtic woman, Catherine Maclennan, told him:

> My mother would be asking us to sing our morning song to God down in the back-house, as Mary's lark was singing up in the clouds and as Christ's Mavis [a bird] was singing yonder in the tree, giving glory to the God of the creatures for the repose of the night, for the light of the day, for the joy of life. She would tell us that every creature on the earth below and in the great ocean beneath and in the air above was giving glory to the great God of creatures and the worlds, of the virtues and the blessings, and would *we* be dumb![13]

No aspect of life was too insignificant, too mundane, not to participate in this great Celtic vision of a world alive with God's presence. Even milking a cow was a hallowed activity:

> Bless, O God, my little cow,
> Bless, O God, my desire;
> Bless thou my partnership
> And the milking of my hands, O God.

---

[12]William R. L. Haley, "The World as Theophany," *Re:generation Quarterly* 3, no. 4 (1997): 25.
[13]Esther De Waal, ed., *The Celtic Vision* (Petersham, Mass.: St. Bede's Publications, 1988), p. 5.

> Bless, O God, each teat,
> Bless, O God, each finger;
> Bless thou each drop
> That goes into my pitcher, O God.[14]

Here is someone who is at home in a world in which the Creator God is involved in everything that he has made, even the fingers that squeeze the cow's teat. I read these powerful prayers with a sense of deep disappointment, for I don't live within that kind of universe. My daily activities more often feel separated from God's immanent rule and partnership with the world than involved in them. Certainly the world may seem more charged with God's glory when, on a frosty morning on the heath, surrounded by bonny highlands, hearing the lapping of the waves, one faces the side of an engorged cow. But in reality my desk, complete with Mac Powerbook and shelves of books, is no less suffused with the presence of God, and God's creative hand is no less necessary for my work, mouse in hand, than if my hand held a cow's teat.

The Celts were able to hold in a creative tension both the idea of God's transcendence as Creator of all things and God's intimate involvement with all creatures. We need this insight; we need this way of living today. A Christian understanding of the universe revels in God's incomprehensible *closeness* to creation, but avoids his *identification* with it, and this is exactly where Christianity and pantheism part company. As Ian Bradley says of Celtic Christianity, "There is no blurring of distinction between Creator and created, no worship of nature . . . but rather a wonderful sense that the whole cosmos is a theophany—a marvelous revelation of the goodness and wonder and creativity of God."[15] This Celtic way of seeing God interacting with creation in daily experience is captured beautifully in St. Patrick's Creed, so clearly born of a life and time in which nature and faith, creation and redemption, were intertwined.

> Our God, God of all men,
> God of heaven and earth, seas and rivers,
> God of sun and moon, of all the stars,

---

[14]Ibid., p. 79.
[15]Quoted in Haley, "The World as Theophany," p. 26.

God of high mountain and lowly valley,
God over heaven, and in heaven and earth and sea
And in all things that are in them.
He inspires all things, He quickens all things.
He is over all things, He supports all things.
He makes the light of the sun to shine,
He surrounds the moon and the stars,
He has made wells in the arid earth,
Placed dry islands in the sea.
He has a Son co-eternal with himself. . . .
And the Holy Spirit breathes in them.

It should be noted that despite the phrase "and in all things that are in them," Patrick cannot be accused of pantheism or even panentheism. He always clearly fences off the divine from created reality. His use of the word *in* is closer to that of Paul in Colossians 2:17 where he speaks of Christ as the one in whom "all things hold together." Nevertheless, the triune Creator's loving, sustaining and purposive involvement with the creation profoundly shapes how Celtic Christianity sees both God and the creation.

Since this world, created by the triune God and redeemed through his incarnate Son, is a sacramental place, God uses created things to reveal himself. It may be a tree, a rainbow, a fleece, a loaf of bread, a cup of wine or a font of water. John Calvin, though he too had his problems with the proper uses of created things in the worship of God, still understood this basic concept of a sacramental universe. Drawing on the examples of the tree of life and the rainbow in Genesis, Calvin wrote:

These, Adam and Noah regarded as sacraments. Not that the tree provided them with an immortality which it could not give to itself; nor that the rainbow could be effective in holding back the waters; but because they had a mark engraved on them by God's Word so that they were proofs and seals of his covenants. And indeed the tree was previously a tree, and the rainbow a rainbow. When they were inscribed by God's Word a new form was put upon them, so that they began to be what previously they were not. . . . Therefore if any philosophizer, to mock the simplicity of our faith, contends that such a variety of colors naturally arises from the rays reflected upon a cloud opposite, let us admit it, but laugh at his stupidity in failing to recognize God as the lord and governor of nature, who according to his will uses all elements to serve his glory.[16]

And here Calvin also suggests a good way to distinguish between what we will call the *sacramental* from a *sacrament*. All created things are sacramental in the sense that as God's creatures they point to, or signify, their Creator, as a great work of art points to the artist. Even more fundamentally, Jesus Christ comes to us as embodied God. In his divine and human natures, he is both the uncreated God and the creature. In Christ this union of God and creature unites heaven and earth, Creator and creation, in an utterly new and unique way. For the believer, the universe is a sacramental place where everything, from the flash of lightning and the crash of thunder (Ps 29) to the industry of the ant (Prov 6:6), from the passionate embrace of husband and wife (Eph 5:31-32) to the sun's slow arc through the sky (Ps 19), shows God's glory and love, and is further hallowed by Christ's own embodiment. As the beloved hymn sings, "He speaks to me everywhere."

A sacrament, however, is a *particular* created thing to which God attaches a word of promise, like the rainbow, which Calvin does not hesitate to call a sacrament. Calvin did make a further distinction between the sacraments of the old covenant and the gospel sacraments, of which there are only two, baptism and the Lord's Supper. They are gospel sacraments for the Christian church because they were instituted by Christ himself and bound to the promise of his own words.

Michael Horton, who is nervous about the attributing the word *sacramental* to all of creation, makes the necessary distinctions:

> A sacrament serves a much greater purpose. It not only discloses God as Creator but as Redeemer, and not only as Redeemer of people in general, but as *my* Redeemer. Furthermore, a sacrament not only reveals, it confers. Through Word and sacrament, God actually gives that which he promises in his gospel. . . . A sacrament is a means of saving grace rather than common grace. . . . It does not simply impart wonder at God involvement in creation, but proclaims and seals divine forgiveness, reconciliation, adoption, justification, and sanctification. Nothing other than the Word, baptism, and the Lord's Supper are given this place by God as a means of grace.[17]

---

[16]John Calvin *Institutes* 4.14.18.

We celebrate the gospel sacraments because the Lord told us to do it and attached his promises to them.

Evangelicals have so emphasized the preaching of the Word that the sacraments have become mere occasional props. Like Walker Percy's fictional Ellen, we are worried when all these "things" get in the way of the pure Word of God. Indeed, if God can save us by faith in his Word, what do we need sacraments for? Frank Senn argues that we need them because "the gospel is not proclaimed by stating propositions. . . . Preaching is not giving a lecture, it is an incanting, a posturing, a storytelling, a proclaiming. The forgiveness of sins is not only promised by sentences, but by sentences joined to a bath, the laying on of hands, and communal eating and drinking." The words may change, but there is no baptism without water, or no Lord's Supper without bread and wine.[18] Just as the Word of God, Jesus Christ, became incarnate in human flesh, so the words of God must also become incarnate in physical reality. Calvin liked to say that in the sacraments God stooped to our weakness. By weakness, Calvin simply meant that we are limited by our physical nature. As physical beings we need more than words to bring us into a relationship with Christ. We need things.

Theodore Beza, Calvin's colleague and one of his greatest interpreters, reflects on why, while the Word of God is sufficient to create faith in Christ, we still need sacraments:

> Since the simple word only strikes one of our senses, while the sacraments involve in addition sight and other bodily senses, and also are distributed with very significant and distinct ceremonies, it is easy to recognize how necessary to us is the help of the sacraments to maintain our faith, since, in a manner of speaking, they cause us to touch with the finger and the eye, and as it were to already taste and actually feel the outcome of that which we await, as if we had it and possessed it already. For this reason, far from despising the holy sacraments, we confess that we cannot sufficiently magnify their dignity and legitimate use.[19]

---

[17]Michael Horton, *In the Face of God* (Dallas: Word, 1996), p. 119.
[18]Frank Senn, *Christian Liturgy: Catholic and Evangelical* (Minneapolis: Fortress, 1997), p. 31.
[19]Theodore Beza, quoted in Christopher Elwood, *The Body Broken* (New York: Oxford University Press, 1999), p. 101.

The blessing of sacramental worship is the thrill and comfort of knowing that God meets us where we are, washing us, feeding us, quenching our thirst for grace. We not only believe it, we sense it, see it, taste it, feel it, smell it and swallow it. What my mind doubts, my mouth tastes as the Lord's goodness. When my faith falters, my fingers can touch the truth.

2

WHAT ARE
SACRAMENTS?

It is significant that in the doctrinal test so important to
American fundamentalists for distinguishing between
authentic Christianity and liberal heresy, the sacraments
are never mentioned. . . . For most American Protestants,
it is a neutral area, an extinct volcano representing no
threat to either side. American Protestantism has to a
great degree become de-sacramentalized.

PHILIP LEE, *AGAINST THE
PROTESTANT GNOSTICS*

Although we will begin discussing the nature of sacraments by
looking at definitions, it will soon become clear that the real issue is not
one of definition but of worldview. Whatever classic definition of the
sacraments you might choose reveals dichotomies: matter and spirit,
visible and invisible, physical and spiritual. It's not that there is no distinction between these aspects of reality but that the distinction opens
up to a great chasm in our worldview that must somehow be overcome
in order to recover our full Christian faith. It is part of my thesis that
this apparent divide in Western Christianity is not a divide at all, but
simply two sides of the same reality of God who "created all things,
visible and invisible" and who took on our real humanity in Jesus
Christ. What I hope to uncover is the essential unity in our understand-

ing and experience of God and our world—a unity that makes sacraments not a theological and philosophical puzzle, but a place where God meets us and where the spiritual and physical come together for our wholeness and our healing.

DEFINITIONS

Throughout this book we will be using various terms that may seem slippery and malleable because of the many meanings they have had throughout history and the many nuances they possess in our various theological traditions. Yet it is necessary to understand each term in its historical and theological milieu.

Sacrament. Get out a Bible concordance, look up the word *sacrament*, and you will not find it. In the Bible you find the church baptizing and breaking bread, but the biblical writers do not analyze or label these activities as sacraments.

Where did we get the term sacrament? The Latin word *sacramentum* was originally a military term describing the oath of allegiance and obedience that a soldier solemnly pledged to his commander. Tertullian (b. about 160) first prominently used this term and applied it to the pledge of faith and allegiance made by candidates for baptism to their Lord.

But the term sacrament, or *sacramentum*, was also used in the Vulgate, the first Latin translation of the Bible. The Vulgate used it in still a different way, to translate the Greek word *mysterion*, or mystery, as in 1 Corinthians 15:51: "Listen, I will tell you a *mystery!* We will not all die, but we will all be changed." However, neither the Latin term *sacramentum* nor the Greek *mysterion* are ever actually applied to the sacraments in the Bible itself. Some scholars think it is possible that the term was later applied to the sacraments because of a vague resemblance they have to some of the mysteries in the Greek religions. Others think that it was simply because they too are "mysteries" of God's grace at work in the world.

Both John Calvin and Martin Luther pointed out that though they used the word *sacrament*, it is not found in Scripture and they did not employ it in its original Latin meaning. All this etymological slipperiness makes it a less-than-precise word to use, but at this stage in time, after a couple thousand years of repetitive usage, we appear to be stuck with it. It is important to understand, however, that we will not arrive at a very precise understanding of the sacraments by delving into their etymology.

One of the earliest and most widely used definitions of the term sacrament comes from St. Augustine: "a visible form of an invisible grace." Twelfth-century theologian Hugh of St. Victor built on it. "What is a sacrament?" he asks. "A sign of a sacred thing," he answers. "Why is a sacrament called a sign of a sacred thing?" he asks. "Because by a visible reality seen externally, another invisible, interior reality is signified," he answers. But "what is the difference between a sign and a sacrament?" he asks. His reply underscores the notion of a sacrament as *effective* sign, the notion that made the technical definition of a sacrament finally possible: "While a sign can signify a thing but not confer it, a sacrament not only signifies but also efficaciously confers. A sacrament simultaneously signifies by institution, represents by similitude, and confers by sanctification."[1] Hugh's great contribution was to offer a distinction between what might be called a general sign, one thing merely pointing to another, and a sacramental sign, which also confers the reality to which the sign points. Here Hugh approaches the concept of symbol, which we shall soon explore.

Calvin quotes Augustine's definition approvingly and then adds his own. A sacrament is "an outward sign by which the Lord seals to our consciences the promises of his good will toward us in order to sustain the weakness of our faith; and we, in turn, attest our piety toward him in the presence of the Lord and of his angels and before men."[2] Following Calvin, many of the major Reformed confessions use the terms *sign* and *seal* to describe the action of the sacraments. These terms come from Romans 4:11 where Paul is talking about circumcision as both a sign and seal to Abraham's faith. Sinclair Ferguson points out that while these terms are used for circumcision in that passage, they well describe the *modus operandi* of all covenant signs, including the sacraments, which are the covenant signs of the church.[3]

The terms *sign* and *seal* also help us understand the two fundamen-

---

[1]Quoted in Michael G. Lawler, *Symbol and Sacrament: A Contemporary Sacramental Theology* (Mahwah, N.J.: Paulist, 1987), p. 33.
[2]John Calvin *Institutes* 4.14.1.
[3]Sinclair B. Ferguson, *The Holy Spirit* (Leicester, U.K.: Inter-Varsity Press, 1996), p. 196.

tal ways in which sacraments "work." As signs they point beyond themselves: the physical realities of water, bread and wine unite us to Christ's great redeeming work. They are also seals in that they convey to us the pledge, or guarantee, of God's grace to us in Jesus Christ. This is also what Hugh of St. Victor wanted to convey by insisting that sacramental signs not only point to their underlying sacred reality, but confer it.

Here, of course, we peer over the edge of the great divide that crosses the Protestant understanding of the sacraments. On the one side are those for whom the sacramental signs merely point to Christ and invite our faith in him but do not involve any action on God's part. On the other side, God uses the signs to point us to Christ and bind us to him. Viewed another way, the issue is whether in the sacraments it is human beings who are doing something by their understanding and action, or it is God who is doing something by his gift and promise. This is the great sacramental divide from which, like the continental divide, the rivers of interpretation flow in one direction or the other. We will walk this divide many times in the course of our study.

This "great divide" between those who understand the sacraments primarily as human actions and those who understand them primarily as God's actions is not widely understood. Protestants tend to locate the great sacramental divide between themselves and Roman Catholics, and Roman Catholics have encouraged this by their refusal to join in table fellowship with others by pointing to their distinctive doctrine of transubstantiation. But the real divide is between those who hold sacraments to be mere signs and nothing more, and those who hold them to be signs *and* seals, signs that bear and confirm God's grace. Another way of stating the division is that on the one side the "ordinances," as they are often called, are means of *expressing faith to God,* and on the other side, sacraments are a means of *receiving grace from God.*

Roman Catholics, along with most Reformed, Lutherans, Anglican / Episcopalians and Methodists are together on the side that teaches sacraments as being mainly God's action, though they may sometimes skirmish about the exact way in which sacraments work. Those churches that have followed the Anabaptist tradition hold that sacraments are no more than signs by which people pledge their faith to

Christ and memorialize their redemption in Christ. This view is probably now the majority view among Protestants today, certainly those who call themselves evangelicals. The present evangelical renaissance is so pervasive in America, at least, that even in my own solidly Calvinist and historically sacramentalist tradition, I find that most ordinary members, and not a few office bearers and pastors, articulate a more Anabaptist than Calvinist view of the sacraments. This may partly be due to the power and persuasiveness of the evangelical media, but as we shall see, it has some deep historical and philosophical roots as well.

Sign and symbol. Everyone who discusses the sacraments from whatever theological point of view uses the word *sign*. Sign means the outward "thing," the material element of the sacrament—water, bread and wine—as it points to the sacred reality. But sacraments are a particular kind of sign that might more accurately be called a *symbol*.

In ordinary language the two words *sign* and *symbol* are used nearly interchangeably. In fact, they have quite different meanings. A sign, according to the *Oxford English Dictionary* is a "mark or device having some special meaning or import attached to it, or serving to distinguish the thing on which it is put." A sign, like a road sign, for example, merely points out the meaning of that to which it points. A symbol is a more complex idea. According to the *Oxford English Dictionary*, it "stands for, represents, or denotes something else . . . especially a material object representing or taken to represent something immaterial." Etymologically, *symbol* comes from Greek words which mean "together" and "throw," thus, to bring together. Symbols do not merely point from one thing to another, they join two things. Paul Tillich's famous distinction still serves us well in their application to the sacraments, "While the sign bears no necessary relation to that to which it points, the symbol participates in the reality of that for which it stands."[4]

Flannery O'Connor relates an incident in one of her letters that points to the problem some people have with the conjunction of symbol and sacrament. In a conversation with novelist Mary McCarthy,

---

[4]Quoted in John E. Burkhart, "The Meaning and Mystery of the Sacraments," *Reformed Liturgy and Music* 29, no. 1 (1995): 7.

she felt "set up" when McCarthy explained that she now thought of the Eucharist as a symbol rather than her childhood understanding of transubstantiation. And if it was a symbol, McCarthy went on, it was a pretty good one at that. O'Connor responded, "If it's a symbol, to h___ with it."[5] O'Connor's truly devout Catholicism might have opened a bit if she had been ready to explore how the Eucharist was a "pretty good" symbol, after all.

The Vietnam War Memorial may serve as a good example of how symbolism works. This starkly imaginative memorial does more than merely point to a war and convey certain facts about it. The names engraved in black granite don't merely give information about those who died in the war—they bring us into the experience. That's why it is surrounded by an eerie silence, while visitors communicate in hushed whispers as they place flowers, write notes and trace names. The very design of the memorial, gouging the turf, listing the nearly countless names, brings visitors back to the experience of a war that gouged our national psyche, aroused our deepest passions and engendered a sense of great loss. While deeply symbolic, it is not a "mere" symbol; it conveys the searing reality of the whole experience of Vietnam.

Michael Lawler illustrates the distinction of sign and symbol with lovemaking: "Making love . . . is a symbol and not a simple sign, for it does not just proclaim the presence of love but also realizes and celebrates that love in representation. So present is love in the ritual of love-making that the ritual, indeed, *is* the love. And because it is the love, the ritual not only makes love present but also incites men and women to appropriate loving action and reaction."[6] It's interesting that even contemporary Roman Catholic sacramental theologians are much more willing to speak of sacraments in terms of their symbolic action. Sacramental theologians Rahner, Schillibeeckx, Lawler, Vorgrimler and Chauvet all speak of the symbolic power and action of the sacraments. In fact, the category of the symbolic becomes a fresh way in which they can discuss the real presence of Christ and the real action of the sacraments without the freight of the Aristotelian category of substance.

---

[5]John W. Healey, "Symbols Are Not Just Symbols," *America*, December 23, 2000, p. 14.
[6]Lawler, *Symbol and Sacrament*, p. 17.

At certain crucial points in his explanation of sacraments, Calvin uses the word *symbol* in much the same way. For Calvin the sacraments were more than signs. They "participate in the reality" of that for which they stand. So Calvin writes,

> From the physical things set forth in the sacrament we are led by a sort of analogy to spiritual things. Thus when the bread is given as a *symbol* of Christ's body, we must at once grasp this comparison: as bread nourishes, sustains, and keeps life in our body, so Christ's body is the only food to invigorate and enliven our soul. When we see wine set forth as a *symbol* of blood, we must reflect on the benefits which wine imparts to the body, and so realize that the same are spiritually imparted to us by Christ's blood. These benefits are to nourish, refresh, strengthen, and gladden.[7]

For Calvin, the physical and natural properties of bread and wine, their ability to strengthen and gladden for example, become part of the symbolic action of the sacrament. The symbols participate in the reality for which they stand. This symbolic connection depends on the ability of the physical sign to bear the spiritual reality, which is why we use bread and wine rather than carrots and Coke.

Brian Gerrish helps us to understand how Calvin and Zwingli could seem to be talking the same language of religious symbol but each be saying something quite different. For Calvin, God uses sacraments as a means to communicate what they symbolize. He constantly reiterates that God does not deceive us when he offers the sacramental gifts to us. For Zwingli, on the other hand, it was precisely the "symbolic" language of the sacraments that enabled him to use their biblically realistic language without meaning it realistically. Zwingli tells us that no one can speak so grandly of the sacraments as to give him any offense, provided the symbolical language was taken for what it is, and no more. For him symbols were always merely symbols. Calvin's position is exactly the opposite. *Because* God uses sacraments as symbols, they *therefore* bestow what they symbolize. "More correctly, because sacraments are divinely appointed signs, and God does not lie, therefore the Spirit uses them to confer what they symbolize."[8]

---

[7]Calvin *Institutes* 4.17.3 (italics mine).
[8]Brian Gerrish, "The Lord's Supper in the Reformed Confessions," in *Major Themes in the Reformed Tradition*, ed. Donald K. McKim (Grand Rapids: Eerdmans, 1992), pp. 248-49.

While we speak of the Christian sacraments in connection with the world of sign and symbol, they are also unique in that they function to communicate the very presence and power of Christ through the Holy Spirit. This is what makes them sacraments, and this separates them from all other symbolic relationships. Christ chooses to touch us with these symbols in a unique way.

Rite and ritual. The terms *rite* and *ritual* are also used in relationship to the sacraments, both positively and negatively, both as descriptive and as pejorative terms, depending on what end of the theological spectrum you come from. Yet these terms can be very helpful in describing precisely what we are doing in sacramental worship. According to the *Oxford English Dictionary*, a *rite* is a "formal procedure or act in a religious or other solemn observance." We may speak, therefore, of the rite of baptism when we are talking about what actually happens in a church when baptism is performed. A *ritual*, on the other hand, is described as something pertaining to a rite, "a prescribed order of performing religious or other devotional service." In other words, the ritual is the specific actions and words of a rite.

It is important to realize that in speaking of a rite or a ritual we are not just talking about those churches that have prescribed liturgies in a book. There are some Christian communities that would claim to have no rites or rituals and would despise what they call ritualism. I have a friend who is very well acquainted with the Vineyard Churches and their founders. While their sacramental life is quite thin, every Sunday the congregation brings food for a huge and joyful dinner after the service. My friend sees this as a ritual that is integral to their life and worship, although they are horrified by the term and would deny that any kind of ritual is happening. When any Christian community from any theological tradition baptizes someone, for example, it is a rite and a certain ritual is followed, whether or not it is prescribed in a book.

The reality that symbols convey comes to be understood and experienced within a *symbolic action*. That symbolic action is known technically as a ritual. In rituals, symbolic meanings are enacted. When we baptize a person, the ritual of immersion or pouring water in the name of the Holy Trinity conveys the symbolic meaning to the individual being baptized and the community. In the ritual of baptism, the water and the words and actions that surround it symbolize the (real) joining of the baptized person to Christ in his death and resurrection, and the cleansing of his or her sin and new identity in Christ.

The importance of rites and the rituals by which we perform them has long been clear to anthropologists, and theologians are beginning to catch on. Our lives are filled with rituals, from birthdays to Christmas celebrations. We rely on these ritual actions to bring order, continuity, and meaning to our existence. As Tom Howard puts it, "We mortal creatures come at reality ceremonially."[9] We are not speaking here only of some "High Mass," but of occasions as ordinary as Sunday dinner or as special as a wedding. A wedding is a good example. Why do we go through all the trouble of the bridal gown, the flowers, the ceremonial march down the aisle? It's not just so much encrusted tradition. The ceremony helps us to see more clearly what is really happening. It's the ideal couple, the man and the woman, who are joined together in a sacred bond before God and human society. "Things come at us in a blur and a tumble generally, but in [a ceremonial act] things are more focused and set in harmonious order."[10] The sacraments always come to us packaged in ritual and rite. We don't just dunk or sprinkle, we don't just eat and drink; we perform these sacraments with certain words and gestures. We enact our redemption ritually, just as a man and a woman enact the fundamental commitments and claims of love in their wedding ceremony. All churches and traditions do this. Someone has suggested that "praise and worship" songs are the sacraments of evangelicalism, just as the altar call was in an earlier era.

In an era in which liturgy and ritual has become increasingly sidelined, evangelicals especially need to recognize the importance of ritual action and symbols in Christian worship. As one anthropologist specializing the importance of ritual graphically puts it, "If you would spay or geld religion, first remove its rituals, its generative and regenerative processes. For religion is not cognitive system, a set of dogmas alone, it is meaningful experience and experienced meaning."[11]

---

[9]Thomas Howard, "Imagination, Rites, and Mystery: Why Did Christ Institute Sacraments?" *Reformed Journal* 29 (March 1979): 19.
[10]Ibid.
[11]Victor Turner quoted in Burkhardt, "Meaning and Mystery," p. 3.

3

SACRAMENTS IN THE BIBLE

The first basic definition of man is that he is *the priest*. He stands in the center of the world and unifies it in his act of blessing God, of both receiving the world from God and offering it to God. . . . The world was created as the "matter," the material of the one all-embracing eucharist, and man was created as the priest of this cosmic sacrament.

ALEXANDER SCHMEMANN,
FOR THE LIFE OF THE WORLD

While the specific sacraments of baptism and the Lord's Supper do not appear until the New Testament, in many ways it is the fundamental worldview of the Old Testament that makes our understanding of gospel sacraments possible.

SACRAMENTS IN THE OLD TESTAMENT

The Old Testament worldview is founded on the assertion that this world is God's creation. The Old Testament begins in Genesis 1 with a great hymn of praise to the Creator. As each succeeding stanza of the hymn unfolds the wonders of the universe, the refrain crescendos with a cry of joy: "It was good . . . it was good . . . it was very good!" The goodness of creation and God's intimate involvement with it is the foundation of the Old Testament worldview.

God did not create the universe to exist in isolation from himself, but wanted to profoundly interact with the material world he had made, and especially with those human creatures who were made in his own image. The first chapters of the Bible picture God's fellowship with human creatures as close and personal, walking with them in the garden in the cool of the day.

Interestingly, God also used physical objects to communicate with the first humans. The tree of life and the tree of the knowledge of good and evil served as physical signs of spiritual boundaries. After the Fall, as human sin separated God from his creatures more and more, the use of physical objects to convey spiritual truth increased. With Noah, God employed the rainbow as a sign of his faithfulness. God called Noah to gaze at this covenant sign and be assured that God would never again destroy the world with a flood. The sign of circumcision functioned in the same way for Abraham. This surgical excision on the male organ, while it was also found in surrounding cultures, became the preeminent sign of the exclusive covenant relationship of the descendants of Abraham. To express his covenant relationship with his people, God is always saying, "Watch this, touch that, feel this, taste that." Created things are God's most common means of expression. As was said earlier, because the world was created by God, it is a sacramental place. God can use anything to communicate his Word and promise or to reveal himself, as in Moses' burning bush.

After the exodus, in the wilderness, where God binds his people into a covenant relationship, these physical, concrete, material signs of God's relationship to his people proliferate. The deepest spiritual issue of the wilderness years, and in fact, of the whole story of God's relationship with Israel, is how can a holy God dwell with an unholy, sinful people? That is God's desire, a desire that echoes through the Scripture, right up to the last chapters of Revelation: "He will dwell with them as their God; they will be his peoples" (Rev 21:3).

This desire of God to dwell with his people is almost always expressed in physical, sacramental ways. The tabernacle, the description of which occupies a central place in the book of Exodus, can be seen as a sacrament of God's relationship with his people. The placement of the tabernacle, the symbolic dwelling place of God in the middle of the encampment, provided a sacramental picture of "the means by which all of life was to be related to God."[1] One of the more ravishing aspects of the tabernacle and the worship which took place in it is its glorious colors, textures and images. The worship of God takes place within the context of the whole creation, and the whole creation, represented in fabric, wood and metal, joins in the worship of the Creator.

In the middle of the tabernacle stood the holy of holies, the place where God symbolically dwelt on the mercy seat between the cherubim. Into this awesome place, the high priest alone could enter, and that only once a year. Surrounding the holy of holies is the holy place, where most of the rituals were performed by priests and Levites. The common people met God at the gates of the holy place. The tabernacle also stood at the very center of the Israelite camp. The Israelites were made holy by their closeness to the holy dwelling place of God in the tabernacle. Outside of the encampment, removed from the holy presence of God, the howling wilderness spread. "What emerges is a picture of an ordered, holy camp with Yahweh at its center, the guardians of his sanctuary in closest proximity (cf. Num. 1:53), the remainder of His people at a greater distance, and all that would defile banished 'outside the camp' (Num. 5:1-4)."[2] God's holiness dwelling among a sinful people was mapped, described and pictured in the physical objects of the tabernacle, and the placement of people around it. The people could *see* the relationship they had with God, they lived it as they walked the lanes of the encampment.

In addition to this relational map, God gave Israel other ritual means of living in his presence, most importantly, the elaborate system of sacrifices that were performed in the tabernacle. While the book of Leviticus describes many different kinds of offerings, it is not always easy to recover their original meaning. One sacrificial ritual stands out from the rest, however, and can serve as an example for us of the sacramental character of Old Testament worship: *Yom Kippur,* the Day of Atonement. Because of its clarity of meaning and purpose, this sacrifice also

---

[1]David Petersen, *Engaging with God* (Grand Rapids: Eerdmans, 1992), p. 32.
[2]S. Westerholm, "Tabernacle," in *International Standard Bible Encyclopedia,* ed. Geoffrey W. Bromiley et al. (Grand Rapids: Eerdmans, 1988), 4:702.

becomes the standard by which the New Testament (especially the book of Hebrews) establishes the meaning of Christ's sacrifice on the cross as the blood that was shed for the remission of our sins.

One of the most important features of *Yom Kippur* for our purposes is the extent to which the material elements—sight, sound and smell—stood at the heart of this key event. The drama of the day unfolded as the high priest, vested in a beautiful robe, with "holy to the Lord" etched in the gold band on his forehead, entered the holy of holies with the censer of incense and the bowl of fresh warm blood from the animal sacrifice while all the people waited outside the tent. As the smoke of the incense, representing the prayers of the people, covered the mercy seat, the high priest splashed the blood on the mercy seat with his finger seven times, and thus made atonement for their sins (Lev 16:16).

Following this there occurred the ritual of the "scapegoat." The high priest laid his hand on the goat's head, confessing over it all the sins of the people of Israel, "putting them on the head of the goat, and sending it away into the wilderness. . . . The goat shall bear all their iniquities to a barren region" (Lev 16:21-22). *Yom Kippur* was a spectacle of the senses, and it comes closest to what we would call an old covenant sacrament.

Commenting on the rites and sacrifices of the Old Testament, it is interesting that Calvin does not hesitate to call them sacraments. "These [rites and sacrifices] were the sacraments of the Jews until the coming of Christ. When at his coming these were abrogated, two sacraments were instituted which the Christian Church now uses."[3] He calls them sacraments because they were instituted by God, they were accompanied by God's word of promise and they pointed to Christ, who is the substance of the sacraments. "There is only one difference: the former foreshadowed Christ promised while he was as yet awaited; the latter attest him as already given and revealed."[4]

This vital sacramental link of Old and New Testaments, of *Yom Kippur* and the cross of Christ, shows us how God has always revealed his saving purposes and confirmed his promises through sacramental

---

[3]John Calvin *Institutes* 4.14.20.
[4]Ibid.

means. "Within this covenant framework," says David Petersen, "the sacrificial system was the means by which God made it possible for a sinful people to draw near to him, to receive his grace and blessing, without desecrating his holiness. . . . By God's provision *through the cult* the covenant relationship could be maintained."[5] They were not mere signs, empty rituals. By God's word and promise, the sacrificial rituals performed what they signified. As one biblical historian puts it, "What saves both Christian [sacraments] and the ceremonial and ritual aspects of Judaism from any tinge or taint of the magical is the strong conviction of the divine authorization of these rites. God is being obeyed by man's fulfillment of his terms, and in obedience to the divine injunction His will is being carried out."[6] Of course, these old covenant "sacraments" were also tied to Christ, for, as the book of Hebrews point out, Christ is the one to whom they point and in whom they are fulfilled.

The prophets of the Old Testament also warn that the old covenant "sacraments" did not automatically guarantee the people's relationship with God. Jeremiah mocked the Israelites invocation, "The temple . . . the temple . . . the temple" (Jer 7:4) as a way of using the temple as a guarantee of God's presence and protection without real faith and obedience. Similarly, the prophets pointed out that the sacrifices were not mere ceremonial actions that guaranteed God's faithfulness, but acts that called forth faith and repentance on the part of the people. By these warnings, they did not dismiss sacramental rituals, but condemned Israel's abuse of them as if they were a means of guaranteeing God's covenant faithfulness while continuing in their own unfaithfulness. Interestingly, God called the prophets themselves to act out their words in sacramental ways, from Ezekiel's burial of his filthy underwear to Hosea marrying a prostitute.

We learn from the Old Testament to expect that God will present and affirm his word and promises by means of physical objects.

SACRAMENTS IN THE NEW TESTAMENT

What connects the sacraments of the New Testament and the Old

---

[5]Petersen, *Engaging with God,* p. 49 (italics mine).
[6]Frank Gavin, *The Jewish Antecedents of the Christian Sacraments* (London: Society for Promoting Christian Knowledge, 1928), p. 21.

should go without saying, except that it's not said enough: The New Testament is mainly a Jewish document. It was written almost exclusively by Jews and was thoroughly anchored in the Jewish worldview. Understanding its essential Jewishness is always the first step to the proper interpretation of the New Testament. As F. Gavin puts it, "A sound Christian definition of sacrament proceeds from the characteristically Jewish premise that the material world is not evil, but good—since God made it and saw that it was good."[7]

It was into this world that Jesus and the apostles were born. As Arlo Duba points out,

> Jesus was nurtured in a Jewish spirituality in which concrete things prompted praise, jogged the memory, reminded one to say "thank you." . . . It is this community in which times such as *Pascha* [Passover] and Pentecost, actions such as lifting up and laying on of hands, sounds such as that of a rushing wind, in short, anything perceived by the five senses, were reminders of the presence and glory of God. In this context it is easy to detect the operation of sacrament in its old and good definition as an outward and visible (or sensible) sign of an inward and invisible grace.[8]

Not that New Testament writers would use that Augustinian definition. For one thing, any split between outward and inward, the visible and invisible, was not part of their Hebrew sense of reality, but was more a product of Christianity's later encounter with the dualism of Greek philosophy. For another, the New Testament writers never bother to define what sacraments are or precisely describe how they work; they did not even have a term that covered both baptism and the Lord's Supper.

From the New Testament record we simply see a baptizing and bread-breaking community. They celebrated the sacraments, but while they could be aware of their profound theological significance, they did not develop a systematic or dogmatic perspective about them. Jesus said "Do this in remembrance of me," and they did it. Jesus said, "Go into all the world . . . baptizing," and they did.

When the New Testament writers do speak of baptism and the

---

[7]Ibid., p. 23.
[8]Arlo D. Duba, "Worship, Daily Life, and the Sacraments," *Reformed Liturgy and Music* 31, no. 1 (1997): 47.

Lord's Supper, they speak of them in surprisingly powerful and active ways. Baptism often functions as a virtual substitute term for regeneration or salvation. In Romans 6, for example, Paul confronts the real question that since Christians are freely forgiven by grace in Jesus Christ, might they therefore sin with abandon? Paul replies, "Don't you know we were baptized into Christ's death and resurrection?" To many evangelicals today that may seem an odd way to answer the question. They might rather respond, "If you're born again, you don't live like that." We tend not to give to give baptism such an identity-defining role in our lives. In Galatians 3:27-28 Paul makes the remarkable claim that in our baptism we are now "clothed with Christ" and are therefore part of a new community in which there is no "Jew or Greek . . . slave or free . . . male or female, for all of you are one in Christ Jesus." If we take Paul at his word, baptism is a radical act by which God incorporates us into Christ and into a new community. Through baptism God redefines us, telling us who we are, and *making* us who we are.

Paul speaks of the Lord's Supper in similarly concrete terms. It is a "sharing in the body of Christ" and a "sharing in the blood of Christ": "Because there is one bread, we who are many are one body, for we all partake of the one bread" (1 Cor 10: 16-17). In other words, in Paul's understanding, the Holy Spirit *creates* deep relationships in the body of Christ by our participation in the Lord's Supper.[9] Paul then goes on in chapter 11 to upbraid the Corinthians for their desecration of the Lord's Supper by their cavalier attitudes toward the poor and their failure to understand its communal depth of meaning. In graphically unsettling terms he describes the consequences of their unholy Communion. "Whoever, therefore, eats the bread or drinks the cup of the Lord in an unworthy manner will be answerable for the body and blood of the Lord. Examine yourselves, and only then eat of the bread and drink of the cup. For all who eat and drink without discerning the body, eat and drink judgment against themselves." That's where we tend to stop, but Paul goes on, "For this reason many of you are weak and ill, and some have died" (1 Cor 11:27-30). In the sacrament something was really happening. Sinclair Ferguson compares the operation of the

---

[9]We will discuss this passage more fully in chapter nine.

Word and the sacraments: "The word never returns in failure, but fulfills its function, either in transforming or hardening (Is. 55:11, Mark 4:10-12). Similarly, the sacraments of the gospel will, in keeping with our response to the ministry of the Holy Spirit [in them], . . . either transform in grace or harden under judgment."[10]

The New Testament does not offer a well-defined concept of sacraments as such, nor are its writers interested in the rites themselves or how they work. The two gospel sacraments simply occur as rites that the church performs at Christ's command and by the power of the Holy Spirit to incorporate converts into Christ and his church by baptism, and re-member their fellowship with Christ and with each other in the supper. Finally, in both sacraments, as they are understood in the New Testament, Christ is their content and their meaning—or to put it in terms of our next subject, Christ is the quintessential sacrament.

---

[10]Sinclair B. Ferguson, *The Holy Spirit* (Leicester, U.K.: Inter-Varsity Press, 1996), p. 199.

4

CHRIST IS THE
QUINTESSENTIAL SACRAMENT

He is the image of the invisible God,

the firstborn of all creation.

COLOSSIANS 1:15

God uses physical things to communicate salvation to humanity. But this is the case only as we recognize Christ himself as the quintessential sacrament. In the human Jesus, who completely shares our creaturely existence, God comes to us and unites himself to us. Jesus' death and resurrection seal all God's promises to us. Everything that we experience and know through the sacraments, we experience and know in Christ. Calvin put it this way: "I say that Christ is the matter or (if you prefer) the substance of all the sacraments; for in him they have all their firmness, and they do not promise anything apart from him."[1] Calvin means that the sacraments are one of the ways God brings us into union with Christ. He is their source, substance and goal. They are the sacraments of Christ.

In what sense is Christ *the* sacrament, the quintessential sacrament? Since Christ is the word made flesh, true God and true man, as he is confessed by the whole church, Christ is the meeting place of God and humanity, spirit and matter, invisible and visible. Paul calls Christ the visible "icon" of the invisible God (Col 1: 15), and analogously, the sac-

---

[1]John Calvin *Institutes* 4.14.16.

raments are visible and material signs to us of the now invisible Christ.

In order to fully appreciate this concept of Christ as the quintessential sacrament, an important biblical and theological principle stands behind it that needs to be highlighted here, and which will be a guiding principle through our entire discussion. Stated very simply it is this: *Everything that happens to Christ happens for us.* Jesus Christ in his incarnation is the new humanity, the new Adam. In him human life and history begins all over again. In him our human destiny is forever changed. In the union of God and humanity in his very being, our human nature undergoes a fundamental transformation.

In Christ, God is creating a new humanity, a new creation. Christ is the second Adam, made of the same stuff as the first. In his incarnation the Son of God unites created humanity with his own divine being. And in that union of divine and human, Christ sets out to transform humanity into a glorious new being, a transfigured humanity. The downward trajectory of divine self-emptying love, and the upward trajectory of human need for God's grace and salvation intersect in Jesus Christ, born at Bethlehem. In him a whole new creation is formed, a new humanity is inaugurated in which we are now sons and daughters of God, partakers of the divine nature, and citizens of heaven. Christ is the prototype of this new humanity in which all his people share by faith and the sacraments.

This begins as soon as Jesus takes on human life. He is circumcised on the eighth day. He is eager to be in his "Father's house" (Lk 2:49). Jesus' baptism unites him with the sinners who follow John into the muddy waters of the Jordan even while John proclaims that Jesus will baptize with the Holy Spirit and with fire (Lk 3:16). He battles the devil in the wilderness like Israel did, and God's angels sustain him (Mk 1:13). Most significantly, at the pinnacle of his earthly ministry, Jesus shines in all his glory as the new human on the mountain of transfiguration, a glory that one day all his brothers and sisters will share in union with him. All through his life, Jesus' faith, his obedience to his Father and his loving service all portray a picture of what this new humanity looks like.

Yet as Jesus himself was constantly aware, it is especially through his death and resurrection that God creates a new humanity by lifting the awful weight of human sin and guilt from our shoulders, vindicating his own righteousness, and disarming the devil and all his hosts. And finally, God inaugurated a glorious new existence for humanity in the resurrection and ascension of Jesus, who as the first fruits assures and even pictures for us the glory which is our destiny in him.

Alasdair Heron, following the pattern of the Eastern Fathers, says that Christ is the "sacrament of union between God and man, of the coming of God to man, and the raising of man to God."[2] In our baptism God unites us with Christ, human and divine, dead and risen, ascended and sitting at God's right hand. In the Lord's Supper, Christ feeds us with his glorious new humanity through the Spirit. Christ is *the* sacrament because, as John Macquarrie says, "There is nothing in them that is not already in him."[3]

Though this is a biblical way of thinking about Christ, it is not necessarily the typical conceptual framework of either Roman Catholics or Protestants today, especially at the popular level. For Catholics, the *church* tends to be the mediator of the graces and benefits of Christ to the people. Christ's salvation is mediated through the apostolic authority of the church's hierarchy which controls the flow of grace and salvation like water from a spigot. For Protestants, especially American Protestants, one's relationship with Christ tends to be based solely on *individual* faith and experience. People are saved when they believe in Christ, and in various ways (defined differently by different groups, from tongues to holy living) show that they have had the experience of salvation. If Catholics appropriate salvation in Christ by the mediation of the church and its sacraments, Protestants appropriate it by means of individual faith which shows itself in various *experiential* rather than sacramental signs. For Catholics, Christ has handed salvation over to the church to manage and distribute. For evangelical Protestants, God has made a general offer of salvation to humanity that individuals can either receive it by "accepting Jesus Christ as their personal Savior" or reject it by failing to believe. In the evangelical "presentation" of the gospel (note the word from the world of sales and marketing rather

---

[2]Alasdair I. C. Heron, *Table and Tradition: Toward an Ecumenical Understanding of the Eucharist* (Philadelphia: Westminster Press, 1983), p. 158.
[3]John Macquarrie, *A Guide to the Sacraments* (New York: Continuum, 1997), p. 37.

than "proclamation," a word from the Bible), God "offers" salvation through Jesus Christ to all. It is up to individuals who hear this divine offer to accept or reject it.

It seems to me that the Bible and the early church fathers spoke very differently about how God's grace in salvation comes to humanity. In the biblical worldview, God decisively acted in Christ so that the whole course of human history has changed. God's action in Christ places every man and woman's relationship to God on a whole new basis. God is reconciled to them. Jesus Christ is Lord of all. All humanity, all of Adam's race, has been regathered into the one new humanity, under the headship of the new Adam. Christ's birth, life, baptism, death, resurrection and ascension was accomplished on behalf of everyone, everywhere. Christ is the one mediator between God and humanity. This has happened apart from any human action or faith. "While we still were sinners Christ died for us" (Rom 5:8). The gospel message given to the church is to announce this new reality that God established in Christ to the whole world.

When in Romans 5 and 1 Corinthians 15 Paul presents Christ as the second Adam, he is not, in my view, merely speaking metaphorically. Paul is saying something essentially true and important both about Christ and about humanity: "As in Adam all die, so all shall be made alive in Christ" (1 Cor 15:22). In Romans 5 he writes: "Just as one man's trespasses led to condemnation for all, so one man's act of righteousness leads to justification and life for all" (5:18). Later, at the climax of his discussion of the painful rejection of the gospel by most of his fellow Jews, Paul envisions God's all-inclusive plan: "For God has imprisoned all in disobedience so that he might be merciful to all" (Rom 11:32). These "all's" may make some people nervous, and scholars have found ways to pare "all" down to mean the elect, or the believers. But we do not have to affirm that all people will be saved in order to affirm that in saying "all" Paul means all—not in the sense that all will then automatically be saved, but in the sense that God's atoning work is accomplished for all, the whole world. Whether all will participate in the reality of this new relationship between God and humanity established in Christ, the new Adam, is another question. But what God has accomplished in Christ for all humanity stands firm as the basis of a full proclamation of the gospel.

Biblically speaking, God does not hand the treasures of salvation in Christ over to the church to distribute and control. Neither does God have his Son die and rise again only to offer a "deal" to humankind, and then wait around to see what they might do. God decisively acts; God does not make offers. God creates something new; God does not tentatively offer a new product to the world in the hopes that it will succeed in the religious marketplace. God's act of reconciliation in Christ changes the world, it transforms history, it makes all things new (2 Cor 5:17). This ultimate act of God in Jesus Christ becomes the core gospel message of the church: *You are reconciled with God by the cross of Christ. In him you have salvation, the forgiveness of your sins, and eternal life.* All this is not because of something we do, but rests solely on what God has done for us by sending his Son to take on our human nature and raise us to God.

Of course we are called to believe it. While God's act of salvation in Christ, the second Adam, includes all of the first Adam's descendants, this does not mean that all will be saved. In the passage quoted above, Paul goes on to say that Christ is making his appeal through Paul, "Be reconciled to God" (2 Cor 5:20). The reconciliation of all has taken place in Christ, but God still demands acceptance and faith in this already accomplished salvation through the preaching of the gospel and, as we shall see, through the sacraments. God appeals to us to believe, as human creatures endowed with freedom, limited as it is by our finitude and sin. We may never fully understand this mysterious nexus of God's sovereign grace and human faith, but we know we are saved by grace *through* faith. Even human faith, as crucial as it may be, is not a work we perform to win our salvation as much as it is a gift of God who through his Holy Spirit opens our hearts. It is not only faith *in* Christ, it is also the faith *of* Christ that saves us.[4] This mystery of God's reconciling all people in Christ, coupled with the call of the gospel to believe it and accept it as the new reality of our lives, is, I believe, the

---

[4]For a good summary and definitive stand on the contentious issue of the objective or subjective genitive in relation to faith, see Richard B. Hays, *The Faith of Jesus Christ* (Grand Rapids: Eerdmans, 2002).

typical way of describing salvation in the New Testament.[5]

Apostolic preaching is not shaped around the announcement of a hypothetical possibility that you will be given salvation *if* you believe in it. It is based on God's stupendous act of reconciliation that through his Son involves all humanity and, through his death and resurrection, reconciles all of humanity to himself. Paul preaches that God's act of atoning work in Christ includes all people, and implores them to believe it, and accept it as the new reality about themselves. "You are reconciled, so be reconciled."

Clearly the New Testament, and especially Jesus himself, also speaks frighteningly about the possibilities of hell, apparently meaning that not everyone will be saved. The awful reality of hell is that it is truly outside the new order God has created in Christ, and this new order is all there will be. The old cannot exist alongside it. God, who respects human freedom, apparently allows for the possibility that some of Adam's sons and daughters who are included in Christ may turn their backs on the truth and reality of what God has done. For them, in the end, the horrible possibility is that they will find themselves (as they have desired) truly outside, cast into the outer darkness, beyond the boundaries of the new created order. This is hell.

Despite that horrible possibility, what God has done in Christ embraces absolutely everyone. That is the substance of the gospel message. We can declare to all people: "Christ has reconciled you to God. God has wiped away your sins in him, offers you eternal life, and has a new and glorious destiny for you." But God does not force his salvation on anyone. The demand of the gospel is to believe, that is, to open your eyes, to live in the new humanity which Christ has accomplished for you within the new community he is creating, his body, the church. Faith means open arms, open hearts, open minds given by the Holy Spirit to our new creation in Christ.

The proclamation of the gospel is not the *offer* of salvation, it is the *declaration* of God's saving work on behalf of every human being. Faith

---

[5]I am aware of the arguments, from outright universalism to theories of how for those who have not heard the gospel or have heard it inadequately all or most might finally be saved. In stating the traditional understanding that salvation depends on faith in Jesus Christ in this life, I am not thereby excluding any of these. The question simply falls beyond the scope of the present work.

is not the acceptance of Jesus Christ as merely *your* personal Savior, as though you were given something to put, like change, in your desk drawer. Faith joyfully trusts in what God has done in Christ, for you and for the whole world. It is basing your whole life, your whole future, on this accomplished fact.

What has all this got to do with the sacraments? I have spent so much time discussing the nature of our reconciliation in Christ because understanding it is fundamental to understanding the sacraments. They are *gospel* sacraments. They are signs and seals of the salvation we have *in Christ*. If one believes, for example, that this salvation is mediated through the apostolic authority of the church, then sacraments become ways in which that grace is controlled and distributed by the church. If a human decision of faith brings about our salvation, then the sacraments become testimonies to a personal faith and devotional aids to the growth of that faith. If, however, reconciliation is accomplished for all people in Jesus Christ as a gift of grace, then sacraments are powerful declarations, alongside the preaching of the gospel, of our new humanity in Christ, which we receive, as we receive the gospel declaration itself, by faith. In the sacraments we acknowledge in faith that *whatever happens to Christ also happens to us*. Baptism plunges us into the waters of his vicarious human life, uniting us and identifying us with this new humanity. The Lord's Supper feeds us with Christ, participating in his perfect human life, death, resurrection and ascension in the bread and the wine.

Christ is the quintessential sacrament, the visible sign of the invisible grace of God. The sacraments Christ instituted are a means God uses to unite us with him and seal all the promises of his grace to us. It is a divinely ordered way for us the share in the reality accomplished for us in Christ.

5

How Do Sacraments Work?

Don't despise *things*. Every *thing* has a soul that speaks to our soul, and may move it toward love. To understand this is the real materialism. People speak of our age as materialistic, but they are wrong. Men do not believe in matter today any more than they believe in God; scientists have taught them not to believe in anything. Men of the Middle Ages, and most of them in the Renaissance, believed in God and the *things* God made, and they were happier and more complete than we. Listen . . . modern man wants desperately to believe in something, to have some value that cannot be shaken. This country in which we live is giving fearful proof of what mankind will do in order to have something on which to fasten his yearning for belief, for certainty, for reality.

ROBERTSON DAVIES, *WHAT'S BRED IN THE BONE*

How do sacraments work? What a typically modern and Western question that is! We tend not to like mysteries, least of all in our theology. We want to take things apart, finger the nuts and bolts, and put it back together again. As might be expected, sacraments operate in a manner we can't disassemble and put back together. They operate at the very boundaries of our understanding. Just as we recognize that the incarnation is a mystery, just as the union of Jesus' divine and human natures is a mystery, just as God's action in history by his providential rule is a mystery, so the sacraments are a mystery. One of the greatest books ever written on the sacrament of the Lord's Supper was Calvinist John Nevin's book called *Mystical Presence*.

The sacraments are mystical. They beggar human comprehension. We cannot fathom how they work or trace the lines from physical element to spiritual power and action. Calvin, who devoted so many pages of the *Institutes* to the sacraments, admitted as much. Speaking of the presence of Christ in the Lord's Supper he says, "Now, if anyone should ask me how this takes place, I shall not be ashamed to confess that it is a secret too lofty for either the mind to comprehend or my words to declare. . . . I rather experience it than understand it."[1]

That being said and fully appreciated, we can still try to understand what we can of this great sacramental mystery at the heart of Christian worship. The boundaries of our understanding of God and his ways should not hinder us from thinking God's thoughts after him right up to the edge of our finite minds.

The question is this: How does God enable us to share in our union with Christ through the sacraments? I suggest that our best answer involves four elements. The sacraments operate (1) by the power of the Holy Spirit, (2) through physical elements, (3) when united with the word and (4) when received in faith. In each case, it is essential to remember that I am not asserting that the sacraments constitute the *only* means by which we are united with Christ. This also happens through the proclamation of the gospel itself, for example. Nevertheless, the sacraments are an important God-given means of that union through the power of the Holy Spirit.

1. WE ARE UNITED WITH JESUS CHRIST IN THE SACRAMENTS THROUGH THE WORK OF THE HOLY SPIRIT.

It has often been alleged that one of the faults of the Heidelberg Catechism (on which I was raised) is that it lacked an adequate theology of

---

[1]John Calvin *Institutes* 4.17.32.

the Holy Spirit. Indeed, if you quickly scan through the catechism, there is only one brief question and answer specifically devoted to the Holy Spirit (Q and A 20). But if you read carefully, the Holy Spirit appears on nearly every page. The Holy Spirit has often been described as the hidden person of the Holy Trinity. The Spirit always seems to be pointing away from himself toward the Father and the Son. The Spirit's whole purpose in the economy of God's salvation is to reveal the Father and the Son to us and to awaken faith in them.

When the Heidelberg Catechism comes to discuss the sacraments, the very first question zeroes in on the work of the Holy Spirit. Question 65: "You confess that by faith alone you share in Christ and all his blessings: where does this faith come from? Answer: The Holy Spirit produces it in our hearts by the preaching of the holy gospel and confirms it through our use of the holy sacraments."[2]

While the relationship of baptism and the Holy Spirit clearly resonates through the New Testament, the relationship of the Holy Spirit and the Lord's Supper are less biblically clear.[3] One important way of seeing the importance of the Holy Spirit in the sacraments is how the liturgical prayers surrounding each of the sacraments culminate in the *epiclesis,* calling the Holy Spirit to unite the recipients to Christ.[4] What Cyril of Jerusalem said of the Spirit in relation to the Lord's Supper pertains to baptism as well: "Whatsoever the Holy Spirit has touched is sanctified and changed."[5] The sacraments have no capacity to affect us in any way apart from the work of the Holy Spirit in awakening and assuring our faith through them.

2. GOD IMPARTS HIS GRACIOUS SALVATION IN CHRIST TO US
   THROUGH THE PHYSICAL ELEMENTS AND RITUAL ACTIONS OF
   THE SACRAMENTS.

Through the physical elements of water, wine and bread, and in the rit-

---

[2]*Psalter Hymnal* (Grand Rapids: CRC Publications, 1987), p. 889.

[3]See a more detailed treatment of the work of the Holy Spirit in each of the sacraments in chapters six and seven (baptism) and chapter ten (the Lord's Supper, especially Calvin's teaching on it).

[4]See, for example, the liturgies for Holy Baptism and Holy Communion in the Presbyterian *Book of Common Worship* (Louisville, Ky.: Westminster John Knox, 1993).

[5]In James White, *The Sacraments in Protestant Practice and Faith* (Nashville: Abingdon, 1999), p. 114.

ual actions and words of the gathered community, God imparts grace and salvation to us in the sacraments. Historical Christian orthodoxy, going back to the early church fathers, is convinced that in the sacraments God is doing something through these ritual signs. They are truly means of grace. I use the word *grace* a bit hesitantly. Historically the impartation of grace in the sacraments took grace to be some kind of substance that could be poured into the soul. Rather, grace is the saving action of the triune God centered in the life, death and resurrection of Christ, which brings us into a new relationship with God apart from any merit on our own. Through the sacraments we partake of this new relationship, which is characterized by forgiveness and adoption as God's children. In that sense they are truly a means of grace along with the preaching of the Word.[6]

This way of speaking is precisely what makes many Protestants nervous today because they doubt whether God *can* use physical elements to convey spiritual reality. That doubt arises from the same old dualistic or gnostic split that has harassed the church through the centuries. Paul's distinctions between the flesh and Spirit, the body and the soul were fundamentally misunderstood in the light of classical philosophical systems. According to his own Hebrew worldview, by "flesh" Paul meant sinful, fallen human life, not human existence itself; and by "spirit" Paul meant this earthly human life filled with and directed by the Holy Spirit, not only some existence outside of this world. These terms were taken in the second-century Greek context to mean something quite different, leading to a dichotomy between matter and spirit, earth and heaven. Reading Irenaeus's warnings in *Against Heresies* (second century), one comes to understand how quickly and how powerfully these anti-material, anti-incarnational gnostic heresies crept into the church—and looking around today, one comes to recognize how stubbornly they have persisted.

Despite certain misgivings, the Reformation tradition (apart from its Anabaptist wing) has never cut the physical elements and the ritual actions themselves out of the spiritual transaction of our union

---

[6]There is a sense in which the Word, preached and read, is also a sacrament. It too is physical—symbols on a page and sounds in our ears that convey God's grace in Christ to us.

with Christ. Listen to the words of the Heidelberg Catechism, which of all the Reformed Confessions tends to most spiritualize the sacraments: "I am washed with [Christ's] blood and Spirit from the pollution of my soul, that is, from all my sins, as certainly as I am washed outwardly with water, whereby the filthiness of the body is taken away."[7] And on the Lord's Supper: "He himself feeds and assuages my soul to everlasting life, as certainly as I receive from the hand of the minister, and taste with my mouth, the bread and cup of the Lord, which are given to me as certain tokens of the body and blood of Christ."[8] Notice especially the tight connection between the water and the spiritual cleansing with Christ's blood, the bread and cup and the spiritual feeding with Christ's body and blood. Clearly, the physical elements are not Christ in some crass physical sense. But just as clearly, Christ comes by means of them. They are crucial in the celebration of the sacrament and not merely tangential to their spiritual meaning and effects.

God uses earthly elements in sacramental rites because we are earthly beings. Calvin often emphasizes that sacraments are aimed at our human weakness, the fact that we are tied to earth and bound by our senses. "The sacraments therefore, are exercises which make us more certain of the trustworthiness of God's Word. And because we are of flesh, they are shown under things of flesh to instruct us according to our dull capacity, and to lead us by the hand as tutors lead children."[9] The very physical, earthbound nature of sacraments remind us that we are creatures of dust.

We are children before a great and unfathomable God. Jesus said that unless we become like little children we cannot inherit the kingdom of God (Mt 18:3). So with the sacraments, we humble ourselves to receive the promises and the grace of God through our human senses. We come to God with all the humility and faith expressed in the words of Psalm 81:10: "Open wide your mouth and I will fill it."[10] In the sac-

---

[7]Heidelberg Catechism, Q and A 69.

[8]Ibid., Q and A 75.

[9]Calvin *Institutes* 4.14.6. Calvin too much degrades human earthly life here, but the point is really about communication from God who is Spirit to human, earthbound creatures.

[10]This was the first metrical psalm memorized by Dutch Reformed children of the last century.

raments we open wide the mouths of our human senses so that God can fill us with his grace in Christ.

Evelyn Diephouse, a Reformed pastor, writes movingly about the importance and power of the physical elements in the Lord's Supper. She remembers how she learned in seminary that in John 6, Jesus' "bread of life" discourse, the words Jesus uses are extremely graphic, "Unless you eat [Greek: gnaw, munch, chew] the flesh of the Son of Man . . . you have no life in you." In contrast, she says, the communion services of her childhood, with their bread in pre-cut, bite-sized pieces, and wine pre-poured into sterile cups, seemed to minimize the physical importance of the elements. "What would have happened if some of them had slurped or smacked their lips? . . . But the strong word John uses to picture us eating Jesus' body offers some basis for thinking about how to balance the docetic tendencies in the Reformed tradition. Our bodies have to be taken into account."[11] She goes on to say that liturgical renewal, with its fragrant loaves of homemade bread, broken and passed in a circle, and large chalices of aromatic wine, has helped focus more on the elements. But still, she asks, what does it mean to "gnaw" on Jesus for dear life?

> My mind shifts again to a vivid tale from the evening news, of one of the survivors of an earthquake . . . in Armenia several years ago. . . . One woman was found alive after four or five days, pinned under a slab of concrete, yet holding an infant who had somehow not been injured. She was not its mother, and unable to nurse it, she had kept it alive by letting it suck on her lip—gnaw on her lip, actually—drawing her own lifeblood to keep from getting dehydrated and using her own flesh for food. Jesus gives us himself as food to keep us alive. It's not very civilized, is it?[12]

As uncivilized as it may sound to eat and drink the body and blood of Christ (a similar criticism came up in attacks by outsiders on the early church as being cannibals), it is impossible to separate the physical elements from their sacramental matrix. To do so would be to destroy the sacraments as physical bearers of spiritual reality.

---

[11]Evelyn Diephouse, "Gnawing Jesus," *Perspectives* (October 1997): 24.
[12]Ibid.

3. SACRAMENTS IMPART GOD'S GRACE IN CHRIST TO US WHEN THESE PHYSICAL ELEMENTS ARE JOINED TO THE WORD.

In the whole spectrum of the Protestant tradition, the two essential means of grace are always *word* and sacrament. When the Reformers insisted on the word and sacrament being bound together, they meant not only the biblical Word but also the *preached* word. In the medieval Catholic tradition, the sacramental liturgies also contained words. The Scriptures were read and the proper prayers were offered. Of course most of this took place in Latin, out of sight of the people, and often even out of their hearing. What few sermons there were had more to do with practical and political matters than with the preaching of the Word of God. It is no wonder that the words uttered by the priest at the moment of consecration, *hoc est corpus* ("this is my body"), accompanied by ringing of the bells, came into the vernacular, down to this day, as *hocus pocus*, a magical incantation.

Calvin is typical of the Reformers in his criticism of the way in which words were used as a kind of magical accompaniment to the sacraments: "We ought to understand the word not as one whispered without meaning and without faith, a mere noise, like a magical incantation, which has the force to consecrate the element. Rather, it should, when the word is preached, make us understand what the visible sign means."[13]

The Reformers believed the sacraments and the word belong together for two reasons. First, the sacraments were signs and seals of the promises of God contained in the gospel. The gospel promise, therefore, had to be heard alongside the sacramental signs and seals so that the sacraments could be properly understood and received. Second, in both word and sacrament together, Christ is given to us to be received by faith in a way that neither word nor sacrament can properly accomplish on their own. Sacraments are not subsidiary accompaniments to the word. They are sometimes described that way because in practice the word *can* function without the sacrament, but the sacrament cannot function without the word. That is true in the sense that the sacraments cannot "speak" to us on their own, but only in the context of the proclamation of the preaching of the gospel. In another sense this inaccu-

---

[13]Calvin *Institutes* 4.14.4.

rately explains the relationship of word and sacrament. Sacraments are given to us by God to enable, strengthen and confirm our humanly weak faith in his gospel promises. Calvin says, "The clearer anything is the fitter it is to support faith. But the sacraments bring the clearest promises; and they have this characteristic *over and above* (italics mine) the word because they represent them for us as painted in a picture from life."[14] Word and sacrament always belong together.

One way of thinking about the relationship of word and sacrament is to think of human communication. Since we are embodied persons, communication is seldom if ever merely a matter of thoughts passing from one mind to another. When we interact with each other, there is "body language"—those telltale gestures and minute movements that convey the true meaning of the words we say. We can all appreciate how in a telephone conversation or e-mail our message can be garbled when the words are divorced from physical gesture. But even our hearing alone picks up signals through the tone of the voice, the clipped or drawn-out phrasing of a sentence, or the gestures of speech that may even belie the words we say. Even the barest form of communication, words on a page, is made up of physical symbols that our eyes see and interpret. In addition, their punctuation, phrasing and poetic structure convey meanings beyond the written word.

Sacraments are God's "body language" to us, his creatures, who live in a physical world. We need them for many of the same reasons we need the body language we described above. But sacraments serve an even more important purpose. They not only explain the word, they confirm it. For the Reformers, the primary need for sacraments to accompany the reading and preaching of the Word of God, was that the word by itself placed more weight on our faith than it had the strength to bear. Sacraments accompany the word because faith is not strong enough to be sustained by the word alone. Sacraments confirm, convey, and apply the word in ways in which the word by itself cannot do. Calvin disparages the creaturely weakness of our faith in God's Word alone as

slight and feeble unless it be propped on all sides and sustained by every

---

[14]Calvin *Institutes* 4.14.6.

means, [or else] it trembles, wavers, totters, and at last gives way. Here, our merciful Lord, according to his infinite kindness, so tempers himself to our capacity that, since we are creatures who always creep on the ground, cleave to the flesh, and, so not think about or even conceive of anything spiritual, he condescends to lead us to himself even by these earthly elements [the sacraments], and to set before us in the flesh a mirror of spiritual blessings.[15]

Both Calvin and Luther saw the need for the sacrament of Holy Communion every Sunday since God gave it to us for the strengthening and confirmation of our faith. In the light of the Reformers' conviction, it is interesting to follow the history of sacramental teaching and practice down to the present day. The Reformed tradition and evangelical Protestantism generally began to exalt the word to such an extent that the sacraments became merely occasional additions. In worship services today evangelical Protestants invariably, and properly, make preaching central every Sunday. But they tend to celebrate the sacraments only a few times a year, or perhaps monthly at best. This reveals a subtle reversal in the thinking of the Reformers. Instead of the close conjunction of word and sacrament, we now have word and *maybe* sacrament, depending on whether it's that day of the month or year, or unless we have too many other things to do, or perhaps it's Mother's Day. Perhaps we don't really believe, as Calvin did, that our faith is so weak as to need sacraments to frequently build it up.[16]

From the Protestant side, one of the persistent problems is the misunderstanding of the nature of sacraments and therefore their relationship to the preached word. It is true that, as Calvin, following Augustine, liked to say, sacraments are visible words. But that is far too minimal an understanding of the sacraments.

First, the sacraments do not merely make the word visible; they make it tasty, aromatic, tactile. They appeal to *all* the senses, not just to the eye. Furthermore, there are actions taking place in the context of the believing community. Peter Leithart points to the inadequacy of the venerable old formulation of sacraments as the intersection of word and element:

---

[15]Calvin *Institutes* 4.14.3.
[16]For more on the frequency of the Lord's Supper, see chapters nine and twelve.

Even if we (rightly) insisted that the word is not a magical incantation but the word preached and believed, this definition is still terribly inadequate. Water in the presence of the word preached does not make baptism; bread and wine over which the words of institution are spoken do not make the Eucharist. . . .

Lacking in these definitions and metaphors is a clear indication that a sacrament requires actions and people as well as words and material objects. Baptism is not water plus preaching, but water that an officiant applies to a subject in the name of the Trinity; the Eucharist is not the word plus bread and wine, but the word plus bread and wine eaten and drunk by the gathered people of God.[17]

Second, the sacraments do not merely make the word available through the senses; they *confirm* the word through the senses. That's why Calvin always insisted they were necessary because of the *weakness* of our faith.

Sacraments confirm our faith in Christ by incorporating us into his body through baptism and by feeding us in the Lord's Supper with the ascended Lord's body and blood.[18] As the Word brings us Christ for our faith to grasp through hearing, so the sacraments bring us Christ for our faith to grasp through seeing and tasting and touching. Robert Bruce, the great sixteenth-century Scottish preacher and fine interpreter of Calvin, preached a sermon on the sacraments in which he explained how the sacrament (in this case the Lord's Supper), while it belonged with the word, was not merely a visible word:

Do you ask what new thing we get in the sacrament? I say we get Christ better than we did before: we get a better grip of Christ now. That same thing that you possess by the hearing of the word, you possess now more largely. For by the sacrament my faith is nourished, the bounds of my soul are enlarged, and so when I had but a little grip of Christ before, as it were betwixt my finger and my thumb, now I get him in my whole hand: for the more my faith grows, the better grip I get of Christ Jesus.[19]

---

[17]Peter Leithart, "The Way Things Really Ought to Be," *Westminster Theological Journal* 59 (1997): 163.
[18]See chapters nine through twelve for a fuller elaboration.
[19]Quoted in Geddes MacGregor, *Corpus Christi* (London: Macmillan, 1959), p. 181 (my translation of the old Scottish dialect).

In the sacraments we get the same thing as we get in the word, we get Christ, but we get him "better" in the sacraments. By "better" Bruce does not mean that we get more of Christ. Both word and sacrament bring Christ to our souls by faith through the Holy Spirit. But in the sacraments we get Christ in a way that is particularly suited to our humanity. We get Christ through water, bread and wine.

4. THE SACRAMENTS ARE RECEIVED THROUGH FAITH.

Faith operates through the sacraments in the same way faith operates in relation to the Word of God. That seems like a simple enough proposition, but it brings us into the heart of one of the deepest controversies of the Reformation. How does faith operate, and what is its relationship to salvation?

God has accomplished our salvation in Jesus Christ for the whole human race before faith receives it. Faith is simply the opening of our eyes and hearts to this astounding truth: that we have been made new persons in Christ. Faith receives, faith grasps, faith trusts what God has done in Christ. Faith does not make it happen, for it has happened long before our faith was there to receive it. In fact, faith is not a human work at all, though it seems to be. T. F. Torrance emphasizes that faith is God's gift of sight to those blinded by sin.[20] It is the opening of the heart by the Holy Spirit. Faith plays no causal role whatsoever. It participates in salvation without in any way displacing the primary work of the Holy Spirit.[21]

The same holds true for the relationship of faith to the sacraments. Calvin said, "[The sacraments] avail and profit nothing unless received in faith," and on this there would be no disagreement from his contemporaries or us.[22] But this does not mean Calvin believes that faith makes the sacraments effective. He makes the comparison of faith and the sacraments to pouring some liquid into a jar. No matter how much you pour, nothing will get in if there is a lid on the jar. We cannot re-

---

[20]Torrance also emphasizes, along with a number of New Testament scholars today, that in Paul especially, faith is not just our faith, but the faith of Christ on our behalf. See T. F. Torrance, *The Mediation of Christ* (Grand Rapids: Eerdmans, 1983), p. 100.

[21]George Hunsinger, "Baptism and the Soteriology of Forgiveness," in *Call to Worship* 35, no. 3 (2001): p. 24.

[22]Calvin *Institutes* 4.14.17.

ceive Christ in the sacraments if faith does not open our souls to him.

But that leads Calvin and others to the next logical question. Does that mean that we are somehow in control of the efficacy of the sacraments? If the sacraments are not received in faith, do the sacraments lose the power of God's promise? Or, as Calvin put it, "Do the wicked, then, by their ungratefulness cause the ordinance of God to be voided and nullified?" For Calvin the answer has to be no. The "force and truth" of the sacrament does not depend on the condition or the choice of the one receiving it. "For what God ordained remains firm and keeps its own nature, however men may vary." The sacraments, consecrated with the word and promise of God, keep their force, but they do not benefit those who do not receive them in faith and obedience. Calvin quotes Augustine here: "If you receive carnally, it does not cease to be spiritual, but it is not so for you."[23] This does not mean, however, that some secret power lies hidden in the elements themselves, or is imparted by the words of consecration upon them. Calvin is clear that it is the Holy Spirit who makes sacraments effective, and the Holy Spirit brings the blessings of Christ where faith receives him.

We cannot receive Christ and his benefits in the sacraments apart from faith. At the same time, faith does not make the sacraments effective. God acts through them, with or without the faith of the celebrant or the recipient, just as God has acted to save all humanity before human faith. Both Augustine and Calvin did not want to suggest that we humans were in control of the sacraments. In 1 Corinthians 11 Paul describes the way the Lord's Supper operates in the disobedient and unloving atmosphere of the church at Corinth. It is not that the sacrament loses its power or efficacy but that it works for their judgment rather than their salvation. For those who receive it without "discerning the body," it becomes the food and drink of judgment. Instead of healing them, it makes them sick (1 Cor 11:27-30).

This issue of the relationship of faith to the sacraments confronts us with another important term in the history of the church's reflection on the sacraments, *ex opere operato* (literally, by the work, worked). I will not detail here the long and convoluted history of the

---

[23]Calvin *Institutes* 4.14.16.

term as it was used by the medieval and Reformation theologians.[24]
For the medieval theologians, the term was used to safeguard the sacraments from the heresies of Pelagianism (the notion that our works of faith merit salvation) and Donatism (the notion that the efficacy of the sacraments depended on the qualities of the officiant). The medieval theologians affirmed that the sacraments were God's work, not ours. They did not depend on us for their effectiveness. The problem is that as this doctrine evolved, the efficacy of the sacraments more and more came to depend on their own inner power and on the church's authorized dispensation of them rather than on God's action. Nicholas Wolterstorff says that for Aquinas the sacraments literally *cause* grace. "The sacraments are not effective *ex opere operantis*, through the activity of the performer; they are effective *ex opere operato*, through the deed performed. The sacrament infuses grace into the soul if it is actually performed and if the recipient does not interpose the obstacle of consciously being in mortal sin."[25] Actually, according to the Council of Trent, lack of faith was among the mortal sins that could block the efficacy of the sacrament, but that was not the real focus of medieval Catholic thinking about the sacraments. As Catholic scholar Godfrey Diekmann puts it: "By the time of the Reformation, the thoroughly sound principle that sacraments effect what they signify [*ex opere operato* in its original sense] . . . had fallen victim, certainly in the popular understanding, to the very Pelagianism which it had tried to overcome. Sacraments had become almost automatic dispensers of grace. They were viewed as *things*, valuable and powerful more or less in their own right, as actions to be performed by man guaranteeing him salvation."[26]

Historically, the Roman Catholic/Protestant impasse over the relationship of sacraments and faith was sometimes more a matter of misunderstanding and emphasis than substance. In its statements the Council of Trent was really battling the concept of "faith *alone*," which they understood to undermine the efficacy of the sacraments in them-

---

[24]For a compact and accurate description of this history, see Nicholas Wolterstorff, "The Reformed Liturgy," in *Major Themes in the Reformed Tradition*, ed. Donald McKim (Grand Rapids: Eerdmans, 1992), pp. 281-87.

[25]Ibid., p. 282.

[26]Quoted in ibid., p. 283.

selves. The Protestants were battling the crassest forms of *ex opere operato* in which they felt that faith had no place at all. Michael Lawler sums up a more complete Roman Catholic understanding of the relationship of faith and sacraments:

> Up to the Council of Trent Catholic theologians unanimously affirm that sacraments are efficacious "by" faith, "in" faith, "in proportion to" faith. In reaction to the theories of the Reformers, Catholic teaching insisted that "faith alone" did not justify, but justified in and through sacraments. This was not . . . to deny the necessity of faith, but only to affirm the efficacy of the sacraments. Orthodox Roman Catholic teaching never considered the sacramental conferring of grace to be independent of faith.[27]

Perhaps Roman Catholics and many Protestants can agree today on the conviction that sacraments ultimately derive their validity and effectiveness from the power and promise of God. Human faith and human readiness to accept God's grace are not the *cause* of a sacrament's effective power; they are, however, the *condition* for the effective reception of the grace of God that is offered in the sacraments. Certainly, many contemporary Catholics and Protestants would agree to that formulation.[28]

For Calvin the operation of faith in the sacraments was tied to the activity of the Holy Spirit. That is why the *epiclesis*, the prayer for the Holy Spirit to make this water, this bread and wine, the sacraments of Christ's grace to us, rather than the words of institution, was for Calvin the central prayer by which the sacraments were constituted and through which the elements were consecrated for God's use. Faith is not directed at the elements themselves, as though they had some kind of magical quality infused in them by the words and works of the officiant. Faith is directed to God, who sends his Holy Spirit to bring Christ to us through the sacramental elements. Michael Horton calls the conjunction of word and sacrament with the fission of the Holy Spirit the true experience of "signs and wonders": "When we are bound by this union of the Spirit with his means of grace (word and sacrament), we are truly engaged in a 'signs and wonders' ministry. The signs are the written and preached Word, the water, the bread and

---

[27]Lawler, *Symbol and Sacrament: A Contemporary Sacramental Theology* (Mahwah, N.J.: Paulist, 1987), p. 43.
[28]Herbert Vorgrimler, *Sacramental Theology* (Collegeville, Minn.: Liturgical Press, 1992), p. 87.

wine. The wonders are the supernatural activities of the Spirit attached to these signs."[29]

But the relationship of faith to the sacraments is not just a one-way street. It is not merely a matter of faith in God and in Jesus Christ, but it is a faith that is exercised *through* the sacraments themselves. The sacraments are not simply opportunities for faith; they are handles for faith to grasp. The sacraments are effective not only *because of* the faith of the recipient, they also *build up* the faith of the recipient. So Donald Baillie says that "instead of saying that the efficacy of sacraments depend on the faith of the recipient, it would be better to say that the sacraments operate through human faith. And faith works both ways. Faith grasps sacraments, and faith is stimulated by sacraments."[30]

Baron Von Hugel talked about the effects of kissing his daughter, "I kiss my daughter in order to love her, as well as because I love her." This is also a remarkable commentary on sacraments. Love requires physical expression. But does a kiss create love? Not exactly, but it is expected that the kisses will cause his love for his daughter to grow. The physical display of affection is the means and instrument by which love grows and increases. The kiss is a "sacrament," an outward and visible sign by which love is given the expression it craves and is given growth and strengthening in itself.[31]

Faith grasps Christ in the sacraments, and faith in Christ is stimulated and strengthened by sacraments. William Temple writes movingly of the faith-strengthening power of sacraments:

> When faith exists as a struggle to believe in spite of empirical and temperamental pressure to unbelief, when the whole life of feeling is dead, when nothing is left but stark loyalty to God as He is dimly and waveringly apprehended to be—then the sheer objectivity, even the express materialism, of a sacrament gives it a value that nothing else can have. And when faith revives its ardor, and feeling is once more aglow, when the activity of prayers spoken and praises sung is again a natural expression of devotion, the rite which is believed to have retained its efficacy when all else failed becomes a focus of grateful adoration to the

---

[29]Michael Horton, *In the Face of God* (Dallas: Word, 1996), p. 140.
[30]Donald M. Baillie, *The Theology of the Sacraments* (New York: Scribner's, 1957), pp. 52-53.
[31]Carroll E. Simcox, *Understanding the Sacraments* (New York: Morehouse-Gorham, 1956), pp. 14-15.

God who therein offered grace . . . to a soul that could receive him in no other way."[32]

Nancy Mairs puts it even more pointedly, "I don't partake because I'm a good Catholic, holy and pious and sleek. I partake because I'm a bad Catholic, riddled by doubt and anxiety and anger: fainting from severe hypoglycemia of the soul."[33]

CONCLUSION

In the Reformation tradition (apart from the Anabaptists), the gospel sacraments are much more than naked signs. They are signs and seals of God's grace to us in Jesus Christ, symbols that carry with them what they symbolize. Already in the Old Testament the Creator freely used created things to communicate his covenant promises to his people. The whole of Israel's worship could be described as sacramental in that so many physical objects, from the tabernacle itself down to the vestments of the priests, were instituted by God to convey his word and his will to his people. The New Testament continues that fundamental way of communication through physical things with the gospel sacraments of baptism and the Lord's Supper. Though they are not called sacraments (which is a problematic word at any rate), nevertheless the way they are described and practiced make it clear that all the blessings of faith and salvation are bound to them. They do not just give outward testimony to our faith and devotion to Christ, or evoke memories of Christ, or serve as devotional aids. They are not merely as someone put it, "God's flannelgraph." They are powerful means of grace that demand our faith in Christ and bolster our faith in him. In the sacraments, accompanied by the word and received in faith, God acts so that his people share in a unique fellowship with Christ himself through the Holy Spirit. In baptism God really and uniquely incorporates us into Christ and makes us members of his body. In the Lord's Supper God really feeds us with Christ, the bread of eternal life.

As it is developed in the Christian tradition, the sacraments operate

---

[32]William Temple, *Nature, Man, and God* (London: Macmillan, 1935), p. 491.
[33]Quoted in Philip Yancey, *What's So Amazing About Grace?* (Grand Rapids: Zondervan, 1997), p. 190.

through the physical elements in their ritual setting, by the power of the Holy Spirit, in unity with the word, and as received in faith. Each one of these is a crucial factor in the correct understanding and practice of the sacraments. We cannot separate the word from physical element that is its sign and seal, or the physical element from the word which gives it substance and meaning, and we cannot separate either from the faith that receives Christ in them through the Holy Spirit.

6

BAPTISM

Introduction and Biblical Background

You are my Son, the Beloved; in you I am well pleased.

MARK 1:11

I don't remember my own baptism. It took place when I was a few months old in an Orthodox Presbyterian Church in Rochester, New York. I don't even know the date. I am told that there was a huge church fight going on in the Christian Reformed Church in Rochester where my parents had been members, so they left and sought peace in the O.P. Church (as they called it) for a time. So, ironically, I was baptized into the unity of the one body of Christ as a result of some rather heated disunity.

I cannot recall my parents talking about my baptism very much, or that any particular significance was placed on it. Of course, we often witnessed baptisms in the large congregation we joined after moving to Grand Rapids, Michigan. They were mostly baptisms of infants, though once in a while an adult was baptized, which, because of its infrequency, seemed quite an event.

Even as a child and young man, one thing I recall about the administration of baptism in our church was the absurdly small amount of water that was used. The minister would barely dip a finger or two in the water and then lightly sprinkle it on the child's or the adult's forehead, as though to avoid getting the carpet wet. This invisible, tidy and almost dry baptism had the effect of making the sacrament seem more remote and unreal, something to think about rather than to revel in. The long didactic liturgy read at each baptism tended to further emphasize the understanding rather than the experience of baptism.

All in all, until I grew up into adulthood my own baptism did not particularly interest me. It was not an important part of my identity. The church was telling me that the really important step was to make Public Profession of Faith. It was then that one became a full "communicant" church member, rather than merely a "baptized member." Though it was meant to highlight the believer's personal covenantal response to God's grace in baptism, this emphasis on the public profession of faith also served to denigrate the importance of baptism as the sacrament of membership in Christ and his church.

It wasn't until I had children of my own that I really began to seriously contemplate my own baptism, and what baptism means. With their baptism I sensed that one of the most important aspects of baptism was God's promises to my children, and my promise to God to bring them up in the Christian faith. I began to pray to God in terms of my children's baptism, and I still do today: "God, they are yours, you claimed them in baptism. Work in their heart by your Holy Spirit and bring them to true faith and guard them from the devices and desires of the evil one." This has been my continuous daily prayer for my children. It is centered in baptism.

Through all this, my own baptism continued to have little personal meaning. I remember as a pastor having some sympathy with an adult who had been baptized as an infant, coming to me and asking to be rebaptized. She described her parents as nominal believers who were just following family tradition and "christening" their child with little personal faith or commitment. I seriously contemplated going along with her request. Part of my sympathy with her position was that I did not remember my own baptism, and it had little meaning for me. It would be a powerful experience, I thought, to consciously enter the baptismal waters as an adult.

It was when I attended my first Easter Vigil that I was struck with the personal significance of my own baptism. The Easter Vigil is part of the Paschal Feast (Christian Passover) which includes Maundy Thursday, Good Friday and, of course, Easter. The vigil, which usually occurs late at night on Holy Saturday, marks the decisive liturgical turning point from Christ's death to his everlasting life, from darkness to light. It begins in darkness until the "new fire" is lit. Then each worshipper lights a candle and passes the light until the light of Christ spreads through the whole congregation. In the procession into the church the joyful cry is heard, "Light of Christ! Thanks be to God!" At the heart of the vigil is the celebration of baptism, which marks our own identity with, and participation in, the death and resurrection of Jesus Christ. The vigil is all about being plunged into the baptismal waters with and in Jesus Christ and rising again to new life in him.

Several adults and children were baptized at the vigil that night. But it was not just their baptism that was celebrated. We were all invited to join with them in renewing our baptismal vows—renouncing the devil and all his works and turning with them to Jesus Christ with our whole hearts. After the baptisms took place, to help us all remember and celebrate our own baptisms, the liturgist took a branch full of leaves, dipped it into the baptismal water, and joyously moved about the congregation, waving the branch and liberally dousing everyone with water. When those drops hit my face, the tears leaped out. At that moment I knew: "I am baptized! I am a member of the one universal, indivisible body of Christ. I am buried with Christ in baptism and raised with him to a new life. I renounce the devil and all his ways, and turn every day to Jesus Christ, to whom I belong, body and soul, in life and in death." My baptism in that little Orthodox Presbyterian Church, which had meant so little to me over the years, suddenly became the defining and identifying moment in my life and has remained so ever since.

Since then, I have introduced the Easter Vigil with its remembrance of baptism to various congregations. I am often amazed at how many people react exactly as I did. Baptism becomes astonishingly real. It is as though this dormant rite, lost to memory, explodes into life again. Even people baptized as adults react with deep feeling to this remembrance of something they experienced perhaps years ago.

We have already addressed some of the issues in the previous chapter, sacrament versus ordinance, the role of faith in relation to sacraments, and we will confront others: the Holy Spirit's role in baptism, and infant or adult baptism. What Paul celebrates in Ephesians 4 as the "one baptism," has become a flash point for fragmentation and disunity.

In this situation, the need for dialogue across the high walls of our traditional boundaries is even more imperative. I believe there is room to build bridges between the deeply entrenched camps. So I invite even the convinced Baptist to stay with me, since I believe, with them and with Paul, that there is only one baptism and that is baptism into Jesus Christ. If we can begin to see at least some of our differences as matters of emphasis rather than principle, and if we can seriously listen to each other, we may all come to a more balanced and flexible understanding of baptism as a result.

In this chapter I will move from a consideration of the Old Testament roots of baptism to a look at New Testament texts on baptism, and in the next chapter I will work toward a constructive contemporary theology of baptism rooted in the biblical and theological tradition.

THE OLD TESTAMENT ROOTS OF BAPTISM

In the Old Testament worldview, water is the realm of chaos. In the beginning the Spirit "swept over the face of the deep" (Gen 1:2). Order emerged from this watery chaos by the power of God's Word, as God's creation came into being. The world became habitable when God separated the waters from the dry land. But the world's existence was still precarious. Water surrounded the creation, held back by God's almighty hand. It was in the sky, held in place by the firmament, and under the ground, ready to spring forth should the Creator lift his hand or blow his nostrils (Ex 15:8).

This is exactly what happened in the biblical account of the flood. The waters came down from above and they rose up from below. The flood destroyed the whole world as the watery chaos erupted. Only Noah and his family were spared as they bobbed above the floodwaters in the ark. Borne up by the ark, the waters of destruction became, for Noah and his family, the waters of salvation. Peter picks up this theme of the saving waters when, after describing the flood, he concludes, "And baptism, which this prefigured, now saves you" (1 Pet 3:21).

This baptismal identification of drowning waters with God's saving purpose reoccurs in the story of the exodus. The children of Israel march through the walls of water on dry land, only to see the waters roar back to destroy the Egyptians. At the Red Sea, God threw horse and rider into the sea. "The floods covered them; they went down to the depth like a stone" (Ex 15:1, 5) The New Testament also understood this event as a prefiguring of baptism. Paul reminds the Corinthians that "our ancestors were all under the cloud, and all passed through the sea, and all were baptized into Moses in the cloud and in the sea" (1 Cor 10:1-2). Paul thinks of the crossing of the sea as a baptismal metaphor, and employs it as a warning against baptismal presumption.

The drowning, destroying, chaotic waters become instruments for the deliverance of God's people. And baptism always carries with it that element of deliverance from the chaos and destruction of sin, a rebirth through water with all its dangers and possibilities.

These key events, all of them soaked in water, are taken up in the great prayer of thanksgiving that is used in so many liturgies of baptism:

> By your invisible power, O Lord, you perform wonders in
>   your sacraments
> and in the history of salvation you have used water, which you
>   have created,
> to make known to us the grace of baptism.
> At the beginning of the world your Spirit hovered over the waters,
> prepared your work of creation, and planted the seed of life.
> By the waters of the Flood you declared the death of sin
> and the birth of a new life.
> You brought the children of Abraham through the waters of the Red Sea,
> and the people, freed from slavery, journeyed toward the
>   Promised Land.[1]

Water was also significant for the Hebrew people for its cleansing qualities. For them, washing with water was a religious ritual as well as a hygienic activity. In order to be the holy people of God they needed to be clean morally and spiritually as well as physically. The laws governing religious ritual in the Old Testament prescribe frequent washings, or lustrations as they are sometimes called. These were prescribed for people in various situations of "uncleanness" (menstruation, contact

---

[1]Max Thurian and Geoffrey Wainright, eds., *Baptism and Eucharist: Ecumenical Convergence in Celebration* (Grand Rapids: Eerdmans, 1983), p. 94.

with an unclean object, etc.) in order to make them ritually "clean."

The spiritual symbolism of this ritual cleansing is especially evident in the ritual bath of the high priest on the great Day of Atonement, the high point of Israel's sacrificial rituals. The high priest was instructed to bathe his whole body in water before putting on the priestly vestments for this day. This was clearly a sign of his cleansing from sin in preparation for standing in the presence of the Holy One of Israel in the holy of holies.

These cleansing rituals were also woven into the fabric of Israel's piety. In that great psalm of penitence, Psalm 51, the psalmist yearns for God's true cleansing:

> Purge me with hyssop, and I shall be clean;
> wash me, and I shall be whiter than snow. . . .
> Hide your face from my sins,
> and blot out all my iniquities.
> Create in me a clean heart, O God,
> and put a new and right spirit within me. (Ps 51:7, 9, 10)

These same cleansing rituals were also highlighted by the Old Testament prophets to portray God's purifying intent for his people. In Ezekiel, as God promises to gather his people back from all the countries where he had scattered them, God says, "I will sprinkle clean water upon you, and you shall be clean from all your uncleanness, and from all your idols I will cleanse you." But the prophet goes on, pointing beyond the outward cleansing with water to the inner reality to which it points: "A new heart I will give you, and a new spirit I will put within you; and I will remove from your body the heart of stone and give you a heart of flesh. I will put my spirit within you" (Ezek 36:25-27). Here, already we begin to see the faint outlines of baptism in the New Testament, an outward washing with water that signifies an inner new life.

In the immediate pre-Christian era and in the first century, the practice of ritual washing became an even more prominent feature of Jewish faith and life. With their emphasis on a return to the true righteousness of the Mosaic law, the Pharisees also practiced frequent ritual washings. Their concern for ritual cleanliness is reflected in some of the Gospel stories about Jesus in which he is criticized because his disciples did not wash *(baptizmoi)* themselves properly before they ate (e.g., Mk 6:1-8).

Another important antecedent to Christian baptism is not found in the Old Testament itself, but in the pre-Christian rabbinical writings concerning the rituals by which proselytes were brought into the Jewish community. In these rituals the images of death and resurrection were often used. The proselyte's conversion to Judaism marked the end of a life of slavery to the pagan gods and the beginning of a new life of obedience to Yahweh, the one true God. Two rituals were especially associated with this conversion: circumcision, and a ritual bath or baptism. It is clear that circumcision was the most important of these rituals, and the one that really marked the passage from death to life. The baptism was a ritual cleansing that took place one week after the "death" of circumcision. It marked the point at which the proselyte was ritually clean and was therefore permitted to engage in Jewish worship.

One important exception to the central importance of circumcision in proselyte conversion were the rituals pertaining to women and girls. They were considered members of the "circumcision," but of course they were not physically circumcised. In the case of women and girls, it was the ritual proselyte bath that marked their separation from the "uncircumcised" life and the whole world of paganism. In the judgment of G. R. Beasley-Murray, while it cannot be proven that proselyte baptism directly influenced Christian baptism, the theology of conversion inherent in proselyte baptism and circumcision was certainly an important factor in shaping Christian thinking on baptism.[2]

THE BACKGROUND AND MEANING OF BAPTISM IN THE NEW TESTAMENT

It is a daunting task to attempt a brief, coherent and accurate statement of the background and meaning of baptism in the New Testament because the New Testament writers themselves do not offer a coherent explanation of baptism. They assume its practice and importance. They describe baptisms and correct mistaken notions about it. They ascribe a number of meanings to baptism, from death and resurrection to

---

[2]G. R. Beasley-Murray, *Baptism in the New Testament* (London: Macmillan, 1962), p. 31.

cleansing from sin, from regeneration to anointing. On top of that, there is a staggering amount of scholarly literature pertaining to baptism in the New Testament, with many competing interpretations of the various texts and of the meaning of baptism itself.

Nevertheless, I firmly believe that there is a discernible thread of common understanding in the New Testament that flows, in turn, into the life and practice of the early church. I also firmly believe that all of us, Catholics and Protestants, Baptists and Reformed, do in fact share "one Lord, one faith, *one baptism*," as Paul says in Ephesians 4:5. We all need to set aside our underlined proof texts, our favorite theologians, and try to meet together in that biblical center from which all our understandings come, and where they can still converge.[3]

John the Baptist and the baptism of Jesus. John the Baptist's baptism of Jesus was the most decisive precursor of Christian baptism and also provides the basic framework in which we understand Christian baptism. All four gospels prominently feature John the Baptist's call to a baptism of repentance in the Jordan. He clearly had an important influence on Jesus, who begins his public ministry as one of John's followers. Most importantly, Jesus himself was baptized by John in the Jordan. We will consider two important questions that help us to understand the relationship of John's baptism and Christian baptism.[4]

1. *What was the nature and meaning of John's baptism?* The origin of John's baptism probably lies in the ritual cleansings of the Jews. It may also have some ties with the practice of proselyte baptism, the washing by which Gentiles became adherents of the Jewish faith. Oscar Cullman affirms with certainty that John the Baptist was involved in this practice of proselyte baptism. If so, "he introduced the revolutionary and—in Jewish eyes—scandalous innovation, that he demanded this baptism not only for the heathen but from all circumcised Jews on reception into messianic fellowship."[5]

---

[3]Two solid classic treatments of baptism in the New Testament are Beasley-Murray, *Baptism in the New Testament;* and Oscar Cullman, *Baptism in the New Testament* (London: SCM Press, 1950), p. 62.

[4]The list of scholarly materials on this issue is immense. For good summaries from differing viewpoints, see G. R. Beasley-Murray, *Baptism;* and James D. G. Dunn, *Baptism in the Holy Spirit* (London: SCM Press, 1970).

[5]Cullman, *Baptism in the New Testament,* p. 62.

In all three Synoptic Gospels and in Acts, John's baptism is called a "baptism of repentance." People came to the Jordan and baptized *themselves* (which was presumably John's practice, since it was the only method of baptism known to Jews of that time). As they were baptized in the Jordan, they gave expression to their repentance, turning away from their sins. This is especially evident in Luke 3 where, following their baptism of repentance, John gives specific instructions to various groups of people, including soldiers and tax collectors. Included in this baptism of repentance was the promise of forgiveness. Mark calls John's baptism a "baptism of repentance for [or into] the forgiveness of sins" (Mk 1:4). The exact relationship between John's baptism and forgiveness is not clear from the texts. We don't know if the forgiveness was tied more to the baptism or to the act of repentance.[6]

Another important aspect of John's baptism is that within this context he proclaimed the coming of the Messiah. "I baptize you with water for repentance, but one who is more powerful than I is coming after me; I am not worthy to carry his sandals. He will baptize you with the Holy Spirit and fire" (Mt 3:11; see also Lk 3:16). This baptism with the Holy Spirit and with fire can best be understood to refer to the double effect of the Messiah's baptism: the gift of the Holy Spirit to those who believe and are obedient, and the fire of judgment (or possibly purification) for those who are not believing and obedient.[7] John declared that he was not the Messiah, and that his baptism was a preparation for and inferior to the messianic baptism. John's baptism pointed to the coming of the one whose sandals he was not worthy to untie.

2. What was the significance of Jesus' baptism by John for our understanding of baptism? It has been traditional, at least from the time of the Reformation, to anchor Jesus' institution of the sacrament of baptism to his Great Commission in Matthew 28:19, "Go therefore and make disciples of all nations, baptizing them." By contrast, the early church fathers commonly anchored the institution of baptism in Jesus' baptism by John. Fredrick Dale Brunner notes that Matthew places the baptismal texts as bookends around his gospel. Jesus ministry begins with

---

[6]For a good summary, see James D. G. Dunn, *Unity and Diversity in the New Testament*, 2nd ed. (Philadelphia: Trinity Press, 1990), p. 152.

[7]For a good summary of this important and difficult text, see Donald A. Hagner, *Matthew 1-13*, Word Biblical Commentary (Dallas: Word, 1993), p. 51.

his baptism by John and ends with his Great Commission to go and baptize the nations. Brunner sees this juxtaposition as significant and gives due place to both. The gifts of God in baptism—the open heaven of justification, the descent of the dove/Spirit, and the declaration of loving sonship—were first given to Jesus at his own baptism by John. Then, at the end of Matthew, they are given to us in our baptism.[8]

It must certainly be significant that all four Gospels begin Jesus' ministry with his baptism by John. What exactly does Jesus' baptism at the Jordan by John reveal about the meaning of baptism?

First, in his baptism Jesus identifies with sinners and begins their liberation. One of the problems posed by Jesus' baptism by John is that John's baptism was a baptism of repentance. How could the sinless one be baptized with a baptism of repentance? That this was a source of some embarrassment in the early church can be seen in Matthew's singular addition of the conversation between John and Jesus concerning Jesus' baptism. John asks, "I need to be baptized by you, and do you come to me?" (Mt 3:14). But Jesus' reply helps us to understand why this had to happen. His baptism by John is to "fulfill all righteousness" (Mt 3:15). This is highly significant. In Matthew's gospel, to "fulfill all righteousness" is the reason for Jesus coming. It explains his incarnation, including his entire life and ministry leading up to his death and resurrection. In Christ and his atoning work the righteousness of God is declared and made manifest (see also Paul in Rom 1). Now this work of fulfilling all righteousness, which began in his incarnation, circumcision, dedication in the temple (and his assumed *bar mitzvah*), continues.

Luke tells us that Jesus was baptized "when all the people were baptized" (Lk 3:21). Luke seems to be emphasizing Jesus' identification with sinners in his baptism by John, which was a baptism of repentance. Jesus, being the sinless one, did not have to repent of sin, but he nevertheless buried himself in the waters of repentance with sinners. In his baptism, Jesus identifies himself as our brother and there begins to assume our sin and guilt. In other words, Jesus' baptism was but one aspect of his total participation in our broken and fallen humanity. It is continuous with his incarnation, anticipates his

---

[8]Frederick Dale Bruner, *Matthew, a Commentary,* vol. 1, *The Christbook* (Dallas: Word, 1987), p. 84.

death and resurrection, and becomes ours through the gift of the Holy Spirit at Pentecost.[9]

Jesus' identification with sinners in his baptism becomes clearer when later he refers to his own death on the cross as his *baptism* (Mk 10:38, 39; Lk 12:50). For Jesus, his baptism by John and his identification with sinners in that act is another step in a baptism, an immersion in human suffering, that ultimately leads to the cross and the resurrection through which he will release us all from sin and death. Jesus' baptism at the Jordan therefore anticipates his death on the cross, his baptism in blood, where he again identifies with sinners by taking the burden of human sin and alienation on himself ("My God, my God, why have you forsaken me?" [Mk 15:34]). Our baptism into Jesus' death and resurrection is possible because Jesus joined the community of sinners, assuming our real broken humanity and not some generic version of it. In the murky waters of the Jordan he committed himself to die on the cross as our brother and our Savior.

In his baptism, Jesus is "ordained" and commissioned for his messianic work on our behalf. But we must also recognize in them a derivative meaning which refers to us and applies to our baptism and our ministry. T. F. Torrance beautifully weaves Christ's baptismal anointing as the Messiah with our anointing as his people. "What happened to Jesus at his baptism . . . was given its counterpart in the church when the Holy Spirit sent by the Father in the Name of the Son came down upon the Apostolic church, sealing it as the people of God redeemed through the blood of Christ, consecrating it to share in the communion of the Father, the Son, and the Holy Spirit, and sending it out into the world united with Christ as his Body to engage in the service of the Gospel."[10] Thus, the Great Commission of Jesus in Matthew 28:19 to "Go into all the world . . . and baptize" becomes the pivot that reaches

---

[9]T. F. Torrance, whose emphasis on the "vicarious humanity of Christ" has done much to renew the emphasis of the early church fathers and Calvin in our day, lays great stress on Jesus' baptism as an essential aspect of Christ's identification with us and our new life in him. He calls attention to *baptisma* as the normal (and possibly newly minted) New Testament term for baptism as opposed to the Greek term *baptismos*, which might have been expected. *Baptisma* refers to the reality signified, pointing to what Torrance calls the "depth dimension, namely our union with Christ, while *baptismos* refers to the rite itself." See Torrance, *Theology in Reconciliation* (Grand Rapids: Eerdmans, 1976), pp. 82-105.
[10]Ibid., p. 86.

back to Jesus' own baptism and forward to the church's one baptism into the one Lord by the one Spirit.

Second, at Jesus' baptism the heavens were opened. It is easy to overlook this little statement contained in all three Synoptic Gospels. Mark's Greek conveys the idea that the heavens were "torn open." The idea is that, in the baptism of his Son, God opens the heavens with his favor and blessing, and showers his love upon the world. In Isaiah 64:1 the prophet cries out, "O that you would tear open the heavens and come down." Well, here God does exactly that. The heavens are torn open at Christ's baptism; God comes down in Christ with grace and favor.

The opening of the heavens also declares to us that in Christ all the spiritual blessings of heaven are now available to all who are united with Christ in baptism. "Wherefore were the heavens opened?" asks Chrysostom. "To inform thee that at *thy* baptism also this is done."[11] At Christ's baptism and at ours, God opens heaven's door to us in grace. We now have peace with God through Christ and in the Spirit, inviting us to commune with him in prayer and worship him in purity of spirit.

Third, at Jesus baptism he is anointed by the Spirit to do God's will. Each of the Gospels says that the Spirit descended upon Jesus like a dove. This, along with the Father's affirmation of sonship points us back to Isaiah 61, where it is prophesied of the messianic servant:

> The Spirit of the Lord GOD is upon me,
>   because the LORD has anointed me;
> he has sent me to bring good news. (Is 61:1)

The Holy Spirit descended on Jesus to mark his ordination and empowerment as God's servant for our salvation. It is only after his baptism (and temptation in the wilderness) that he bursts into ministry. John the Baptist promised that the coming Messiah would "baptize you with the Holy Spirit." Peter preached on Pentecost, "Repent, and be baptized . . . in the name of Jesus Christ . . . and you will receive the gift of the Holy Spirit" (Acts 2:38). So throughout the New Testament, baptism and the gift of the Holy Spirit belong together.

For us, baptism is God's pledge and gift of the Holy Spirit's presence in our lives and also our ordination and empowerment by the

---

[11]Quoted in Bruner, *Matthew,* p. 89.

Spirit to the ministry of the kingdom. In our baptism we are named as Christians, *Christ*-ians. In explaining why he is called Christ and we are called Christians, the Heidelberg Catechism says that Christ means "anointed one," and we are, by faith, partakers in his anointing (Q and A 32). According to Athanasius, the descent of the Spirit on Jesus at his baptism "was a descent upon us because of His bearing our body; and it happened . . . for our sanctification, that we might share in his anointing."[12]

Finally, the Father voices his approval and sonship. The voice from heaven thunders, "You are my Son, the Beloved; with you I am well pleased" (Mk 1:11). This message carries echoes of Psalm 2, "You are my son; today have I begotten you," which served as such a crucial messianic text for the early church. In the Father's voice we hear both a loving affirmation and a solemn proclamation. The Son is the Father's priceless gift to the world, and in this person everything that God is and everything that God does is now revealed in human flesh. As the voice of God says at Jesus' transfiguration, "Listen to Him!" (Lk 9:35).

If we again follow the principle of identification with Jesus, then the voice speaking at his baptism can also be heard at ours. Jesus was already eternally the Son, but at his baptism, this was affirmed to him and to everyone else. In our baptism the Father also says, "You are my beloved son (or daughter)." Of course, God's affirmation of Jesus' sonship at his baptism and his affirmation of ours is not the same. Jesus was God's only begotten Son. We are God's sons and daughters by his gracious adoption through Jesus Christ, who assumed and transformed our fallen humanity. Still, as the New Testament affirms over and over, we are children of God, we have all the rights and responsibilities of sonship,[13] and by the Spirit we cry with Jesus, "*Abba*, Father." Here we approach the heart of what our baptism means, and we first see it in the baptism of Jesus. In the Jordan's waters Jesus joined the broken and sinful human family. In doing so, we became his brothers and sisters so that the Father's voice at Jesus' baptism also speaks to us.

Some biblical theologians question this connection between Jesus'

---

[12]Quoted in G. W. H. Lampe, *The Seal of the Spirit* (New York: Longmans Green, 1951), p. 6.
[13]I use the more accurate term *sonship* advisedly, since in biblical times only sons received the father's inheritance. Today we understand God's inheritance belongs to all his children.

baptism and ours. The problem is that nowhere (with the possible exception of 1 John 5:6) does any New Testament writer *explicitly* bring together Jesus' baptism and Christian baptism.[14] While we recognize such apparent parallels, and such profound theological connections between the two, why is this connection not made in the Bible itself? One answer may be that Paul and many of the other writers of the New Testament wrote their epistles before the Gospels were written. As baptismal doctrine developed, Jesus' baptism by John gradually assumed a more crucial meaning and role, and was therefore so widely and significantly reported in the Gospels, which are, after all, also deeply theological statements of the meaning of Christ's life.[15]

The whole work of Jesus Christ, his incarnation, baptism, ministry, death, resurrection and ascension, form the matrix of salvation into which we are baptized. His baptism, at which he identified with sinners, was anointed by the Spirit, and was commissioned to do the Father's will of sacrificial redemption, sets forth that total redemptive act which is the foundation of Christian baptism. In our baptism we are united with Jesus who united himself with us sinners in his baptism. In and through our baptism we share in the whole of Christ's "vicarious humanity,"[16] his sonship, his obedient life, his atoning death, his resurrection and his new humanity in communion with the Father.

Baptism in the Epistles and Acts. While we find no systematic explanation of the meaning of baptism in the New Testament, a reading of the Epistles and Acts show that baptism was deeply established in the life and practice of the church even when it was only a few weeks old. That in itself, is a remarkable fact, and it strongly affirms the im-

---

[14]Beasley-Murray, *Baptism*, pp. 64-65.
[15]Speaking of Jesus' baptism, T. F. Torrance writes: "The early Church regarded that, not as Jesus' adoption to be the Son of God, but as the public proclamation of his Sonship, pointing back to his birth from above of the Spirit, to be the Savior of the world, and pointing forward to his death on the Cross when he was to fulfill the whole work of atoning redemption" (*Theology in Reconciliation*, p. 85). Commenting on Torrance, Elmer Colyer says "we have to think 'stereotypically,' holding together as a single yet differentiated reality and event: (1) Jesus' vicarious baptism on our behalf in water and the Spirit at the Jordan, (2) Jesus Christ's baptism in blood in his death and resurrection, and (3) the baptism of the church in Christ's Spirit at Pentecost uniting the church with Christ in his vicarious baptism (in [1] and [2]) in our behalf" (*How To Read T. F. Torrance* [Downers Grove, Ill.: InterVarsity Press, 2001], p. 264).
[16]A term used by T. F. Torrance throughout his writings.

portance of baptism in the New Testament.

One of the most striking features of the New Testament's understanding of baptism is the way in which the term is used almost interchangeably with conversion, regeneration and salvation itself. "This is why, in the New Testament, the same effects are attributed to the sacraments and to the word, or to faith, which is evoked by the word (Jn 17:20; Rom 10:17; Eph 1:13)."[17] When the New Testament strikes the note of baptism, all the overtones of the great chord of God's salvation can be heard.

We will look at the teaching of the Epistles and Acts under seven main themes: (1) Baptism unites us to Christ's death and resurrection; (2) Baptism into Christ involves us in a new society, the church; (3) Baptism operates through faith; (4) Baptism into Christ means the washing away of our sins; (5) Baptism is the sign and seal of our regeneration; (6) Baptism and the gift of the Holy Spirit are inseparable; and (7) Baptism is the circumcision of the new covenant.

1. Baptism unites us to Christ's death and resurrection. Of all that Paul says about baptism, perhaps the most memorable and important are his remarks in Romans 6:1-11, where he identifies baptism as our participation in the death and resurrection of Jesus Christ. "Do you not know that all of us who have been baptized into Christ Jesus were baptized into his death? Therefore we have been buried with him by baptism into death, so that, just as Christ was raised from the dead by the glory of the Father, so we too might walk in newness of life" (Rom 6:3-

---

[17]Roger Beckwith, "Church and Sacraments in Christian History," in *Evangelical Essays on Church and Sacraments,* ed. Colin Buchanan (London: SPCK, 1972), p. 25: "Thus regeneration comes through the word of faith in John 1:12f; James 1:18; 1 Peter 1:23-25, and through baptism in John 3:5; Titus 3:5. The gift of the Spirit comes through faith in Gal. 3:2, 14; Eph. 1:13, and through baptism in Acts 2:38. Remission of sins and a clean heart come through faith in Acts 13:38f; 15:9, and through baptism in Acts 2:38; 22:16, Eph. 5:26; Col. 2:12f. A share in Christ's death and resurrection comes through faith in Col. 2:12 and through baptism in the same passage and in Rom. 6:3-11. The putting on of Christ and of sonship comes through faith in John 1:12; Gal. 3:26, and through baptism in Gal. 3:27. Salvation comes through faith in Eph. 2:8, and through baptism in Tit. 3:5, I Peter 3:21. Fellowship with God in the church comes through the word in 1 John 1:3, and through holy communion in 1 Cor. 10:14-22. It is noteworthy how often both kinds of teaching occurs in the same book, and even in the same passage (Acts 2:39; 19:4f, Gal. 3:26; Col. 2:12f). When word and sacrament are viewed as a unity, as in the New Testament, the same effect can be attributed to both without contradiction and without difference in meaning, and this is what is evidently happening in the passages listed above."

4). While this is probably the fullest and deepest statement of the meaning of baptism in the New Testament, it is certainly not the simplest.

In the immediate context of this passage Paul is dealing with a moral question. Some people evidently believed that since "grace abounded" (Rom 5:20) over all their sins by faith in Jesus Christ, they could go on to sin with impunity. They could "continue in sin in order that grace may abound" (Rom 6:1) Nonsense! says Paul. Why not? Paul answers, "You were baptized into Christ Jesus." Note, Paul's reply is not, "you were saved," "you believed," or "you were born again," or even, "you have the Holy Spirit," but simply, "You were baptized in to Christ Jesus." Within this immediate context, it is important to remember that whatever else Paul says here about baptism, he is answering a practical and an ethical question. He is not constructing a theology of baptism. He is mainly interested in what baptism means in the Christian's daily life, a baptized way of living.

Still, for all the practical force of Paul's argument, he evokes powerful images that shape our understanding of baptism. Paul is talking about water baptism as a rite which fundamentally changes how we act and how we think of ourselves by identifying us with Christ in his death and resurrection.

But what does it mean to be baptized into Christ, and especially into his death?

If the immediate context of the statement is the specific ethical question about continuing to sin, the broader context goes back to chapter 5, where Paul makes the compelling connection between the first and second Adam. Adam represents all humanity in its fallen sinfulness that leads to death. Christ, who is the second Adam, represents all of humanity in their original righteousness and holiness to which he restores them. "If, because of the one man's trespass, death exercised dominion through that one, much more surely will those who receive the abundance of grace and the free gift of righteousness exercise dominion in life through the one man, Jesus Christ" (Rom 5:17).

So when Paul speaks of baptism into Christ Jesus in Romans 6, he is carrying over into it the implications of Christ as the second Adam from chapter 5. Baptism into Christ defines our new corporate identity in Christ, who is the second Adam, the new human. By baptism we are new humans beings in the new Adam. Baptism makes real in our experience and through faith what God *has already done* in his Son, whom he has chosen to be the firstborn of many brothers and sisters in a new creation.

And what does this baptism into Christ's death involve for us? It means our death. "You were baptized into his death" (Rom 6:2). Christ's death was a historical event that he alone experienced and accomplished. But his death on the cross is also the central event of human history. In his death and resurrection the tectonic plates of history shifted, and there was a seismic shift in world power. Where once death reigned through sin, now life reigns in Jesus Christ. Where once humans existed under the domination of the powers of evil, they now exist under the reign of Christ. When Paul says that we are baptized into his death, he means that we are baptized into this new reality, this historical event and everything that his death has accomplished in the disarming of the powers and the release of the captives from the prison of the tomb.

In the very next verse Paul deepens the imagery, "Therefore you have been *buried* with him by baptism into death." As Jesus' burial was the last step of his dying—"crucified, dead, and buried," as the Apostles' Creed says—so our burial in baptism is the true mark of our absolute death to the old life of sin and death. Behind Paul's vivid language of burial likely rests the powerful symbolism of immersion, our "drowning" in the water of baptism. Death marks the end of a life—in this case, life under the domain of sin. Christ's death on the cross marks the end of sin's grip on humanity. Because we are baptized into Christ's death, we now must consider ourselves "dead to sin and alive to God in Christ Jesus" (Rom 6:11).

But Paul does not leave Jesus or us in the grave. He adds the obvious conclusion that as Jesus was raised from the dead, "so we too might walk in newness of life" (6:4). Paul does not clearly state here that we rise with Christ *in baptism* as we are buried with him in baptism. It is safe to assume, and most commentators agree, that Paul is continuing the idea of baptism here. This is especially borne out if we compare Romans 6 with Colossians 2:11-12, where Paul clearly links death *and* resurrection to baptism, with almost the same words as he uses here. Perhaps one point Paul wanted to make in Romans is that our death with Christ in baptism is not quite the same as our resurrection with Christ in baptism. We experience our death in Christ every day as we respond to Jesus' invitation to "take up your cross and follow me." But our resurrection, and with it the restoration of all things, lies in the future. What is most evident about our lives now is that we live under the shadow of the cross; but even there, because we are united with Christ in baptism, we live in the joy and freedom of Christ's resurrection and "walk in newness of life" (Rom 6:4).

While we might like Paul to spell out a little more exactly what he means by our being baptized into Christ's death and buried with him in baptism, he certainly presents it as a defining moment in the life of Christians. It determines who we are and how we ought to live.

It is also important to see how Paul links our death and resurrection with Christ in baptism with the renunciation of sin. We do not renounce sin as a secondary act, after we are baptized, or merely in response to our baptism. Baptism and renunciation of sin are all part of the same reality, which is why many ancient baptismal liturgies include the renunciation of the devil and all his works. Baptism marks a decisive turning away from sin and the devil, and a turning to Jesus Christ who died and rose again for us. Our baptism into Jesus Christ marks our movement from the kingdom of darkness and death into the kingdom of light and life. To go on with a life of careless sin is a contradiction of our baptism, and a contradiction of our new identity in baptism.

2. Baptism into Christ involves us in a new society, the church. In the New Testament, baptism not only defines our personal identity by uniting us with Jesus Christ; it also defines our social identity. We become members of a new community called the body of Christ. This community sets aside all human divisions and hierarchies, and places everyone on equal footing under the Lord Jesus Christ.

In Galatians, Paul most clearly describes this new community in relation to baptism. Here Paul debates the so-called Judaizers, Jewish Christians who were advocating that in addition to faith in Christ they needed to follow the law of Moses, with a particular emphasis on circumcision. By insisting on circumcision even for Gentile Christians, they were asserting that the gospel was not enough, the law of Moses also had to be obeyed.

At the heart of his letter to the Galatians, Paul answers this threat to the faith. The Mosaic law, he says, was only a guardian, or tutor, until Christ came. But now that faith has come, we are no longer subject to a disciplinarian, for in Christ Jesus we are all children of God through faith. "As many of you as were baptized into Christ have clothed yourselves with Christ. There is no longer Jew or Greek, there is no longer slave or free, there is no longer male and female; for all of you are one in Christ Jesus. And if you belong to Christ, then you are Abraham's offspring, heirs according to the promise" (Gal 3:27-29).

Again we meet the term "baptized into Christ." But whereas in Romans 6, Paul used the analogy of death and resurrection, here he uses the analogy of clothing: in baptism we are clothed with Christ. It is possible that this analogy comes from the practice that we know from the first century but cannot prove was present in the New Testament church, that at baptism a person would strip off the old clothes, step into the waters of baptism, and emerge to put on a new set of clothes.[18] Whether or not this is what Paul had in mind, the image is still vivid. In baptism we put off the old self like dirty clothes, and put on a new self. We dress ourselves up as Christ, for we are now identified with him.

Paul quickly adds that this new wardrobe places us in a new social reality as well. In this new society there is no longer "Jew or Greek . . . slave or free . . . male or female . . . for all of you are one in Christ Jesus" (Rom 3:28). It is important to note that Paul is not merely talking about the fact that we are members of a new church, or that we all share in a common belief. Baptism defines a new social reality. To live within the traditional social boundaries and hierarchies would be to deny our baptismal identity.

Many commentators regard this verse as a part of an early Christian baptismal liturgy. It is repeated in other letters of Paul with slight variations (see 1 Cor 12:13; Col 3:11; 1 Cor 7:17-28). So we can imagine candidates for baptism either saying or being told at the time of their baptism that this rite marked their entry into a new social order in which all the old hostilities and divisions are gone. There is also some evi-

---

[18]Richard Longenecker, *Galatians*, Word Biblical Commentary (Dallas: Word, 1990), p. 156.

dence that it was used to express the new Christian ideal in exact opposition to the three benedictions with which a devout Jew began his
prayers every day: "Blessed be He that did not make me a Gentile . . .
a slave . . . a woman."[19] Christ, and more particularly Christian baptism, strips all this away like old clothes. It is not circumcision with its
racial and sexual limitations that defines us; it is baptism. In baptism
we are now one community in Christ—Jew and Gentile, slave and free,
male and female. Baptism not only creates a new identity of the individual Christian, but it places him or her into a community. This new
community of the baptized functions in a radically different way than
any human community.

   3. *Baptism operates through faith.* Another important aspect of the
preceding text in Galatians is the way it closely links faith and baptism:
"For in Christ Jesus you are all children of God *through faith.* As many
of you as were *baptized* into Christ have clothed yourselves with
Christ" (Gal 3:26-27). The same juxtaposition between baptism and
faith is found in Colossians 2:12 where Paul says, "When you were buried with him in baptism, you were also raised with him through faith."
Both these texts show that Paul can use the words Christ, faith and
baptism almost interchangeably, and everywhere it must be assumed
that baptism works hand in hand with faith.

   As Richard Longenecker warns, however, baptism and faith are not
synonymous. Baptism is not just another way of believing. Nor should
they be confused with each other, as though "baptism serves the same
function as faith and so makes faith unnecessary, or conversely faith
serves the same function as baptism and therefore makes baptism unnecessary."[20] Faith does not make me a child of God in Christ. I receive
that dignity by God's gracious adoption in Jesus Christ. Faith simply
recognizes and trusts that this is who I am by God's act of grace in
Christ his Son. As Beasley-Murray puts it,

   The significance of baptism is the *objective fact* to which it witnesses, the
   historic event of redemption and the present gift that it makes possible,
   embraced through faith in that God who acted and yet acts. Through
   such an alliance of faith and baptism, Christianity is prevented from

---

[19]Ibid., p. 157.
[20]Ibid., p. 156 (italics mine).

evaporating into an ethereal subjectivism on the one hand and from hardening into a fossilized objectivism on the other. The two aspects of Apostolic Christianity are preserved in faith-baptism.[21]

Faith functions in relationship to baptism in exactly the same way it functions in salvation. In baptism faith accepts the gift of union with Christ with a believing heart.

4. Baptism into Christ means the washing away of our sins. The most obvious symbolic meaning of baptism is washing. When Ananias is about to baptize Paul, he says, "And now why do you delay? Get up, be baptized, and have your sins washed away, calling on his name" (Acts 22:16). As water washes our bodies clean, so the water of baptism cleanses us from the filthy stains of sin. Here we must also note that the water of baptism is linked to the blood of Christ. It is the blood of Christ that cleanses us from sin so that baptismal cleansing has as its basis the once-for-all cleansing that Christ accomplished on the cross.

Right from the beginning, in the baptism of John the Baptist, remission of sins was associated with baptism (Mk 1:4). And of course, Jesus' other "baptism," the baptism of his death on the cross as he refers to it in Mark 10:38, won for us the complete remission of our sins. On Pentecost, the thousands of converts at Peter's great sermon were told that they must be baptized in the name of Jesus "so that your sins may be forgiven" (Acts 2:38). Throughout the New Testament baptism is the sign and seal of the washing away of sin.

Because baptism signifies the washing away of our sins, it also calls us to a new way of life. We must not jump back into the mud like a newly washed puppy. Paul argues that the Corinthians cannot live like their pagan neighbors precisely because in baptism they were "washed" and "sanctified" (1 Cor 6:11). In the same way Peter and the writer of Hebrews use baptism as an "appeal to God for a good conscience" (1 Pet 3:21; see also Heb 10:22). Peter even says, "baptism . . . saves you," but not as "the removal of dirt from the body, but as an appeal to God for a good conscience, through the resurrection of Jesus Christ" (1 Pet 3:21). When Peter says that baptism saves you, he is not talking merely about the rite itself, but identification with Christ's new

---

[21]Beasley-Murray, *Baptism*, p. 153.

humanity that baptism signifies and seals. Since baptism is a sign and seal of our cleansing from sin, not only at the moment of baptism but all through our lives, it serves as a potent and immediate appeal before God for a clear conscience and is a constant reminder of our calling to live a godly life. Christ won my forgiveness on the cross. My baptism so declares it and calls me to live the baptized life.

Of course, baptism in and of itself does not automatically confer forgiveness. Paul compares the Corinthians to the Israelites who were "baptized into Moses in the cloud and in the sea" (1 Cor 10:2). Yet they were "struck down in the wilderness" (v. 5). His point to the Corinthians is that they cannot presume on their baptism. It does not guarantee their salvation. It is only baptism coupled with faith and obedience that truly assures our hearts of salvation. Baptism points us to Christ, awakens our faith, and stimulates us to obedience. Calvin wonderfully captures the profound interrelationship of baptism, faith and obedience:

> We must realize that at whatever time we were baptized, we are once for all purged for our whole life. Therefore . . . we ought to recall the memory of our baptism and fortify our mind with it, that we may always be sure and confident of the forgiveness of sins. . . . For Christ's purity has been offered to us in it; his purity ever flourishes; it is defiled by no spots, but buries and cleanses away all our defilements.[22]

Christ alone cleanses us, but our baptism is his own seal of that cleansing, giving us his assurance of it and calling us to faith and obedience.

5. *Baptism is the sign and seal of our regeneration.* In the New Testament, baptism is also a sacrament of regeneration or rebirth. In Titus 3:5 Paul calls baptism "the water of rebirth," and in John 3:5 Jesus speaks of being "born again by water and the Spirit." (Some also add 1 Peter 1:3-5, "a new birth into a living hope," on the basis of the whole epistle being an extended baptismal instruction.) The crucial question is the exact relationship between water baptism and regeneration by the Holy Spirit. Is baptism merely a particularly apt and graphic way of expressing what it means to be born again, does baptism in some sense effect our regeneration, or is there some other way of under-

---

[22]John Calvin *Institutes* 4.15.3.

standing the relationship? Is there a middle way?

It seems odd to many Protestant evangelicals to think of baptism and regeneration in such close proximity.[23] They tend to think of regeneration as a personal spiritual event that takes place when they believe, while baptism is the public and sacramental sign and seal of that regeneration. It seems to me that it is perfectly legitimate, from all that the New Testament has to say about baptism, to see a strong relationship between baptism and regeneration without identifying the two.

It might be helpful to think of it this way: regeneration has both cosmic and personal levels. On the cosmic level it points to the new creation that God has established in Christ, and into which he desires to include everyone and everything: "Through him God was pleased to reconcile to himself *all things* . . . making peace through the blood of the cross" (Col 1:20). On the personal level, regeneration involves my personal participation by faith in that new creation: "So if anyone is in Christ, there is a new creation" (2 Cor 5:17). In that moment of my participation by faith and baptism in the new creation in Christ, I am born again into that new life. I become part of that new creation. Being personally born again also entails that I begin to live the new life into which I have been born from above. Regeneration begins with God's great act of giving rebirth to his creation through Christ, then it involves my personal experience of being born again, not by some particular experience, but by simply receiving by faith the gift of the new creation. Baptism bridges these two levels of regeneration.

6. Baptism and the gift of the Holy Spirit are inseparable. In the New Testament baptism and the gift of the Holy Spirit are almost always found together. Jesus himself received the Spirit when he was baptized,

---

[23]There have been those (mainly Roman Catholics, some Anglicans and Orthodox, and, interestingly, Abraham Kuyper [a Dutch Calvinist]) who say that baptism brings about regeneration, a position that has been called "baptismal regeneration." Those whom the church baptizes are to be regarded as born-again people, such is the regenerating power of baptism. Evangelical Protestants react against such a direct connection between baptism and regeneration. In direct contrast, they often make a distinction between the merely baptized person and the truly "born-again Christian," by which they mean a person whose life has truly been converted and transformed by the Holy Spirit, which can be demonstrated in some experience. Most Baptists demand of the person baptized a testimony of faith and evidence of regeneration and sanctification before baptism. For them, baptism is the sign of a regeneration that has *already* taken place.

and John the Baptist prophesied of him that he would baptize with the Holy Spirit. In Acts, which we shall discuss more fully below, the gift of the Holy Spirit is almost always connected with baptism.

In a number of key passages, Paul also ties the gift of the Holy Spirit with baptism. He often links the baptismal washing with the work of the Holy Spirit in the same breath. In Titus 3:5, Paul speaks of the "water of rebirth *and* the renewal of the Holy Spirit." In 1 Corinthians 6:11, he writes, "But you were washed, you were sanctified, you were justified in the name of the Lord Jesus Christ *and* in the Spirit of our God." In 1 Corinthians 12:13 the link appears again, "For in the one Spirit we were all baptized into one body—Jews or Greeks, slaves or free—*and* we were all made to drink of one Spirit."

What exactly is the relationship between baptism and the Holy Spirit? In some traditions (Roman Catholic and Orthodox) the relationship is so close that the Holy Spirit is sacramentally conferred at baptism or at confirmation (often through the laying on of hands or anointing with oil). In other traditions (especially among the Pentecostals) the real focus is not so much on baptism itself, but on the gift of the Holy Spirit, often in an ecstatic experience entirely separate from baptism. In the Heidelberg Catechism from the Reformed tradition, the deep connection between baptism and the Holy Spirit is always present but never fully explained: "Christ has appointed the outward washing with water, and has joined therewith this promise that I am washed with his blood and Spirit" (Q and A 69). All six of the catechism's questions and answers on baptism refer to the work of the Holy Spirit.

One clear conclusion that we should draw from these biblical passages is that the Holy Spirit is the one who accomplishes in our hearts and souls those things that baptism signifies—our incorporation into Christ, our cleansing from sin and our sanctification. Baptism itself cannot incorporate us into Christ, wash us of our sins or regenerate us. But that does not mean that baptism and the gift of the Holy Spirit are separate entities, running on different tracks. God promises his Holy Spirit in conjunction with our baptism to bring all the gifts and graces of Christ into our human experience. To suppose that at baptism God directly confers the Holy Spirit on people errs in making the Spirit captive to human actions. The Holy Spirit is free as the wind "that blows where it wills" (Jn 3:8), and cannot be captured by sacramental rites. On the other hand, God promises his grace *and Holy Spirit* in baptism. It is not an empty sign, but as a sacrament, it carries with it that which it symbolizes.

How can we understand the gift of the Holy Spirit in baptism, avoiding the instrumental understanding on one side and the purely symbolic on the other? The book of Acts can be instructive in understanding the relationship between baptism and the Holy Spirit. While the baptism and the gift of the Holy Spirit are always closely related in Acts, Luke describes various sequences in which this happens. The Holy Spirit may be given after baptism (as to the Samaritans in Acts 2:38; 8:15), before baptism (as to Cornelius in Acts 10:44-48) and with baptism (as to Paul in Acts 9:17-18, and the Ephesians in Acts 19:5-6). There is no invariable formula precisely because the Holy Spirit is not controlled by human actions. Nevertheless, the apostles and the early church expected baptism and the gift of the Holy Spirit to be powerfully interconnected. Edmund Schlink's comment is apropos:

> Even though the act of Baptism and the gift of the Holy Spirit do not coincide in time, according to the reports of Acts, they are so intimately related that the baptized cannot remain without the effects of the Spirit and the one filled with the Spirit cannot remain without Baptism. Even though the Spirit is not in every case given to the believer *through* Baptism, He is nevertheless given in a necessary association *with* Baptism.[24]

In 2 Corinthians 1:21-22 Paul adds another term to the relationship of the Holy Spirit and baptism: "But it is God who establishes us with you in Christ and has anointed us, by putting his *seal* on us and giving us his Spirit in our hearts as a first installment." Similarly, in Ephesians 1:13-14, Paul says, "In [Christ] you also, when you had heard the word of truth, the gospel of your salvation, and had believed in him, were marked with the *seal* of the promised Holy Spirit; this is the pledge of our inheritance toward redemption as God's own people, to the praise of his glory." What is this seal with which believers are marked and by which they are promised the Holy Spirit? Is baptism the seal, or is the

---

[24]Edmund Schlink, *The Doctrine of Baptism* (St. Louis: Concordia, 1972), p. 65.

seal merely a metaphor for the gift of the Spirit? While the opinion of scholars is mixed, often according to their theological tradition, many have come down on the side of identifying baptism as the seal of the Spirit,[25] and I would agree. In these texts Paul seems to give a brief but sweeping description of the entire process of the believer's initiation into Christ—from conversion, to faith, to baptism and the reception of the Spirit. If this is the case, then we have another indication of the close relationship of baptism and the gift of the Holy Spirit in which baptism and the Holy Spirit's activity in the life of the believer function together as a seal or guarantee of their future inheritance. In baptism, Christians are sealed; that is, they are marked with the sign that they are God's property, and the Holy Spirit affirms that truth in their hearts and lives.

It is clear from this brief overview of the New Testament that baptism and the gift of the Holy Spirit belong together. The gift of the Spirit may not always coincide in time with baptism, but the two cannot be divorced from one another. It is always water *and* the Spirit.

7. Baptism is the circumcision of the new covenant. In Colossians 2:11-12 Paul brings together baptism and circumcision in such a way that they seem closely related, if not successive, signs of God's covenant: "In him also you were circumcised with a spiritual circumcision, by putting off the body of the flesh in the circumcision of Christ; when you were buried with him in baptism, you were also raised with him through faith in the power of God, who raised him from the dead." This text has been a battleground for exegetes. Some insist that Christ's "circumcision" here only refers to his death, and that Paul does not introduce the idea of baptism until verse 12. Others see Paul as referring to Christ's death as the "circumcision of Christ" in the same sense as Christ's death was his "baptism" (Mk 10:38). In this case, Christ's death is the true circumcision, and the fulfillment of the meaning of circumcision in the old covenant, the stripping away of the sinful flesh. When Paul talks about the circumcision of Christ as his death, he means, according to Michael Green, that "this was no partial and ritual setting aside of evil . . . by removing the foreskin; but rather a total and

---

[25]See especially Geoffrey William Hugo Lampe, *The Seal of the Spirit* (London: SPCK, 1967), pp. 46-63.

actual victory over evil itself through the cross."[26] The cross was Christ's real circumcision *and* it was his real baptism, as he himself referred to it. Since Paul brings baptism and circumcision so closely together in Christ, we can also understand him to correlate them in our lives as well. "So it is very natural for Paul in this passage to draw together the covenant marks of circumcision and baptism and to relate them both to the supreme events from which they derive their meaning and efficacy, the work of Jesus on the cross at the mid-point of redemption history."[27] We now participate in that circumcision of Christ's death through the new covenant sign of baptism.

The major problem with this line of thought, however, is that Paul is battling the "Judaizers" who insist on continuing the practice of circumcision for Gentile believers, and Paul refused to bow to their demand. But it was not because circumcision had no enduring significance. Paul clearly shows its *spiritual* significance in Colossians 2:11. He refused to allow the continuation of actual circumcision because it ultimately meant salvation by the works of the law (see Gal 2—4). So it is quite in line with Paul's thinking that while baptism superceded circumcision as the covenant sign, the two still have a deep spiritual and metaphorical connection.

Baptism in Acts. In Acts, the sequel to his Gospel, Luke follows the storm track of the gospel as it breaks out across the world. He tells us the story of how the ministry of Christ is continued in and through his church in the power of the Holy Spirit. By its very nature Acts does not so much offer us a theology of baptism as a description of the practice of baptism in the apostolic church. Luke weaves the characteristics of New Testament baptismal practice into the story of the church's spread to "the ends of the earth" (Acts 1:8).

Acts displays several more distinctive features of baptism in the New Testament. First, baptism and conversion are closely linked in Acts, so that people are baptized as soon as possible after conversion. In a surprising number of cases baptism is the very first thing done to new converts. While in the church today great care is often taken to in-

---

[26]Michael Green, *Baptism: Its Purpose, Practice, and Power* (London: Hodder and Stoughton, 1987), p. 87.
[27]Ibid.

struct candidates for baptism and to discern whether their conversion is authentic by its fruits in their life, in Acts baptism takes place quickly and, it seems, with little or no preparation.

One reason for this was undoubtedly the rapid advance of the church. Philip, for example, converted the Ethiopian eunuch while he was on his way home from Jerusalem (Acts 8:27-40). Nobody was going to provide for his baptism in the palace of Queen Candace of Ethiopia. In many cases of conversion and baptism there was no infrastructure for instruction and no church organization to receive candidates. We find that as the church matured into the first and second centuries, more time and care was taken in the instruction of baptismal candidates.

Still, we have to wonder whether this quickness to baptize didn't have something to do with the theology of baptism that Luke and the apostles held. Certainly baptism was closely tied to conversion, the moment of belief in Christ. The closer the event of baptism was to the actual conversion, the more impact it might have on the new believer. But the quickness of baptism also says something about its importance and its meaning. At his or her baptism in the name of Jesus, the new believer both confessed the name of Christ and invoked the name of Christ. It is this relationship with the Savior, the Lord, which is the heart of baptism for Luke in Acts. To understand the meaning of baptism in Acts we have to look beyond the rite itself to the binding relationship to Christ that it signified. The old life is over, its practices renounced, and a new Lord has taken his place in the convert's life. If baptism were not so important, it could wait. As soon as a person believes, he or she is baptized because baptism is the mark of conversion, the seal of identity, the incorporation of the convert into Jesus Christ. Because it was so vitally important in the apostolic church, it had to be done as soon as possible.

Second, another rather surprising element in several accounts of baptism in Acts is the baptism of entire households (Cornelius, Acts 11:14; Lydia, 16:15; the Philippian jailer, Acts 16:31; and Crispus, Acts 18:8). Modern readers of the New Testament tend to be unprepared for this phenomenon of household baptism, and it has therefore been the source of much controversy.[28] Baptists tend to minimize its importance, while advocates of infant baptism want to find in it a clear example of paedobaptism in the New Testament. The issue is not really the baptism of infants and children because we do not know for a fact whether they were included in the "household," though they certainly may have been. At any rate, these household baptisms seem strange to our modern understanding of faith and conversion that places such importance on individual decision. The households likely included not only family but also slaves and others who were regarded as under the authority or patronage of the person who was the main focus of conversion. Did every one of these people in the household give a personal confession of their faith in Christ? We don't know, though some would insist they had to for their baptism to be valid. The important issue in these household baptisms, then, is the sociology of salvation that they imply.

We cannot understand this phenomenon of household baptism apart from appreciating the underlying Jewishness of the whole New Testament. In the Jewish way of thinking, one's relationship to God is not merely individual, but social. It naturally includes the household. In the Jewish mindset, God works as he has always worked, according to the social structures he himself creates and blesses—clan, household and family. It is interesting that in many mission situations today where Christianity encounters cultures where the social structures of the family and the clan are deeply imbedded, baptism often involves whole groups. The chief, the head of the clan, or the family head becomes a believer, and all those under his authority (usually) follow. Rather than seeing this as an aberration from the normative individual response to the gospel (in Western culture), Acts suggests that we should see it as the way in which God by his Spirit naturally works through the social structures he has created.

Finally, we find little indication in Acts of *how* people were baptized. While some insist that the word *baptize* means "to immerse," scholars point out that it is clearly used to describe other modes in Greek. Given the astonishing variety of places and times of baptism, for example, it would stretch credulity to imagine that a deep pool would be available on every occasion in every house. A good case can be made for baptism by both immersion and affusion, or pouring. Ultimately, it seems to

---

[28]See chapter eight, "Infant Baptism."

me, the mode is not as important as the meaning. It is getting from one side to the other, not the depth of the water that counts.[29]

SUMMARY

One cannot come away from even a cursory reading of the New Testament without sensing the extraordinary importance of baptism for the Christian faith. Faith, salvation and baptism are so deeply interwoven that they are virtually indistinguishable. Baptism, with its roots in the Old Testament, is the sacrament that marks our incorporation into Christ through which we are also heirs of all the benefits of his redeeming work. T. F. Torrance celebrates the close identification of Christ with the church's act of baptism: "Thus whenever the church in obedience to the command of Christ baptizes specific individuals with water in the name of the Father and the Son and the Holy Spirit, it believes that Christ himself is present baptizing with his Spirit, acknowledging and blessing the action of the Church as his own, fulfilling in the baptized what he has already done for them in the fruit of his finished work."[30]

---

[29]In the practice of baptism today, however, I think its sacramental nature is best highlighted by using as much water as possible according to the circumstances. There is an exciting return to immersion among non-Baptist churches, even for the baptism of infants and young children. I believe that immersion, where possible, is the best means to express the meaning of baptism.

[30]Torrance, *Theology in Reconciliation*, p. 87.

7

A Theology and Practice of Baptism for Today

We thank you, Almighty God, for the gift of water.

Over it the Holy Spirit moved

in the beginning of creation.

Through it you led the children of Israel

out of their bondage in Egypt into the land of promise.

In it your Son Jesus received the baptism of John

and was anointed by the Holy Spirit as the Messiah,

The Christ, to lead us, through his death

and resurrection, from the

bondage of sin into everlasting life.

BOOK OF COMMON PRAYER, HOLY BAPTISM,
PRAYER OF THANKSGIVING OVER THE WATER

A few years ago I worked on a committee to produce a new baptismal liturgy for my own Reformed denomination. It was instructive to all of us that as our work advanced, we necessarily became involved in deep discussions of all the main points of Christian doctrine. The meaning of baptism is so central to the Christian faith that if I were to fully explain the meaning and implications of baptism to a new convert, she would have a rich and deep understanding of the whole Christian faith and life from that discussion alone.

If we have learned anything from our look at the biblical background of baptism, it is that to talk about baptism is to talk about salvation. Baptism is the prism through which all the light of God's grace in Jesus Christ passes. If baptism is so central to the Christian faith, and if it is the focal point of so many basic Christian truths, we can understand why it's also a flash point for controversy. At the same time, if we hope to come to deeper unity in the faith and in the church, then certainly one fruitful place to begin is in our understanding of baptism. In baptism our journey of faith begins, and as those sharing "one Lord, one faith, one baptism," we must try to walk that journey together.

In order to build a common understanding of baptism, I will begin with a definition and then proceed to explain its component parts.

> In baptism, God, by water and the Spirit,
>   incorporates us into the new creation in his Son, Jesus Christ,
>   and joins us to Christ's body, the church;
> to this gift we respond in faith
>   and seek to shape our lives more and more to this new identity we
>   have in Christ.

This definition highlights several important truths about baptism. While I treat some of the same concepts here as in the last chapter on the Bible's teaching on baptism, in this chapter I will deal with them from a more theological, ecclesiastical and practical perspective.

1. The central action of baptism belongs to God. This, it seems to me, is fundamental to any understanding of baptism that rings true to the language of the Bible and the witness of the church through the centuries. Of course, we have stumbled over this issue before; and it continues to divide Christians regarding baptism and the sacraments in general. On the one side there are those who affirm that God acts through the sacraments, though there is great disagreement as to exactly how. On the other side are those who argue that sacraments function only as vehicles of human action and human faith. I wonder whether we can all agree, at least, that it is a matter of both God's action *and* human faith. To bridge this sacramental divide we will need to make sure that neither side of the equation, God's activity or ours, is lost. Still, one or the other must have priority.

This issue first surfaced in a division between factions during the Reformation, and it is important to have a grasp of this history to understand the profound issues involved which still divide Christians today.[1] To put it all too briefly, Luther and Calvin virtually agreed that in the sacraments God acted through visible signs and seals for our faith to grasp. Zwingli and others believed that the sacraments are mainly expressions of human faith in God's actions through Christ. For Calvin and Luther, baptism is about what God is doing and promising to us; for Zwingli, baptism is about what humans are doing and promising to each other and to God.

John W. Riggs summarizes the way major Reformers agreed on the priority of divine activity in baptism:

> What we have seen in Luther, Zwingli and Calvin studies is that each of these Reformers came to distinguish baptism itself, grounded in God's immutable promise of grace, from the proper appropriation of baptism, which always inheres with acceptance of that promise. [Calvin, however], holding these two issues together, demands that baptism, as God's *testimony* which evokes and nourishes faith, must take priority over baptism as *appropriating* God's baptismal promise through public initiation into the mysteries of Christ by public initiation into the community.[2]

Zwingli, in spite of the fact that he desperately wanted to maintain the priority of God's activity in baptism, ended up with the Anabaptists by emphasizing human over divine activity in baptism. In his "Commentary on True and False Religion" (1525), he characterized baptism mainly as a sign of obligation, resorting to an appeal to the ancient meaning of *sacramentum* as a soldier's pledge or oath. He saw baptism as a confession of faith by which the baptized persons obligated themselves to the Lord in the presence of the congregation. This is at the heart of Zwingli's radical reinterpretation of the sacraments, which set him at odds with the church fathers, the medieval scholastics

---

[1]For a good summary of these historical developments, see John W. Riggs, "Reformed Thoughts: On Baptism and a Rite of Christian Initiation," *Reformed Liturgy and Music* 19, no. 4 (1985): 179-83; and Edmund Schlink, *The Doctrine of Baptism* (St. Louis: Concordia, 1972), pp. 97-105.

[2]Riggs, "Reformed Thoughts," p. 181 (italics mine).

and his own contemporaries in the Reformation.[3] Even though he eventually came to see the significance of baptism as a sign of the church by which it designated the baptized person as its member, he still did not recognize any activity of God in and through baptism.

The Anabaptist movement rose within the Zwinglian circle of influence and was built on Zwingli's humanistic scholasticism. Hubmaier, one of the leading Anabaptists following Zwingli, denied that baptism can wash away sins and understood baptism as a human duty and testimony. Thomas Münzer, another leading Anabaptist and follower of Zwingli, wrote, "This water does not confirm or increase faith, as the scholars of Wittemburg [Lutherans] are saying . . . nor does the water save." On the contrary, baptism "is a sign of the fact that one has died to sin and must have died to sin, that one must walk in newness of life, and that one will surely be saved if one conforms to the proper sense of faith through the inner Baptism."[4] The baptism with water and the baptism of the Spirit are thus separated, with water baptism merely confirming the evidence of Spirit baptism, which is always inward and spiritual. While I do not claim that there is a uniform understanding of baptism among Baptists (who by their very nature and church structure affirm strict congregational independence), it's safe to say that this is the view held by the majority of Baptists today.

Roger Beckwith analyzes the Anabaptist insistence on centering baptism in human faith and human action:

> It was not until the rise of the Anabaptists . . . with their insistence that no one is eligible to be baptized until he has already been regenerated by God's Spirit, that the activity of the candidate for baptism became the centre of attention in the sacrament, and began to be stressed in a way that excluded the activity of . . . God himself. The activity which God had traditionally been held to exercise in baptism is now located outside and prior to the sacrament: a new significance was therefore sought for the sacrament and this was found in the activity of the candidate, bearing witness to what God had done through other means.[5]

---

[3]Schlink, *Doctrine of Baptism*, p. 101.
[4]Ibid., p. 102.
[5]Roger Beckwith, "Church and Sacraments in Christian History," in *Evangelical Essays on Church and Sacraments*, ed. Colin Buchanan (London: SPCK, 1972), p. 23.

In a truly biblical and catholic expression of Christianity, God's action always comes before human response. Our salvation in Christ comes by God's act "while we still were sinners" (Rom 5:8). Our election in Christ takes place "before the foundation of the world" (Eph 1:4). God is always the initiator. God's acts then form the basis of the human response of faith and call forth faith. Baptism is another way God has established, alongside the proclamation of the gospel, in which his new creation in Christ is presented and affirmed to us. The new creation is not only proclaimed for our ears to hear and explained for our minds to comprehend; in baptism it is poured over us, and we are inundated in it. In baptism, the very same gospel that comes to us in the word splashes over us by water in a way that especially suits our humanity. In the waters of baptism God solemnly declares: "I have made you new creatures in Christ. I did this before you decided anything; in fact, while you were still sinners Christ died for you." To this proclamation in water of God's gracious and saving act, we are called to respond, both at that moment and all our lives long, with faith and commitment.

Neville Clark speaks for many but certainly not all biblical scholars when he says, "There is little doubt that the New Testament view of baptism is of a rite that is effective rather than merely symbolic. It brings the disciple into union with Christ too deep and realistic for words [to] adequately describe it; it has objective significance."[6] All this reminds us of our earlier general discussion of the sacraments. God has chosen certain physical objects—in the case of baptism, water—to convey the sign and seal of his grace to us. By God's word and promise, baptismal water carries with it the blessings of our incorporation into Christ, our regeneration in him, and our forgiveness from sin. The water of baptism is instrumental in effecting these things in the lives of believers and their children. By calling baptism instrumental I do not mean that baptism guarantees union with Christ, or invariably effects it. I do mean that under the normal circumstances of personal faith we gratefully receive these blessings from God through the instrumentality of the sacrament.

2. *We are baptized by water and the Spirit.* The New Testament itself

---

[6]Neville Clark, *An Approach to the Theology of the Sacraments* (London: SCM Press, 1958), p. 32.

raises the issue of the relationship between baptism by water and the Spirit. John the Baptist declares of Jesus, "I have baptized you with water; but he will baptize you with the Holy Spirit" (Mk 1:8). Yet water baptism does not end when Christ pours out his Holy Spirit on the church. Baptism involves both water and the Spirit, but how?

Water is the sacramental sign, the visible word by which the Holy Spirit, through faith, brings us into union with Christ. Of course, water by itself, even in the setting of the sacrament, has no independent efficacy. In baptism the Holy Spirit uses water to help evoke faith and assurance. Peter called upon the believers on Pentecost to repent and be baptized. "Repent, and be baptized every one of you in the name of Jesus Christ so that your sins may be forgiven; and you will receive the gift of the Holy Spirit" (Acts 2:38). It is remarkable how in this passage repentance or faith, water baptism, forgiveness of sins and the gift of the Holy Spirit are presented as correlative aspects of one's entrance into a relationship with Christ.[7]

Baptism by water and the Spirit are two sides of the same reality. In our baptism by water, the Holy Spirit presents to our faith our union with Christ and all its benefits by sheer grace. But does one have a certain priority over the other? George Hunsinger thinks so: "Water baptism is best understood as the fulfillment of Spirit baptism. Dominically appointed, it is the normal consequence of Spirit baptism. Spirit baptism can be and is (in principle) efficacious without water baptism, but water baptism is not efficacious without Spirit baptism."[8] Again, we see that this relationship of water and the Spirit is parallel to that of the Word and the Spirit. "Both are objective signs; in both cases the Spirit unfolds and applies their meaning, and he effects in believers the reality to which they point."[9]

H. Wheeler Robinson, a prominent Baptist theologian agrees that "believer's baptism is always baptism in the Spirit of which water baptism is the outward expression."[10] In our baptism by water and the Spirit, the regeneration that we have in Christ, our being "born from

---

[7]Sinclair B. Ferguson, *The Holy Spirit* (Leicester, U.K.: Inter-Varsity Press, 1996), p. 195.

[8]George Hunsinger, "Baptism and the Soteriology of Forgiveness," *Call to Worship* 35, no. 3 (2001): 18.

[9]Ferguson, *The Holy Spirit*, p. 198.

[10]Quoted in Beasley-Murray, *Baptism*, p. 277.

above" (Jn 3:3), is declared, demonstrated, promised and sealed to us. T. F. Torrance writes,

> [Regeneration] is sacramentally enacted as an image and likeness of the birth and resurrection of Christ. Our regeneration does not take place at baptism, *or* when we first believe. Our regeneration has already taken place in Christ. It belongs to the peculiar nature of Baptism that it promises us a redemption which has already been accomplished in Christ; and therefore in Baptism the end is given to us in the beginning. . . . When we look into the waters of Baptism we see our faces reflected in it, not very clearly, but very brokenly. In the Sacrament of Baptism we see the image of our regeneration only, as it were "in a glass darkly," in an enigma. It is essentially a sacramental mystery which under the veil of water directs us back to the work of our renewal which has once for all taken place in Christ, and directs us forward to the day when we shall see Jesus face to face and become like Him.[11]

Still, baptism does not effect regeneration, for that can only be accomplished by the Holy Spirit. "It is not, of course, the rite that regenerates" says Torrance, "but in Baptism our regeneration in Christ is declared, and shown forth, and promised: it is *sacramentally* enacted as an image and likeness of the birth and resurrection of Christ."[12] Baptism is the true pledge from God that the person baptized has been born again into the new creation in Christ by the Holy Spirit. But it is like a seed that only germinates when it is nourished in the water of repentance and the sunshine of faith.[13]

3. Baptism is the sign and seal of our incorporation into Christ. In baptism God acts, and what God has done is embodied in Christ. God's answer to the human predicament of sin and death was to join the human race in order to lead humanity back to its true destiny as adopted sons and daughters of God. T. F. Torrance emphasizes the importance of the incarnation in our understanding of baptism:

> While Baptism is usually spoken of only as the Sacrament of our incorporation into Christ, it is ultimately grounded upon the fact that in Jesus

---

[11]T. F. Torrance, *Conflict and Agreement in the Church* (London: Lutterworth, 1960), p. 131.
[12]Ibid.
[13]Michael Green, *Baptism: Its Purpose, Practice, and Power* (London: Hodder and Stoughton, 1987), p. 56.

the Son of God incorporated Himself into our humanity. . . . That is to say, alongside the important fact that Baptism is the Sacrament of the death and resurrection of Christ [the early church] laid down the important fact that Baptism is the Sacrament of Incarnation, the Sacrament of Nativity, as it was sometimes called.[14]

Christ's incarnation, baptism, death and resurrection and, finally, ascension to the right hand of God mark the pathway by which we follow him to our glorious destiny as his people, his body. God comes down to us in Christ, assumes our fallen creatureliness, redeems it and raises it to glory. The work of Christ incarnate is quite simply the action by which God saves the creation.

In our baptism, we are incorporated into Christ, which means that we are given a share in his perfect human life. In that bond of baptism, again, whatever happens to Christ happens to us. In his birth, Christ bound himself to our fallen human nature; in our baptism, we are bound to his glorious new humanity. In his baptism he became the perfect penitent on our behalf, and in doing so he received the Spirit and heard the Father's voice of approval. In our baptism we turn from sin (to which the great traditional renunciations testify) and receive our adoption as God's beloved children. In Christ's full Spirit-anointed human life, he reversed our rebellion by responding perfectly to the Father with love and obedience. In our baptism we receive the renewing power of the Holy Spirit, who calls us and enables us to live a new and obedient life. In his death, Christ bore the penalty for human sin to fulfill God's mercy and justice. In our baptism we die to sin and pass through the gates of death. The baptismal font becomes our coffin. In his resurrection, Christ conquers sin and death and overcomes the powers of evil. In our baptism, we rise to share with him in his new and eternal life which begins in the baptismal waters but which we will fully inherit when he comes again in glory. In his ascension, Christ comes into his rightful place as the firstborn of the new creation at the right hand of God in glory and honor. As baptized people we "sit with him in heavenly places" (Eph 2:6) and reign with him in the true dominion God created us to share with him over all creation (Gen 1:26). In our baptism we are anointed into the anointed One, and we share in all his anointing as prophet, priest and

---

[14]T. F. Torrance, *Conflict and Agreement*, pp. 117-18.

king. Baptism is sometimes called "christening." That, it seems to me, is exactly what happens in baptism—we are christened, we are made Christ-ians, we are identified with Christ.

Baptism is also, therefore, a sacrament of identity. It confers a new identify on us. Who am I? I am a new creature in Christ, sharing in his new humanity, set free from sin and death by his death on the cross, risen with him to eternal life, and ascended with him to the heights of glory and honor. I am not what I appear to be, but my life is "hidden with Christ in God," and when he is revealed, then I too "will be revealed with him in glory" (Col 3:3-4). At Jesus' baptism, the heavens opened, the voice of God spoke, and the Spirit descended. So in our baptism into Christ, heaven opens upon us, God smiles on us, and in his Son says, "You are my beloved sons and daughters." And the Spirit descends to renew us and empower us.

It is commonplace today to emphasize the importance of a positive sense of identity for mental and spiritual health. Apart from the sometimes ridiculous exaggerations of self-esteem, particularly with children (everybody wins at every game, and every attempt at a drawing must be praised as though it were a museum masterpiece), the exaggerations tend to prove the original truth. Our sense of identity plays a key role in our behavior, our psychological health, and our spiritual well-being. Baptism, as a sacrament of identity, says to us every day, you are a son or daughter of God. You are loved. In your identification with Christ, the true and perfect human, God is well pleased with you.

One of the ways the Bible conveys this crucially important sense of identification with and incorporation into Christ is the way in which it speaks of our being baptized in the name of Jesus, or, in Matthew 28:19, "into the name of the Father and of the Son, and of the Holy Spirit." Frederick Dale Bruner points out that "into the name of" comes from the world of banking and means "to the account of," or "into the possession of": "And thus by baptism . . . believers come under new management. They are transferred to a new 'company'. . . they become members of God's own family. . . . That is why baptism is no little thing: it gives God. It is Christendom's formal and effective ceremony of a person's officially becoming a child of God."[15]

---

[15]Frederick Dale Bruner, *Matthew: A Commentary* (Grand Rapids: Eerdmans, 2004), p. 1100.

If there is an *opus operatum* (a finished work) of baptism, it is this: we are united with Jesus Christ in his new humanity. We are baptized into his finished work in which from birth to baptism, from temptation to crucifixion, from death to resurrection, he not only restored us to fellowship with God, but brought about our adoption into God's family, and will finally make us "participants of the divine nature" (1 Pet 1:4).

4. Incorporation into Christ also means incorporation into his body, which is the church. When Luke describes the first great burst of church growth on Pentecost, he says, "So those who welcomed his message were baptized, and that day about three thousand persons were added" (Acts 2:41). Added to what? What is assumed here is clarified in verse 47, that they were added to the new community, the church. In several key passages on baptism, Paul also demonstrates the close connection between baptism and the church. In 1 Corinthians 12:13 he writes, "For in one Spirit we were all baptized into one body—Jews or Greeks, slaves or free." And in Galatians 3:27 he links baptism, being clothed in Christ, and the community or body of Christ in which there is neither Jew or Greek, slave or free, male or female. Clearly, baptism is both incorporation into Christ and the entrance into the church, which is his body. The two are inseparable.

The common concept of the body of Christ is not as clearly understood as we might think, especially in our individualistic culture. In Paul's thinking, Christ is not only an individual person, he is a corporate identity. In 1 Corinthians 12:12 Paul writes, "For just as the body is one and has many members, and all the members of the body, though many, are one body, so it is with Christ." Paul does not write, "so it is with the church" but "so it is with Christ." Since Paul is clearly talking about the life of the church here, we can see how closely Paul holds Christ and his church, or body, together. The church is Christ's corporate identity.

Christ is preeminent. He is "head" of the body (Col 1:18). In baptism we are not baptized into the church first of all, but into Christ, who includes the church, his body. Beasley-Murray makes this point well: "The believer is engrafted into the Body because he is united with Christ in his saving work by the Spirit; the reverse is never contemplated in the New Testament."[16] Still the body is so closely identified with the head that Paul can use the terms *Christ* and *the church* virtually interchangeably.

Consequently, we must always understand baptism in its ecclesial context. Baptism places us in a personal relationship with Christ, since we are baptized into Christ, and it places us at the same time in a corporate relationship with all the other members of the body, all other Christians, both on the local and the universal levels. In our baptism, says Beasley-Murray, "We are called to recognize therefore that a purely private relationship to Christ cannot exist. . . . *Koinonia* is a key term of the Christian life, connoting fellowship in the Holy Spirit with Christ and with his saints, and it takes its rise in baptism to Christ and the Body."[17]

In its practice, the church has not always held these two dimensions of baptism together very well. Among the historic Reformation churches there has sometimes been a tendency to make baptism, particularly the baptism of infants, a family affair rather than a church affair. As a pastor I find myself resisting the requests of families that Pastor so and so, who is the grandfather or the uncle come in to "do" the baptism. Innocent as it may be, it tends to make baptism into a family matter rather than an incorporation into Christ and his church, sending some wrong signals about the meaning of baptism. The same is true, it seems to me, for the practice in some churches of baptism outside the regular worship services of the gathered community.

On the other side of the Reformation, some Baptists and other "free" churches seem to have lost all sense of baptism as membership in the church. Baptism tends to be seen merely as a sign of personal faith, and either membership in the church is not relevant to it, or the church has no category of formal membership. They tend to say that one is baptized into the real and true body of Christ, and not onto the membership rolls of a local church. Strangely, the same churches sometimes demand rebaptism for those whose baptism is deemed not to comply with the specific standards (such as immersion) of their particular church. In this case, they seem to deny any sense of catholicity in bap-

---

[16]Beasley-Murray, *Baptism*, p. 281.
[17]Ibid., p. 282.

tism and focus only on the specific practice of that local church.

Separating baptism and church membership recalls the venerable distinction between the visible and invisible church. There may be a certain truth in this distinction in that the church is both the "invisible" church, that is, the church universal in all times and all places, and the "visible" church, that is, the concrete manifestation of God's people in local congregations today. But we should take care not to escalate a distinction into a divorce. Baptism includes us in both the universal and invisible reality of the church and in its visible, earthly manifestations.

It is no surprise that our current difficulties in coming to a common understanding of the biblical meaning of baptism correspond to the current crisis in ecclesiology.[18] If we don't really know what baptism is we don't really know what the church is either. It seems to me that we will not recover a solid ecclesiology until we recover a solid biblical understanding of baptism, which is our incorporation into the body of Christ. Perhaps, since the sacraments are the classic marks of the true church, along with preaching, we should expect that they will point us toward a better understanding of ecclesiology as well.

Baptism is a visible act by which we are joined with the visible church. As Beasley-Murray puts it, "The church is on earth as well as in heaven . . . and they, the members of the Body, are very visible; bap-

---

[18]Kevin Offner offers a cogent analysis of the ecclesiological crisis with reference to the sacraments. "In my opinion, the deepest divide that separates Christians . . . is between those who understand the 'church' as primarily *invisible* and those who understand 'church' as primarily *visible*.

"On the one hand, a majority of charismatics, Protestant evangelicals, and the many parachurch groups they have spawned, argue for seeing the church first and foremost as *people*. The Church is comprised of those people whom God has saved (and is saving), that is, Christians. . . . Church structure, liturgy, authoritative leadership—and even sacraments—are all negotiable. The primary non-negotiable (besides the authority of the Bible) is the salvation of people.

"On the other hand, Roman Catholics, the Orthodox, and those Protestants in denominations that are self-consciously aligned with Reformation ecclesiology emphasize the visible, sacramental nature of the church. The church is people, yes, but it is *more* than this. The church is an institution, a "thing," the Bride of Christ that is seen and known by its sacraments, liturgy, and authoritative leadership. Christians are not Gnostics, who must always spiritualize the church, rather, the Incarnation assures us that the body and matter are good. God reveals himself to his people not only in the spiritual preaching of Scripture but in the physical presence of the sacraments; and he leads his people not only spiritually from heaven but through his ordained human authorities, who teach and discipline with his authority" ("Two Ways of Understanding the Church," *Re:generation Quarterly* 3, no. 4 [1997]: 11).

tism as a visible act is a fitting mode of representing the action of Christ by his Spirit in constituting the Body of Christ *on earth*. The outward act of baptism, witnessing the outward entry into the Church, should coincide with the baptism of the Spirit *and incorporation of the believer into the Body of Christ.*"[19] That is the ideal, but how it may be understood, communicated and practiced remains one of the most difficult problems for a theology of baptism in the church today.

It seems to me that to try to overcome this apparent tension between the baptism in the Spirit and baptism into the body of Christ by appealing to the purely spiritual nature of baptism and an invisible (elect) church is too radical a solution and must be avoided. This tendency fits the overall bent in many churches today toward a sectarian "pure church" ideal. The church is, however, the *body* of Christ. It exists in the physical world for everyone to see. It is not a merely a concept, but an institutional and physical reality. It is not some perfect, pure and invisible ideal of true believers, but the real and flawed body of Christ that is being sanctified by the Spirit. Paul, after all, called the Corinthians with all their aberrations, disunity and sins "the saints." Are all members of the visible church true believers in Jesus Christ? Of course not. And there is no way of guaranteeing that every baptized person is or will be a true believer in Christ. The wheat and the tares grow together until the harvest in the church as well as in the world (Mt 13:30). Baptism unites us, by water and the Spirit, into the body of Christ that is both visible and invisible, local and universal, at the same time. We presume that all who are baptized are spiritually united with Christ unless and until they, by their unbelief and unrepentant sinfulness, show themselves otherwise to the very end of their lives. Finally, this is a judgment only God can make.

5. Baptism calls forth and builds up our faith. It is everywhere assumed in the New Testament that baptism calls forth faith. Baptism, all by itself, does not confer our incorporation in Christ. Like grace itself, it is always acts "through faith" (Eph 2:8).

As important as faith is to baptism, baptism is not merely a reflection of our own faith commitment. The danger of understanding baptism as an expression of our faith is that we are thrown back on our

---

[19]Beasley-Murray, *Baptism*, p. 284 (italics mine).

own subjective experiences, actions and decisions. The function of faith is precisely to turn us away from depending on our own resources and toward depending on God's grace in Jesus Christ. But if baptism is an expression of the vitality of our faith, we are only left with our own heart's motivations, slippery and fickle as they always are. It is understandable with this view of baptism that people may want to come back again and again for baptism, claiming that in the previous experience they did not really believe.

The New Testament understanding of the relationship of faith and baptism is that we are incorporated into Christ in baptism, and faith responds to it. Baptism is not primarily a response and follow-up to faith; faith is our response to baptism. We believe through and in our baptism. With his strong biblical and Reformed understanding of the vicarious humanity of Christ, T. F. Torrance focuses on the faith and faithfulness of Christ rather than on the faith of the recipient of baptism. "Baptism tells us that in our believing we do not rely on our own faith but on the vicarious faith of Christ which in sheer grace anticipates, generates, sustains, and embraces the faith granted to those who are baptized."[20]

Faith operates in baptism, and in the sacraments generally, in almost exactly the way it operates in relation to the Word of God. The Word is, in a sense, also a physical thing; it is signs and symbols on a page, sound waves heard with our ears. Baptism (and the Lord's Supper) operates in the same way as the signs (words) used in the preaching of the gospel. Through the preached or written word of the gospel, Christ is made known to us through the Holy Spirit. So, through baptism, Christ is also made known. Faith, by the power of the Holy Spirit, accepts the word and the sacrament, believes it and trusts in it. The life of faith (which I understand to include repentance) surrounds baptism. According to Beasley-Murray, "Faith is needful *before* baptism, that Christ and his gospel may be truly confessed in it; *in* baptism, to receive what God bestows; and *after* baptism, in order to abide in the grace so freely given and to work out by that grace what God has wrought within."[21]

---

[20]T. F. Torrance, *The Mediation of Christ* (Grand Rapids: Eerdmans, 1983), p. 100.
[21]Beasley-Murray, *Baptism*, p. 274.

Because baptism is a once-in-a-lifetime event, the response of faith continues on from the moment of baptism. No matter when it takes place, we spend the rest of our lives believing through our baptism. Just as faith receives the gracious gift of baptism in the first place, so faith returns to baptism over and over, taking new strength through it. I have always taken strength from the often-told story about Martin Luther. In the trough of spiritual depression, he would turn to his baptism as a physical sign of God's grace in Christ. "I have been baptized!" he would shout through the dark shroud of doubt and fear. This is a perfectly proper and wonderful way to "use" our baptism. God has given us this physical sign and seal, this landmark on our journey, precisely so that our faith might cling to it. Of course, we are not depending on baptism itself, but on Christ with whom we are united in baptism, and with God's word of promise, which gives baptism its validity. But baptism is a God-given handle by which our faith embraces Christ.

We discover faith's deepest meaning in that through it we take refuge from our own frailty and instability in the unswerving love of God. So baptism is not so much the declaration of our faith as a refuge in Christ's faithfulness, a sign and seal that begins, not in our decisions, but in God's prior decision in Christ. T. F. Torrance, remembering how he taught his daughter to walk, offers this lovely illustration of how God's faithfulness overlaps and under girds our faith: "I can still feel her tiny fingers gripping my hand as tightly as she could. She did not rely on her feeble grasp of my hand, but upon my strong grasp of her hand which enfolded her grasp of mine within it. That is surely how God's faithfulness actualized in Jesus Christ has laid hold of our weak and faltering faith and holds it securely in his hand."[22]

6. Our baptism gives us an identity which shapes our lives. Baptism is not only a spiritual act by which we are identified with Jesus Christ and his body, the church; it is a moral act. In baptism we cross over from death to life, from the dominion of Satan to the reign of God, from slavery to freedom.

We have already seen the power of baptism to shape our ethical lives in Paul's startling response to the assertion of some in the church at Rome that they could presume on God's grace by continuing in a life

---

[22]Torrance, *Mediation of Christ*, p. 93.

of sin: "Do you not know that all of us who have been baptized into Christ Jesus were baptized into his death?" (Rom 6:3). How can a baptized person go on carelessly in sin? In the same way Paul draws out the social ethics of baptism when he says in Galatians 3 that for "as many of you as were baptized into Christ . . . there is no longer Jew or Greek . . . slave or free . . . male or female." Because baptism unites us with Christ, it also redraws the shape of our lives in him.

The earliest liturgies of baptism that we have from the second century show us that this turning away from evil and turning to Christ was a central feature of the baptismal liturgy. In the *Apostolic Tradition* of Hippolytus from around A.D. 215, just before the baptism takes place after an all-night vigil, the bishop applies the oil of exorcism to the candidate. "And when the presbyter takes hold of each one of those who are to be baptized, let him bid him renounce, saying: I renounce thee Satan, and all thy service and all thy works. And when he has said this, let him anoint with the Oil of Exorcism, saying: Let all evil spirits depart from thee."[23] The liturgy of baptism was also a liturgy of exorcism in which demonic power was cast out in the powerful name of Jesus, and the candidate solemnly renounced the devil and all his works. But even more, in baptism, the candidate turned to Christ as to the rising sun, dedicating himself or herself to obedient and loving discipleship. This liturgy of baptism makes it clear that it is not merely a rite of entrance and welcome; through it we become passengers on the ark over the floodwaters destruction (1 Pet 3:20-21), and pass through the sea from slavery to freedom (1 Cor 10:1-2). Baptism marks nothing less than the beginning of the journey to new life.

Francis Ford Coppola's *The Godfather, Part 1*, ends with an unforgettable scene that centers on baptism. Michael Corleone, who has reluctantly taken over the godfather role from his dead father, is in church for his child's baptism. The priest invites him to make his solemn renunciations of the devil and all his works on behalf of the child, to which he responds three times, in words that echo off the walls of the largely empty church, "I renounce them. I renounce them. I renounce them." Graphically interspersed with these renunciations at baptism

---

[23]Max Thurian and Geoffrey Wainwright, eds., *Baptism and Eucharist: Ecumenical Convergence in Celebration* (Grand Rapids: Eerdmans, 1983), p. 7.

are bloody scenes of Michael's *capos* carrying out revenge killings that wipe out a rival "family." The scene is shocking precisely because it reveals exactly what Paul is talking about. In Michael's world of the *Cosa Nostra*, violence and revenge are part of the code by which they live. But these cruel acts of mob justice obscenely deny the new identity baptism gives us.

Interestingly, the renunciations were not included in the baptismal liturgies of the Reformers. Perhaps they seemed too magical for them. More likely, because they lived in the pervasive world of Christendom, rather than as a minority in a pagan world, it was thought to be unnecessary and overly superstitious. The Roman Catholic, Orthodox and Anglican communions have always retained them. But in our day there is a marked return to the renunciations, even in the major denominations of the Reformation. This return probably derives from the fact that we see much more clearly today, in our post-Christian culture, that baptism is a decisive turning from the realm of Satan and his powers to the kingdom of our Lord Jesus Christ. It is solid and healthy liturgical practice to use these renunciations whenever the congregation practices baptism, or whenever there is a renewal of baptismal vows. It welds together our deliverance by grace with a commitment to continue to fight evil in our lives and in the world. I was reminded of this again when I recently attended an Ash Wednesday service. When the ashes were imposed, along with the familiar words, "Dust you are and to dust you shall return," these words were added (from the *Anglican Alternative Service Book*): "Turn away from your sin and follow Christ." It was like a friendly slap in the face that said to me, "Wake up, remember you are baptized and to whom you belong!"

Our turning from sin and turning to God in baptism is not a matter of our becoming worthy of our baptism, as though the fulfillment of our obligations validates our baptism. We come back to our baptism often as weak and failed sinners, finding in it again the promise of God's grace and forgiveness. The New Testament makes clear that God has already accomplished our renewal by the power of the Holy Spirit. Paul makes clear in Ephesians 2:10 that we are "created in Jesus Christ for good works *which God prepared beforehand to be our way of life.*" Beasley-Murray says that at the heart of the Paul's baptismal theology "lies the conviction that baptism witnesses not only to a *cleansing* from guilt of sin, but to a *release* from the power of sin. The old existence has been ended by the might of the Redeemer; henceforth the baptized lives by the power of divine grace, in communion with the Risen Lord, and in the possession of the Holy Spirit."[24]

The baptized life comes into sharper focus when we remember Paul's characteristic way of approaching the subject of Christian ethics. For Paul it is never "Act this way and you will prove yourselves to be Christians." Rather, it is always "Act this way because this is what you are; this is your identity given to you in baptism, which is the sign and seal of your conformity with the Lord Jesus Christ. You have been buried with Christ in baptism and raised with him to new life" (Rom 6:3-4). "So you also must consider yourselves dead to sin and alive to God in Christ Jesus" (Rom 6:11). When Paul talked about the gift of the Holy Spirit, he always encouraged people to "walk by the Spirit" (Rom 8:4-11). I think it was Oscar Cullman who neatly captured Paul's way of moral instruction: "The indicative always precedes the imperative." The indicative of baptism always precedes and shapes the imperatives of the "law of Christ." We seek to live out what we already are in Christ.

CONCLUSION

It seems more and more apparent to me that the pregnant moment of Jesus' baptism by John contains the whole meaning of our baptism. Jesus, the only Son of the Father, the firstborn of all creation, comes to the muddy brown waters of the Jordan. But remarkably, the holy one, the Messiah, is simply one of the crowd of penitents who come for baptism. There he is one of us in John's baptism of repentance.

In his baptism by John, however, his true nature and the wonder and glory of our identification with him is also revealed. The heavens open, and the voice of God thunders, "This is my beloved Son." And suddenly we realize that God is not only speaking to his Son, and to the bystanders, but to us. In his Son, who has identified with us all in the waters of baptism, we become God's adopted children. Shedding the filthy clothes of our fallenness and sin, we assume a new identity as the

---

[24]Beasley-Murray, *Baptism*, p. 287.

sons and daughters of God.

In Jesus' baptism, the Holy Spirit descends. We too, in our baptism, receive the promise of the gentle, empowering Spirit. We are given the Spirit "who raised Jesus from the dead" (Rom 8:11) to gently convict us of sin and lead us on our journey of discipleship.

Everything we receive in baptism is already wonderfully pictured for us in the baptism of Jesus. Frederick Dale Bruner sums up the paradigmatic quality of Jesus' baptism for believers:

> When believers are baptized they are given two immense gifts—the blue sky of the Father's justifying grace above them ("you are my priceless child"), and the nuclear yet gentle power of the Dove Holy Spirit within them—they are, in theological terms, justified and sanctified (cf. 1 Cor. 1:2; 6:11). Great things happen to the baptized, and the greatest is the gift of the Father and of the Holy Spirit through discipleship to the Son.[25]

Ralph Wood described a baptism in which he participated that forever changed his perceptions about the sacrament.[26] A former student approached him while he was giving a lecture at a rural Baptist congregation. Would he accompany him to prison to baptize one of the prisoners who was related to members of the congregation? Reluctantly, he agreed.

On the way to the prison Wood learned that this was no ordinary prisoner. He was in prison for one for the crimes our society is least willing to pardon. "In a drunken stupor this man had molested his ten-year-old daughter. He had thus committed this triple violation—of the girl's sexual integrity, her filial trust, her moral innocence." Wood confessed that his suspicions grew with every mile to the prison. Just another jailhouse conversion, he thought. The pastor of the church told him something that assuaged some of his doubts. The real turning point in the man's conversion came when a few weeks before, his wife and daughter visited him in prison in order to offer their forgiveness. It was then, freed from the burden of his sin and its guilt, that this molester got on his knees and begged the mercy of both God and his family. Wood comments, "Surely, I thought, this is the true order of salvation: our repentance is always the consequence and not the condition of divine grace."

---

[25]Bruner, *Matthew,* 2:1100.

[26]The following true story was related in *The Christian Century,* October 21, 1992, pp. 925-26.

The baptism turned out to be an event for which "joy would be too tepid a word." Wood felt he was as close to the New Testament experience as he had ever been.

A guard escorted the prisoner from behind a fence that was topped with razor wire. His family was not able to attend because their broken-down car failed yet again. There was just the three of us, with the guard looking curiously on. To the strumming of the chaplain's guitar, we sang a croaky version of "Amazing Grace." We did not balk at declaring ourselves wretches. After a pastoral prayer, the barefoot prisoner stepped into a wooden box that had been lined with a plastic sheet and filled with water. It looked like a large coffin, and rightly so. This was no warmed and tiled First Baptist bath, with its painted River Jordan winding pleasantly into the distance. This was the place of death: the watery chaos from which and to which, in rightful wrath, he almost returned it.

Pronouncing the Trinitarian formula, the pastor lowered the new Christian down into the liquid grave to be buried with Christ and then raised to life eternal. Though the water was cold, the man was not eager to get out. Instead, he stood there weeping for joy. When at last he left the baptismal box, I thought he would hurry away to change into something dry. I was mistaken. "I want to wear these clothes as long as I can," he said. "In fact, I wish I never had to take a shower again."

Later on, sitting in the afternoon sun, Wood listened to this newly baptized Christian explain why this baptismal water was too good to dry off. "I'm now a free man. I'm not impatient to leave prison because wire cannot shackle my soul. I know I deserved to come here, to pay for what I did. But I also learned here that someone else has paid for all my crimes: my sins against God."

Wood concludes,

The wonder that I witnessed on this Saturday could prove a sham. The repentant molester may return to his old habits, destroying both himself and others. It will take careful and prolonged nurture in the faith to free him from such bondage. But I believe it wrong to insist—as many voices would insist—that this man's family should never have forgiven him, that to do so was to sanction his violence, indeed to collude in rape. I believe that this mother and daughter brought a dead man back to life. Their act of forgiveness opened him to the one reality by which our common slavery to sin can be broken, the power of salvation in Jesus Christ.

8

INFANT BAPTISM

"Let the little children come to me . . .

for it is to such as these that the

kingdom of heaven belongs."

MATTHEW 19:14

In the minds of many people, everything that I have written so far about baptism depends on whether I am talking about adult baptism or infant baptism. Even those who are convinced that infant baptism is biblical tend to make an implicit assumption that infant baptism is somehow different from adult baptism. As we turn to the issue of infant baptism, I want to make clear at the outset that everything I have said about baptism so far applies to infant baptism as well. There are not two kinds of baptism, one for infants and one for adults, with different premises. There is but one baptism, into the name of the Father, the Son and the Holy Spirit. If infant baptism cannot be supported on the same basis and with the same understanding as adult baptism, then it is unacceptable.[1]

One major area of disagreement regarding baptism, which we dis-

---

[1]Reformed theologian George Hunsinger takes a somewhat different position on whether infant baptism and adult baptism are identical. Responding to Karl Barth's rejection of infant baptism, he affirms the priority of adult baptism as the norm. However, "Infant baptism may be regarded as a proleptic form of adult baptism. As a displacement of adult baptism it is an abnormality that must be rendered intelligible because of its deeply entrenched status in historic ecclesial practice." He uses the categories of propleptic faith, faith as a representation of something in the future as if it already existed, and *koinonia*, the "eschatology of participation between the candidate and the community over time" (Hunsinger, "Baptism and the Soteriology of Forgiveness," *Call to Worship* 35, no. 3 [2001]: 23).

cussed in the last chapter, was whether baptism is an ordinance mark-
ing a *believer's* profession of faith, or a sacrament that is a sign and seal
of *God's* act of grace. This distinction is inextricably connected with the
legitimacy of infant baptism. Obviously, infants are not baptized in rec-
ognition of their own faith. In fact, to those who do not accept it, infant
baptism displays all the worst tendencies of the "sacramentalists." It
smacks of an *ex opere operato* efficacy, since the faith of the baptized infant is not involved. It appears to tear baptism apart from that with
which it is always tightly woven in the New Testament—faith, and
conversion. And finally, it appears to rest on fairly complicated, if not
tenuous, scriptural grounds.

My purpose in this chapter is not to present a detailed new case for
the baptism of infants, though I am personally convinced that the practice can be defended and should be allowed, even encouraged. The fact
is, there is no air-tight case for infant baptism. If we had a clear statement from Scripture one way or the other, the matter would have long
since been resolved.

Nor do I intend to cover all the arguments that have been put forward over the centuries. It has all been done before, and better than
what I could ever do.[2] My purpose, rather, is to briefly rehearse some
of the principles underlying reasons that many Christians practice infant baptism and then to present a position that might help us move
beyond the barriers to a mutual acceptance, if not to a common practice.

The primary objection to the baptism of infants, beside the lack of
clear biblical evidence, is the fact that in infant baptism one of the most
important aspects of New Testament baptism is missing: conversion
and the profession of faith in Jesus Christ. How can we justify taking
an infant, who has not made, nor is capable of making, any decision of
faith; who has not even heard, much less responded to the gospel, and

---

[2]The best detailed arguments *for* infant baptism are John Calvin *Institutes* 4.14; Joachim
Jeremias, *Infant Baptism in the First Four Centuries* (London: SCM Press, 1960); Joachim
Jeremias, *The Origins of Infant Baptism* (London: SCM Press, 1963); and Geoffrey W.
Bromiley, *Children of Promise* (Edinburgh: T & T Clark, 1979). And *against* are Kurt Aland,
Did the Early Church Baptize Infants? (London: SCM Press, 1962); George Beasley-Murray,
Baptism in the New Testament (New York: St. Martin's Press, 1962); Karl Barth, *Teaching of the
Church Regarding Baptism* (London: SCM Press, 1948); R. E. O. White, *Biblical Doctrine of
Initiation* (London: Hodder & Stoughton, 1960).

mark him or her for life as a child of God in the name of Jesus? How can this be true to the biblical teaching about baptism, and how can it be fair to the child?

In the New Testament, baptism usually took place upon a person's confession of Jesus Christ as Lord. In fact, it happened with what seems to us immoderate haste. There were no pre-baptism classes, no doctrinal instruction, no waiting periods. The main idea seemed to be to get them wet in the baptismal waters as soon as possible. This biblical conjunction of conversion/confession of faith is so strong that it is easy to misunderstand baptism as a result. Even though confession of faith and conversion are closely tied to baptism and are required of adults, baptism is not a sign and seal of a *human decision*. Geoffrey Bromiley is right when he finds no support in the New Testament "for the idea that baptism is a sign, witness, or expression of what the baptized person does, even though that person be an adult making the required profession of faith. Profession of faith certainly is to be seen as the prerequisite but it is not the thing signified in and by the sign."[3] The focus of baptism is on God. Baptism is a sign and seal of what God is doing and has done in Christ and to the baptized individual, not a sign of that individual's faith. In sharp contrast to the Lord's Supper, in which people "take and eat," people do not baptize themselves. They *are* baptized. It is, in that sense, a passive experience. It is possible to pay so much attention to the profession of faith in baptism that we lose sight of the one to whom the profession points and into whose name we are being baptized. In baptism, as in salvation itself, human activity can only be a response to God's prior grace. That, in itself, is not an adequate defense of infant baptism, but it does at least lay a foundation on which to build one.

Digging under the church's reasons for the practice of infant baptism, we discover its Old Testament foundations. The covenant God made with Abraham was between "me and you, and our offspring after you" (Gen 17:7). The covenant sign (or sacrament, as Calvin would call it) was circumcision, which was administered to adults who came into the covenant community, and to the children of the covenant community on the eighth day. Children were assumed to be a part of the

---

[3]Bromiley, *Children of Promise*, p. 106.

covenant community from the beginning, and they were encouraged to participate in its feasts and rituals as soon as possible.

One common misunderstanding of the inclusion of children in the old covenant is that the covenant with Abraham was primarily a matter of racial identity. If you were a child of Abraham by blood, you were a member of the covenant. In the new covenant, the argument goes, our covenant membership now does not depend on the blood of family lines but on the blood of Jesus Christ.

This can hardly be the case, however. The infamous "Judaizers," who opposed Paul's preaching of grace and insisted on the circumcision and adherence to the Mosaic law, were insisting on the circumcision of *Gentiles*. The issue, obviously, was not one of blood or race, but of keeping the law of Moses. Besides, the covenant with Abraham was never a purely racial covenant anyway, since it always aimed to include Gentiles. But even when non-Jews were included with the covenant people, in the practice of proselyte baptism, their children were included as well, just as God had told Abraham.[4] This shows that even the Jews did not consider covenant membership a purely racial matter, and that their inclusion of children was not simply a matter of racial continuity.

We are more likely to find the reason for the inclusion of children in the covenant community, not in the concept of racial identity, but in the Jewish and Old Testament concept of the family. God created us to live in families, and as with all that God does, there is a reason for it. One reason for the family in God's scheme of things is to provide a setting in which the truth and experience of his covenant love might be passed on from generation to generation. Psalms and Proverbs are filled with injunctions to parents "to teach their children; that the next generation might know [God's mighty deeds], the children yet unborn, and rise up and tell them to their children" (Ps 78:5-6). The Passover and other festivals purposely included children so that they might learn who they were and commit their lives in faith to the covenant God of Israel.

God uses the family structure he himself created and blessed to be an important means by which the faith is passed from generation to generation. Family is not the only means of accomplishing this, to be

---

[4]Jeremias, *Infant Baptism*, pp. 37-38.

sure. As Jesus said, God can make children of Abraham out of stones (Mt 3:9). But he usually doesn't. All Christians, whether or not they believe in infant baptism, tend to agree on the importance of the family in passing on faith. To put it very personally, and I hope not too crassly, it is inconceivable for the Jew, not to mention the Christian, to imagine that God would say to a mother and father, "I love you, and you are members of my covenant family, but we will have to see about the kids." God embraces our children with us.

It seems to me that this is exactly how Peter, speaking to an audience of Jews, expresses it on Pentecost. "For the promise is for you, for your children, and for all who are far away, everyone whom the Lord our God calls to him" (Acts 2:39). The promise to which he refers is the prophesy of Joel that he quoted in his Pentecost sermon and that is fulfilled before them that day with the promised outpouring of God's Spirit in Jesus Christ. "The promise is for you," the hearers of this message, Peters says, "and for your children." Why would it be also for their children? Because this was what anyone who was steeped in the old covenant would expect. And Peter goes on, "and for all who are far away, everyone whom the Lord our God calls to him." Family is not the only means for passing on the promise and calling people to faith. When the gospel is proclaimed, many outside the covenant community will hear it and respond with faith. For Peter this was not some new arrangement, but it was what was already promised to Abraham, whose faith in God's covenant promise would bless "all the families of the earth" (Gen 12:3). As new believers are added from the nations in accordance with God's promise, then, as Bromiley puts it, "there is no reason whatever to suppose that God changes course and begins to deal only with individuals in isolation."[5]

It seems to me that many of the other biblical arguments for infant baptism make sense, depending on whether one sees this kind of profound connection between the old and new covenants. For example, no one can prove that the "household baptisms" of Acts did or did not include infants and children. It could have been all adults, and it could have been that each and every person believed individually. But if one starts with the premise of the family as a primary way in which God

---

[5]Bromiley, *Children of Promise*, p. 24.

brings people to faith, as does Peter in Acts 2:39, then these household baptisms are at least consistent with apostolic understanding and practice. The same holds true for the appeal to Paul's claim that children of a believing spouse were "holy" (1 Cor 7:14). Whether or not one finds in them any conclusive argument for infant baptism, they make sense only within that old covenant framework of God's working within households and families, which the apostles apparently assume.

Again, this is not to say that God does not work apart from families. Many are called to faith in Christ totally apart from the faith of their biological family. Some families do not know Christ in the first place. Other families provide only an inadequate or even a distorted understanding of Christianity which hinders rather than helps their children's understanding of the faith. It also remains true that the church is a new community, a new family, which supersedes the biological family. When Jesus' mother and brothers try to get him to come home with them, believing that he has gone too far and has gotten himself in way over his head, Jesus replies by gesturing to the gathered crowd, "Here are my mother and my brothers" (Mk 3:34). The biological family is superseded by the family of faith. Whether it is administered to infants or to adults, baptism is God's gateway into the new family created by his grace, brothers and sisters in Christ who are members of his body.

Nevertheless, the family remains a primary means by which faith is passed on through the generations. Jesus, after all, was also raised in a family, and none of us would want to deny that his immersion in the faith on Mary's knee had a profound effect on his devotion to his Father in heaven. Peter acknowledges it on Pentecost, and we acknowledge it today in our churches. And why not? God created families, as fragile and broken as they are, precisely to carry that freight of faith.

Another strong indication for the validity of infant baptism is the continuous testimony of the church to the practice of infant baptism almost from the beginning. We ought to be cautious of placing too much weight on this, however, for as one opponent of infant baptism wryly observes, "To rest one's case . . . upon the basis of what has always been done is little better than a policy of despair."[6]

Granted, we do not have any clear instances of infant baptism in the

---

[6]J. K. Howard, *New Testament Baptism* (London: Pickering and Inglis, 1970), p. 93.

New Testament or in the first century, but the testimony of the wide, almost universal practice of infant baptism comes thick and fast after that. Around A.D. 215 the Roman theologian Hippolytus set down church practice in a document called *Apostolic Traditions*. It refers to infant baptism as though it has always been practiced. He calls it an "unquestioned rule" that "first, you should baptize little ones. All who can speak for themselves should speak, but for those who cannot speak, their parents should speak, or another who belongs to their family." Before Hippolytus we have very little explicit evidence of infant baptism. Origen, who was born into a Christian family in A.D. 185, comments on Romans 6:5-7 saying, "For this reason the Church received from the apostles the tradition of baptizing children too."[7] What is striking is that if the first century or so of silence on the issue meant that it was not practiced, such a decisive change in the apostolic practice in the second century would certainly have sparked heated debate and discussion. There is none. It is as though it had always been the case. The best way to interpret the near silence of the first century or so, then, is mutual and universal assent.

The very first instance of controversy comes with Tertullian (A.D. 160-220). In his *de Baptismo* (205), Tertullian expresses some doubts about the practice of infant baptism. He does not allege what would have been the clinching argument: that it does not come from the apostles. He argues instead that infant baptism imposes too great a burden on godparents. They might die and not be able to fulfill their responsibilities. So baptism ought to be postponed. He is also concerned that undesirable tendencies might appear in the children which will belie their baptismal vows. The same is true for unmarried young adults and widows, who should wait until they are married or have clearly committed themselves to sexual continence. Tertullian's concern was really for church purity, and this concern would arise often in relationship to baptism throughout the history of the church. It is important to note, however, that the issue for Tertullian is not the *validity* of infant baptism, but its wisdom under the circumstances. Ten years later, in fact, he gladly affirms infant baptism in another writing.[8]

---

[7]Jeremias, *Infant Baptism*, p. 65.
[8]Ibid., pp. 81-86.

After Tertullian, and for some of the same reasons he expressed, we discover that baptism was sometimes delayed into adulthood. Again, the reason was not to question the validity of infant baptism, because the delay occurred even among those who were converted as adults. The issue was the mistaken idea that baptism was considered such a mark of change that post-baptismal forgiveness for sin was sometimes called into question. It was for that reason, and not for any doubts about the validity of infant baptism, that some born into Christian families were not baptized.

Apparently, some Christians did question infant baptism. There is some evidence of Christian families who for a number of generations did not baptize infants. Two of the church's greatest theologians, Basil the Great and Gregory of Nyssa, were not baptized until they were adults even though they belonged to a family that had been Christians for generations. Interestingly, neither Basil or Gregory themselves ever argued against the practice of infant baptism. Where there were differences of opinion on this matter in the church, it was considered a matter of personal or family choice.[9] That, as I will argue later, gives us a hint as to how to handle the situation today.

The universal practice of infant baptism continued right on into the Protestant Reformation. Almost all the churches that came out of the Reformation continued the practice of infant baptism and strongly defended it. Only the Anabaptists argued against it, since it was clearly not in agreement with their understanding of baptism as a sign of the testimony of faith. In the twentieth century, however, some strong and important voices have come out against the practice, especially Karl Barth and Jürgen Moltmann. Interestingly, these come from the European situation where state church arrangements created the danger of nominal church membership by baptism. Under that system anyone within a geographical area or parish had a "right" to baptism and often was baptized regardless of any real faith or involvement with the church.

In America, the historic denominations of the Reformation continue the practice freely, while Baptists, Pentecostals and independent or Bible churches limit themselves to adult baptism. In many cases, these

---

[9]T. M. Lindsay, "Baptism: the Reformed View," in *International Standard Bible Encyclopedia*, ed. Geoffrey W. Bromiley (Grand Rapids: Eerdmans, 1979), 1:421.

churches do not accept infant baptism as a valid baptism at all (both for its mode of sprinkling rather than immersion and for the baptism of infants) and insist on re-baptism for anyone who wants to join their fellowship or even to be considered a "born again" Christian.

It is often insisted that one must be able to give testimony to a moment or time of conversion in order to be baptized. Even in those churches that do not practice infant baptism, however, there is an apparent level of discomfort with the idea that their children before "conversion" do not have a relationship with Christ and his church. In most of these churches, babies are "dedicated" to the Lord, which some have impishly called their "dry cleaning." It is also a rather common feature in Baptist churches that children as young as five and six years old are baptized upon their profession of faith. It seems to me a bit of a stretch to see these baptisms as valid just because they follow upon conversion and profession of faith. One imagines the conversion on mother or father's lap as the little one "accepts Jesus Christ as their Lord and Savior." But faith at that stage in life is so immersed in the family's life and identity that it hardly qualifies as conversion in the usual way in which the term is used, a radical transformation of life and commitment. For many who grow up in Christian families, all their faith decisions are interwoven with family structures and identities. Few can claim that their faith is a purely independent decision. As T. M. Lindsay puts it,

> [The Baptists'] demand for such a conscious, intelligent, strictly individualist act of faith sets aside some of the deepest facts of human nature. . . . Is it possible in all cases to trace the creative effects of the subtle imperceptible influences that surround children, or to say when the slowly dawning intelligence is first able to apprehend enough to trust in half-conscious ways? It is a shallow view of human nature that sets aside all such considerations and insists on regarding nothing but isolated acts of knowledge or of faith.[10]

I doubt any of us, Baptist or paedobaptist alike, really wants to rigidly fix the efficacy of the sacrament to the time of its administration. I can well imagine someone who was baptized upon conversion and profession of faith as a young person, who later comes to a much fuller

---

[10]Ibid., p. 423.

and deeper experience of the Spirit and regards this as their true conversion. Should such persons be baptized again? Unfortunately, they sometimes are.

On the other end, we must all admit as well that there are many who were baptized both as adults and infants who later abandon their faith. Baptism is not a guarantee of salvation, either because we were baptized and raised in a Christian family or because we were baptized upon repentance and faith. As Paul says to the Corinthians, the Israelites were "baptized into Moses in the cloud and in the sea. . . . Nevertheless God was not pleased with most of them, and they were struck down in the wilderness" (1 Cor 10:2-5). With this pointed example, Paul warns the Corinthians—and us—not to presume upon baptism. Baptism only lives and breathes in the air of faith. That faith may be present before baptism, or it may come after baptism, but it always looks back on baptism as a sign and seal of incorporation into Christ's death and resurrection.

Where infant baptism is practiced, it must necessarily involve the faithful commitment and involvement of parents and the entire Christian community in the child's Christian upbringing. There can be no room for the careless baptism of infants where real commitment to raise the children in the ways of Christ and of his church are lacking. There is no parental "right" to baptism. Pastors and elders must learn to say a firm "no" when that right is claimed by those who have only a passing or distant relationship with the church.

Churches need to emphasize to those baptized as infants that their baptism ultimately demands their personal profession of faith. In baptism God says "yes" to the covenant child. In their later Public Profession of Faith, or confirmation, he or she responds to God's "yes" with their own "yes" of faith and commitment. When, after infant baptism, the church looks for the emerging faith to be expressed, the link of baptism and faith is preserved.

At the outset, I affirmed the principle that infant baptism is not valid unless it is the very same as the baptism of adults. There is no unique institution called "infant baptism"; there is only one baptism. The problem remains that however you look at it, in infant baptism there appears to be an additional feature that distinguishes it from adult baptism, and that is, that parents or some other responsible person, along with the whole congregation, stands in for the baptized person to affirm faith in Christ. Doesn't this proxy character of infant baptism make it fundamentally different from the baptism of adults? The bottom line is that someone makes the choice on behalf of the infant, which is not the case for adults.

This idea of the expression of faith by proxy seems rather odd to us, especially in our modern American religious context with its strong emphasis on the personal and independent decision of faith. The fundamental issue here is the nature of baptism and its relationship to human faith. If we are assuming of an adult baptism that it is primarily a testimony to that person's prior faith and conversion, then we have a serious difference between the two forms of baptism. But we have affirmed all along that, while the association of faith and baptism is an important one, baptism is primarily a sign and seal of God's action in Christ for the person baptized. The sacrament points to God's faithfulness more than to human faith. In that sense, infant baptism beautifully pictures what all baptisms are really about: God's act to save us in Christ "while we were yet sinners" (see Rom 5:8). We are all helpless sinners saved by grace.

Nor is the idea of parents and godparents and the whole congregation speaking for the child (or, we might also say, the child speaking through them) as odd as it may appear at first glance. When parents speak for their children in baptism, it naturally and beautifully expresses a simple fact of human life. Parents make all kinds of decisions for their children, where they will live and go to school, what they will eat, who they will associate with. Even more fundamentally, parents decide, as Joshua did, "As for me and my house, we will serve the Lord." This does not remove the child's own responsibility to decide also, but it acknowledges and honors the ways in which that decision is made. As Michael Green says,

> There is nothing at all artificial about the idea of the child speaking through its [parents or] sponsors. It is not only a regular legal device, but it is in fact the way in which little people develop in a home. They learn from the climate about them. And if that [climate] is one of repentance and faith, in which Christ is honored as Lord, then there is every reason

to expect that they will exhibit the same qualities. Just as there is no known moment in the natural life of a child when consciousness starts, so it is with many in their spiritual lives. They have never known a time when they did not trust and obey the Lord who is worshipped by their parents and comes at his own initiative in baptism to offer them the precious gifts of new birth, membership in his family, pardon for sin, and the indwelling of his Holy Spirit.[11]

While there are some specific aspects of infant baptism that do not occur in the baptism of adults (i.e., the proxy confession of faith by parents or other sponsors along with the congregation), I do not believe that this constitutes a different kind of baptism. What we can say about the baptism of any adult we can say about the baptism of any child. In both cases we look for the fruits of faith and repentance after their baptism. In addition, both infant and adult baptism occur in the context of a believing community that promises to uphold the one who is baptized by prayer, support and mutual discipline; and members reaffirm their own baptism as they witness the baptism of another.

Along with a defense of infant baptism, I also want to assert that we should not insist upon it. It is an issue over which Christians legitimately disagree, and we need to make room for that disagreement in our congregations. I am impressed that in the end of his book in which he strongly defends infant baptism, Geoffrey Bromiley offers the following among his guidelines: "Since no direct mandate for infant baptism exists no absolute rule should be imposed on the congregation."[12]

My own congregation is, I think, typical of many in North America today. Though it is part of a denomination that is confessionally Calvinist and therefore teaches and practices infant baptism, the congregation is made up of people from many Christian backgrounds, including independent Bible churches, Baptists and Pentecostals. As pastor, I freely teach, defend and practice the baptism of infants. But I do not insist that everyone has to agree or that all children of church members must be baptized as infants. I find that even within families, couples who come from varying backgrounds have to compromise one

---

[11]Michael Green, *Baptism: Its Purpose, Practice, and Power* (London: Hodder & Stoughton, 1987), pp. 91-92.
[12]Bromiley, *Children of Promise*, p. 109.

way or the other. I know one family in which some children were baptized and some are not. I admit that all this is a little difficult to explain in the class I teach for Public Profession of Faith to young people. But this kind of mutual regard and tolerance is necessary over such an issue over which there is no absolute biblical mandate. I also find that we learn from each other. Baptists express respect for the covenantal aspects of the faith they learn in the practice of infant baptism. Paedobaptists learn to stress to their children the importance of their faith-response to baptism.

I would expect the same kind of respect and tolerance to occur in Baptist churches. To insist on the re-baptism of those who were baptized as infants, even when they have clearly lived a life of faith and obedience to Christ, is disrespectful of the faith of others and makes a mockery of the "one baptism." In discussing this with Baptists in England, I was pleased to find that they are much more accepting of the validity of infant baptisms than most of their American counterparts. I suspect that one of the reasons is that the impetus for cooperation and toleration is greater in a society where Christians are clearly a minority, as they are in Great Britain. In such a situation, Christians refuse to let baptism, of all things, divide them. I hope it will not take a similar decline in numbers of professing Christians to bring about a similar tolerance regarding baptism in our own country.

9

THE LORD'S SUPPER

Introduction and Biblical Background

Was ever another command so obeyed . . .

GREGORY DIX

I have come a long way from those Communion Sundays I describe in chapter one when my brother and I watched the solemn enactment of Holy Communion from our perch in the balcony. While we poked each other and giggled at some of the seeming absurdities of sight and sound, the clink of a thousand glass cups into their receptacles and the nervous coughs of the ladies, we also knew something very special was going on. That sense of holiness, that expectation of heaven touching earth, has never left me.

THE UNDERGROUND COMMUNION

Another celebration of the Lord's Supper sticks out in my mind, partly because it was completely "unauthorized," even clandestine, and therefore all the more exciting, and partly because of the personal simplicity of its celebration that helped me see the Supper in a new light. While in seminary in the heyday of the countercultural 1960s, my wife and I became involved in what was then called an "underground" church. We were all members of various Reformed Churches, but we held a common aversion—looking back, I see that it was often a snide and superior aversion—to the way things were done in the "institutional" church. We rather vainly called our little underground church

"The Church of the Acts," thinking we were reenacting the purity of those heady early days of the church. We experimented with everything from the hymns to the liturgy—we came up with some awful innovations—and, inevitably, the sacraments. One Sunday evening we stole away to a farmhouse and secured the services of a like-minded minister in order to have a real New Testament celebration of the Lord's Supper rather than one of those churchy, funereal Communion services we all despised.

I don't remember much about it except that we all stood in a circle and passed a lovely pottery chalice of wine and a fresh-baked loaf of grainy bread to each other, and each person said to the next, "The body of Christ for you," or "The blood of Christ for you." While this may not seem so striking, this was the first time I drank from a common cup and broke off a piece of bread from a loaf and did so at the invitation of another ordinary Christian. What struck me so poignantly at that moment was the simplicity and power of the shared cup and loaf. This is what the sharing of the body and blood of Christ are all about, I thought. It's people who care about each other sharing in the perfect loving sacrifice of Jesus Christ. That was it—no profound insight into the "real presence" or the meaning of the "anamnesis"—just the power of *koinonia* (fellowship) in the body and blood of Christ.

Hot Dogs and Holy Communion

Another experience of the Lord's Supper that profoundly touched me happened just a few years ago at the Hope Rescue Mission in South Bend, Indiana.[1] For many years our congregation has taken its turn with others to offer a meal and a brief service at the Hope Rescue Mission here in South Bend. Since it usually took place on a Sunday night, we recently decided to make it our regular evening service. At seven o'clock, a number of church folks show up to serve the meal; and at around eight, about thirty or forty members of our congregation join the residents for a worship service.

Then one month we discovered that our regularly scheduled evening Communion service would conflict with our service at the

---

[1]Adapted here with permission, Leonard J. Vander Zee, "Hot Dogs and Holy Communion," *Perspectives* 11 (1996): 24.

mission. I began to think about the possibility of having Communion at the mission, but I knew it could be controversial. I brought it up at an elders meeting. Now here was a real exercise in creative church order interpretation. Our church order welcomes baptized Christians who have made a profession of faith and actively trust in Christ as their Savior to the table. But this was way beyond the welcome of some visitors in *our* church.

As the elders discussed the issue, we wondered how many of the residents were baptized and had made a profession of faith at some time in their lives and what that meant to them. Even more we wondered how many of them would consider themselves as Christian believers. Of course, we couldn't answer those questions, but someone mentioned that according to Calvin, Communion is God's way of bending to our weakness. Another elder from a Methodist background remembered that John Wesley had called Communion a "converting ordinance," meaning that it serves not only to build the faith of believers but may help convert and renew those who are teetering on the edges of faith.

After much discussion, we decided to go ahead and seek the mission's permission to have a Communion service, which they gladly allowed. We also decided that we would make it very clear that not everyone was expected to participate and that those who chose not to were welcome to observe and pray and to see God's love for them in the sacrament even though they did not participate. We also emphasized that baptized Christians were to come forward despite whatever sin or trouble they found themselves in and receive this sacrament as a sign of Christ's grace and strength for them.

After a meal of hot dogs and mixed vegetables, the assorted men, women and children made their way upstairs for the service. It was held in a kind of storefront room filled with old folding chairs and lit by long strips of fluorescent bulbs. In front was a badly out-of-tune piano. There were about seventy-five men, women and children, about a third from our own congregation.

We began with the usual round of songs, prayer and a short sermon. I explained the meaning of Communion. Then I placed bread and grape juice on a beat-up old card table in front of me. I didn't know quite how to proceed, so I blurted out those familiar words, "Lift up your hearts." I was surprised to hear a strong response, "We lift them up to the Lord," even though we had given out no written material at all. At these words a strange and holy quiet descended. It was as though someone had entered the room unseen but whose presence was now felt by all.

After the words of institution, I spoke from memory the words of Jesus in Matthew 11: "Come to me, all you who are weary and heavy laden, and I will give you rest. Take my yoke upon you and learn from me, and you will find rest for your souls, for my yoke is easy, and my burden is light." My voice was cracking and my eyes misty as I finished these words, looking out at the assorted crowd of blacks and whites, grizzled old men, tired-looking women and sleepy children with their knit caps, old winter coats, pockets stuffed with all their earthly belongings, all here to spend a night out of the cold.

Then they began to come forward; first just a few, then a long line formed. Strangely quiet under the buzzing fluorescent light, they moved slowly toward the little card table. With what seemed to me a great solemnity, they placed their hands open in front of me, and I said, "The body of Christ for you." One old man with a yellowing white shirt and old black narrow tie opened his mouth for me to place the sacrament in his toothless mouth.

Hot dogs and Communion at the Hope Rescue Mission. I will always think of the body of Christ now with this scene in mind. Doctors and housewives and professors in nice shoes and brightly colored sweaters shuffling to the table together with men and women who hadn't changed clothes for days or weeks. The sophisticated smell of after-shave mixed with the sharp scent of dirty socks and stale smoke. People whose lives seemed all together sharing the same loaf with people whose lives were broken and tattered. We were all one body, for we all ate from the same loaf.

I will never see most of these people again, but I will always remember that meal. I don't know what happened to them the next day. Some, no doubt, continued their journey to the next town, some drifted back to the bar and others hustled for jobs. But now they had been fed, not just with hot dogs but with the body and blood of Christ.

Before the service I sat at a table to share a hot dog with a couple who were evidently traveling together. I tried to get some conversation going, but they must have felt it wasn't much use to tell what their life was like to a stranger—and a preacher at that. There was a weary look in their eyes, a note in their voices that seemed to say it would always be this way. What could I know about their lives? Were they married or had they met that night?

As I served communion, there they were in front of me, hands open. Now they looked into my eyes as they had not before. Now we were not just strangers whose lives scarcely touched, but children of God remarkably bonded together in the love of Jesus. Maybe I just imagined it, but somehow it seemed to me that the despair that had clouded their eyes had given way to a look of tender hope.

MINISTER ON THE OTHER SIDE OF THE TABLE

For me one of the barriers for the full enjoyment of the Lord's Supper is that most often I am the officiant at the table. This can be a wonderful experience, as I have pointed out, but I find it also keeps me from fully entering into the sacramental awareness I long to have. There are the words and gestures to think about, the signals that have to be given to the servers, and even the worry that the elder assigned for bringing bread that day may have unwittingly brought a loaf smeared with oil, or a loaf like a bag of crumbs. Petty concerns, to be sure, but they cannot be overlooked. Whenever I'm on vacation, or whenever I have an extended time away from my parish duties, I always try to find a place to worship where I know the Lord's Supper will be celebrated. There is a deep hunger to come to the table as an ordinary recipient.

In many churches I have visited, the practice is that the congregation comes to the front to stand or kneel as they receive the bread and cup. I love to sit there and watch these perfect strangers, young and old, fat and svelte, dressed in Anne Taylor or Target. Here they come, one and all, saint and sinners, bored and intent. And I will join them at the table, sharing the one loaf and the one cup.

The strange thing is that on almost every occasion when I come to the table in some strange church, I end up fighting tears. It happens at various points in the liturgy, but I find that two old prayers offered just before the Communion especially move me. One is found in both the Roman Catholic and Anglican services: "I am not worthy to receive you, but only say the word and I shall be healed." The other is Episcopalian: "We do not presume to come to this Thy table, O merciful Lord, trusting in our own righteousness. . . . We are not worthy so much as to gather up the crumbs under Thy table." I don't know what it is that touches me so deeply. In part, it's the powerful personal confession these prayers evoke, and in part it's the reality of the fact that I am about to receive the Lord himself. Sometimes the tears come when the bread is laid in my hand, or pressed in, as on one recent Sunday, by an earnest server, looking straight into my soul it seemed, saying, "The body of Christ keep you in everlasting life." The sheer physicality of it—the touch, the smell, the jostling bodies, the silver or ceramic chalice—envelopes me in the embrace of grace, and does so again and again.

Sure, I am bored sometimes, or distracted, or offended by a banal sermon, or put off by an annoyingly sing-song liturgical voice. But the wonderful thing about the Lord's Supper is that its benefit does not depend on my feelings at the time, but on the Lord's promise of his personal presence made known in the bread and wine.

THE LORD'S SUPPER IN THE BIBLE

Unlike baptism, there is no question at all about where the Lord's institution of the Supper as a sacrament takes place. The three Synoptic Gospels and Paul all give prominence to that last meal Jesus ate with his disciples just before his death. Here, they all tell us, Jesus called his disciples—and by extension all of us—to remember him in the sharing of the bread and the cup. But while we all recognize *where* Jesus instituted the Supper, we diverge widely in our understandings of *what* his words mean. What did he mean, "This is my body. . . . This is my blood?" What did he mean when he called us to remember him in this way?

A Jewish meal. We cannot begin to understand the meaning of the Lord's Supper without reckoning with the fact that, before everything else, it is a Jewish meal. John Macquarrie recalls a fond memory from his years of teaching at Union Theological Seminary in New York. He was invited on the eve of Shabbat to supper at the home of Rabbi Abraham Heschel, the great Jewish theologian. At the beginning of the meal, in the warm light of the Shabbat candles, the host took a loaf of bread in his hands and said the brief prayer, called in Hebrew the *berakah*, which means blessing, or thanksgiving. "Blessed are you, Lord God, king of the universe, you bring forth bread from the earth." The rabbi then broke off a piece for himself and distributed the rest to the guests around the table. Macquarrie recalls that at the end of the meal there were more extended thanksgivings. The host took a cup of wine, known as the "cup of blessing" (see 1 Cor 10:16), and said a similar *berakah:* "Blessed are you, Lord God, king of the universe, you create the fruit of the vine."

Macquarrie says that this scene could hardly fail to remind him of Jesus' last meal with his disciples on the night before he died. "It is quite possible that he used much the same prayers at the Last Supper as I was now hearing from Abraham Heschel . . . [I]n Heschel's apartment I had a vivid sense of that Last Supper at which was instituted the Lord's Supper or eucharist, a word which itself means 'thanksgiving.'"[2]

Because the Gospels describe the Last Supper as a Passover meal, we tend to forget that it was also a meal. Eating and the etiquette of the table were deeply significant in ordinary Jewish life, and textured with religious meaning. Among Jews in Jesus' day, *who* you ate with was as important as *what* you ate and *how* you ate. Since eating was an act of fellowship and acceptance, to eat with sinners was to accept them as friends and companions (Mk 2:15-16).

The several Gospel accounts of Jesus feeding large multitudes of people also provide us with a deeper understanding of the Lord's Supper. In these meals at the seaside and hillside, Jesus enacts the ritual of the Jewish meal, blessing and breaking the bread. Reading back from Jesus' resurrection meals with his disciples, through the Last Supper, to these miraculous feedings, we cannot help but see the connection. Just as Jesus miraculously fed the famished multitudes, he feeds our hungry souls with "the bread of everlasting life." Chapter 6 of John's Gospel makes this connection very explicit. It takes place when the Passover was near (Jn 6:4). After Jesus miraculously feeds the multitude, they follow him in a kind of feeding frenzy, wanting to make this

---

[2]John Macquarrie, *A Guide to the Sacraments* (New York: Continuum, 1997), p. 101.

miraculous giver of food their king. It is then that Jesus explains the spiritual significance of his feeding, "I am the bread of life. Whoever comes to me will never be hungry" (Jn 6:35).

That Last Supper in the upper room before Jesus' death should be seen in connection with all the other memorable meals at which he was a guest and a host. Every time believers gather around the bread and wine, Jesus again lovingly extends his table fellowship to sinners, lavishly feeds them with the living bread, and accepts them as his friends.

When Paul and the Gospels tell us that Jesus "*took* the bread . . . *blessed* . . . and *broke* it," it is important to realize that these three terms defined an ordinary Jewish table blessing.[3] This Jewish blessing was also taken into the early church. Justin Martyr's *Apology* from around A.D. 150 describes the Lord's Supper this way: "And when the president has given thanks and all the people have assented, those whom we call deacons give to each one present a portion of the bead and wine and water over which thanks has been given [Greek, *eucharistenthentos*, literally, 'the thanked upon or blessed upon']. . . . And we call this food 'thanksgiving' [Greek, *eucharistia*]."[4] So, this extraordinary meal of Jesus' body and blood is consecrated like every daily meal with the blessing or thanksgiving to God. In understanding the Jewish blessing, we will better understand Jesus' words at the Supper and their meaning for us in the sacrament.

The Jewish blessing, or *berakah*, was more than just a perfunctory grace before the meal. It was an important ritual of faith. When the bread was raised and broken, the blessing or thanksgiving that was spoken carried in it the idea that this bread was eaten as God's gift. It was "received with thanksgiving," the words Paul uses in good Jewish fashion in 1 Timothy 4:4 to say that everything received with thanksgiving is sanctified to the recipient.

But the significance of the Jewish blessing for Jesus' words goes even deeper. As Alasdair Heron points out, "Coming as it did at the beginning of the meal, the blessing and thanks offered over the bread ex-

---

[3]Joachim Jeremias, *The Eucharistic Words of Jesus* (London: SCM Press, 1966), p. 109. It should also be noted that at the Passover meal these same words were said later, after the preliminary course and the first section of the liturgy of the Seder.

[4]Thurian and Wainwright, *Baptism and Eucharist*, p. 112. Thus, *Eucharist* is one of the most ancient terms with which we can designate the Lord's Supper.

tended to cover the whole meal that was to follow."[5] The whole meal was offered to God in thanksgiving, and then given back to them by God for their use. The bread becomes the locus of meaning for the whole meal. It was all consecrated in the bread.

Heron further points out that the sharing of the bread meant that in this meal isolated individuals were drawn into a single community: "For the Jews, as for other ancient peoples, the shared meal had a profound religious and human significance of which we in our largely secularized and functional outlook have almost wholly lost sight. Those who ate together were bound together by that simple sharing. . . . The meal itself established a bond between those who shared in it: it did not merely symbolize the bond, but actually constituted it."[6] So in blessed and broken bread the whole meal was consecrated, and in its sharing a community was formed.

While this may seem rather insignificant in itself, it takes on new meaning in the light of Jesus' words at the Last Supper. Jesus took the bread, uttered the words of blessing to God as at every meal, and then said, "This is my body." Jesus thus links the blessed bread and his own self. Just as the bread was received as God's gift and shared between them, so now, in his death, Jesus is given to them by God. Now they were to eat the bread blessed with thanksgiving as Jesus, God's gift of eternal life to them.

Furthermore, since in Jewish thinking the bread included the whole meal, so the bread included the whole Christ—his incarnation, his life of obedient service and everything that he was about to do for them in his redeeming death and resurrection. When Jesus linked the blessed and broken bread and his body, he very likely meant that this bread represented his whole person as God was now giving it to them. And in eating and drinking it together, they would have fellowship with him and with one another.

A Passover feast. While this was a meal, it was not just an ordinary meal. Jesus' last meal with his disciples, according to the Synoptic Gospels, was a Passover meal. John's Gospel does not give us an account of the Last Supper, but it does set Jesus' death clearly within the context

---

[5]Alasdair I. C. Heron, *Table and Tradition* (Philadelphia: Westminster Press, 1983), p. 25.
[6]Ibid.

of the Passover (Jn 19:14). Also in John's Gospel, John the Baptist refers to Jesus as the "Lamb of God," which many interpreters take to be an identification of Jesus with the Passover lamb. The Passover setting was so strong that by the end of the first century, if not before, the Christian celebration of Good Friday/Easter was called the Christian Passover (see also 1 Cor 5:7-8).[7]

As described in Exodus 12 and 13, the seven-day Feast of Unleavened Bread wrapped around the Passover meal itself to provide a setting for this great commemoration of the deliverance of the Hebrew slaves from Egypt. The instructions for that first Passover involved the killing of the spotless lamb or kid, the smearing of blood on the lintel and doorposts of their houses, and the meal of roasted lamb with its explanation to the children of the Lord's salvation of his people from slavery. As time went on and historical circumstances changed, the Passover ritual also evolved somewhat, but the basic elements of slaughtered lamb, the rehearsal of the great story and the seven-day Feast of Unleavened Bread remained.

Exactly how do the words and actions of Jesus in the Gospels fit into the Passover ritual? For example, while the disciples are told to procure a lamb for the feast (Mk 14:12-16), the lamb itself is never mentioned by Jesus at the meal. Even more importantly, how do Jesus' words over the bread and wine, "This is my body . . . this is my blood" fit into the Passover ritual?

The Passover meal itself has four main parts: (1) the preliminary course, at which a word of blessing for the feast is spoken, some hors d'oeuvres are eaten, and the main meal is placed on the table; (2) the Passover liturgy in which the Haggadah, or explanation of the meal, is given by the *paterfamilias* or host, with the first part of the Hallel (Ps 111—113) and the second cup of wine; (3) the main meal, with the blessing of the unleavened bread (first bread eaten), the eating of the

---

[7]Scholars disagree on whether the Last Supper can truly be called a Passover. Michael Welker says, "At the core, the whole discussion of the New Testament scholars observes the tension that on the one hand, the longer Lukan text (Luke 24:14-20) 'clearly takes its orientation from the flow of the Passover meal,' while on the other hand, the text with clearly the earliest historical origin, 1 Corinthians 11:23b-25, 'evinces no reference to a Passover meal.' . . . We should thus reckon with the fact that *two traditions* are to be found in the New Testament material, and that they are bound together in a relationship of tension" (*What Happens at Holy Communion* [Grand Rapids: Eerdmans, 2000], p. 51).

meal and the blessing of the third cup; and (4) the conclusion, hors d'oeuvres with the second part of the Hallel (Ps 114—118), and the fourth cup.[8]

With this basic structure in mind, we can begin to reconstruct Jesus' words and actions at the culminating Passover meal with his disciples. According to the Gospel accounts, Jesus took a loaf of bread, and after blessing it, broke it and gave it to them, and said, "Take; this is my body" (Mk 14:22). The characteristic words of the table blessing (bless, break and give) show that this action could only have taken place at the blessing of the bread at the beginning of the main meal, just after the Haggadah. It is more difficult to determine when exactly in the Seder Jesus spoke the words around the cup of wine, since there were four cups at the Passover. Both Luke and Paul say that these words came with the cup "after the supper," and Paul calls it the "cup of blessing" (1 Cor 10:16). This points to the third cup, called the "cup of blessing," which came after the meal. It is also important to notice that the Haggadah, or instruction, comes before both of these elements of the meal. Jeremias believes this may have been the point at which Jesus instructed the disciples concerning the special meaning of this Passover in relation to his coming death, preparing them for the words over the bread and the cup.[9]

The Passover sacrifice. When, in Exodus 12, the child asks the father about the meaning of the feast, the father responds, "It is the Passover *sacrifice* to the Lord." The lamb was offered, and the blood placed on the doorposts and lintels of the houses so that the "the Lord will pass over that door" (Ex 12:23). Clearly, the blood of the lamb provides for the salvation of the firstborn of Israel but did not protect the Egyptian firstborn. By the time of Jesus the sacrificial element had become even more explicit. In fact, this was the only sacrifice that was performed by the offerer, who slaughtered the lamb himself in the temple under the supervision of the priests.

When Jesus and his disciples met that night for the Passover meal, the roasted lamb lay prominently at the center of the table. Yet the Gospels never mention the lamb except in the disciples' preparation

---

[8]Jeremias, *Eucharistic Words of Jesus*, pp. 85-86.
[9]Ibid., pp. 59 and 219.

for the supper. Jesus' words over the bread and the cup seem to have nothing to do with the lamb that was so central to the Passover meal. Is the lamb forgotten, or do we have to somehow reckon with its unspoken presence?

Jeremias suggests that Jesus explained some or all of this sacrificial meaning to the disciples during the Passover Haggadah, so that when he finally blessed and broke the bread, and blessed and poured the third cup, what he was doing would be clear to them. There is evidence that others also added their own words to the traditional Haggadah.[10] This is a tantalizing possibility, but we have little evidence for it.

Jeremias is on firmer ground, however, in pointing out how the Gospel writers call attention to the sacrificial nature of the Passover lamb through Jesus' words at the supper. Remembering that Jesus originally spoke these words in Aramaic, Jeremias convincingly shows that when Jesus said "This is my body and blood, given, poured out for you," the words are rich with sacrificial meaning. They point to the two parts of the sacrifice, body and blood, that are separated from each other at the point of the ritual slaying.[11] In addition, in Matthew and Mark, Jesus says over the cup, "This is my blood . . . that is poured out for many." These words, Jeremias argues, are picked up from Isaiah 53, that great servant song of the lamb that willingly goes to slaughter. At its climax, the prophet says that "he *poured* himself out to death, and was numbered with the transgressors; yet he bore the sin of *many*" (Is 53:12). Here again, Jesus' words, reminiscent of Isaiah 53, point to his sacrificial understanding of what he was offering his disciples in the bread and the wine.

Remembering what we pointed out before regarding the blessing of the bread in an ordinary meal, the blessing of the wine at this Passover meal takes on special meaning. When the head of the family says the blessing over the bread and breaks off a piece and hands it to each person at the table, it means that each one *"is made a recipient of the blessing by this eating."* The same is true of the cup of blessing. Drinking from it mediates a share in the blessing that has been spoken. So when Jesus gives the blessed bread and cup to his disciples at this

---

[10]Ibid., pp. 60-61.
[11]Ibid., pp. 220-25.

Passover meal, he means that they now share in the blessed meaning of the bread and cup, and *"that by eating and drinking he gives them a share in his atoning death."*[12]

At this final and fulfilling Passover, Jesus is the only Son of God, the firstborn. But instead of a lamb being offered on his behalf, as it was for the Israelites, he willingly becomes the lamb of God who is offered for all the other sons and daughters of God so that the angel of death passes over them and they are delivered from the bondage of sin and death. In the words over the bread and the cup, Jesus infuses the Passover with this new meaning and shares it with his disciples. Heron summarizes this new meaning:

> The bread is received as a gift from God; and Jesus himself is God's gift. By its sharing the group are gathered into a new community; and through Jesus a new community is brought into being. As the "bread of affliction" it is a memorial of the deliverance from Egypt . . . and Jesus now tells his disciples to repeat what he has done for his remembrance. Each of these three moments connected with the Passover bread is thus taken up and transformed in a new perspective which is defined by reference to Jesus himself. In the giving of the bread, he is given; in the sharing of the bread, he is shared; in the whole action, he will be remembered in the strong sense that what he was and did will come to bear afresh upon the present time and the new future.[13]

The sacrificial overtones implicit in the Gospels become explicit in Paul. He boldly claims that Christ is the Passover sacrifice: "For our paschal lamb, Christ, has been *sacrificed* for us. Therefore, let us celebrate the festival" (1 Cor 5:7-8). In addition, Paul places sacrifice and the Lord's Supper side by side when he says that drinking the cup is a "sharing in the blood of Christ" and eating the bread is a "sharing in the body of Christ" (1 Cor 10:16-17). He then goes on to say that the children of Israel ate the sacrifice which made them "partners in the altar" (10:18). Paul seems to be making a comparison between the sacrificial feast of the Israelites and the sacrificial character of the Supper. In both cases, the participants share in the sacrifice and in the benefits of that sacrifice.

---

[12]Ibid., pp. 232-33.
[13]Ibid., p. 28.

John's Gospel, while it does not have an account of Jesus' last Passover meal with his disciples, nevertheless sees Jesus' death in the context of the Passover. Jesus' discourse on the bread of life in John 6 takes place at the Passover (Jn 6:4). Also, according to John, Jesus' crucifixion took place on the "day of Preparation for the Passover" (Jn 19:14), that is, the day preceding the night of the meal, the day on which the lambs were ritually slaughtered in the temple. Of course, this causes some chronological problems between this and the synoptic accounts, which say Jesus' death took place on the day after, but our focus should be on John's purpose in setting Jesus' crucifixion on the day of preparation. John clearly wants his readers to see Jesus' death on the cross as the true sacrificial lamb occurring while the Passover animals are slaughtered in the temple.

This sacrificial aspect of the Lord's Supper through its associations with the Passover comes through in the church's earliest liturgies as well. Hippolytus gives an example of a common eucharistic prayer. It reads, in part, "Remembering therefore his death and resurrection, we offer to you this bread and cup, giving you thanks because you have held us worthy to stand before you and minister to you."[14] The word "offer" shows that the Lord's Supper clearly has a sacrificial aspect for Hippolytus. But what is being offered, and what does offering mean? The bread and cup are not offered to God as a propitiatory sacrifice in themselves, but as gifts of bread and wine the people have brought and which are then given back to them as the body and blood of Christ. With the bread and wine the people also offer their praise and thanksgiving (*eucharistia*) in response to God's grace. Christ's self-offering, represented in the bread and wine on the table, are received by the people and then "offered" to God in thankful remembrance of Christ's one atoning sacrifice.[15]

Passover and remembering. Luke and Paul tell us that Jesus said that we should "do this in remembrance of me." We see what this remembering involves through the lens of the Passover, which was above all a meal of remembering. God instituted it precisely for the

---

[14]In Wainwright and Thurian, *Baptism and Eucharist*, p. 114.
[15]A proper understanding of the Lord's Supper as a sacrificial meal is more fully developed in chapter three.

purpose of searing the memory of his deliverance into the minds of the Israelite people. "This day shall be a remembrance for you" (Ex 12:14). But this remembering was not merely recalling that something happened way back when. The Jewish Mishnah says, regarding the Passover, "In every generation a man must so regard himself as if he came forth himself out of Egypt. . . . He brought us out from bondage to freedom, from sorrow to gladness, and from mourning to a Festival-day."[16] The feast is not merely a historical reconstruction but is a way of making the past event present and of making each participant in the meal a slave freed by God's mighty hand. The Passover rituals were not merely recalling an event, they were a "re-presentation, making present the past which can never remain merely past but becomes effective in the present."[17] When the Israelites remember the Exodus, they are participating in it.

This quality of Passover remembering greatly affects how we understand the remembering we are called to do in the sacrament of the Lord's Supper. The Septuagint accounts of the original Passover use the Greek word *anamnesis* to translate the Hebrew "remembrance," and this is the same word used in the Gospels for Jesus' command that the Supper be done "in remembrance of me." So when we remember Jesus in the Lord's Supper, it is more than a recollection of the events of the night he was betrayed or of what he did for us on the cross. It is a remembrance *by participation*. To the question posed in the old Negro spiritual, "Were you there?" we can respond at the Lord's Table with a firm "Yes!" When, in the words of institution, Jesus offers the bread and wine as his body and blood, it is for me. Remembrance means I participate in his death and resurrection as I receive the bread and the wine.

As we hear the story of that first supper over and over in our worship, it becomes our story, our memory; we were there. Allen Verhey describes this remembering at the Lord's Supper as owning the stories as our own. "This remembering involved 'pleading guilty' to the death of Jesus, but also a sharing in that death and in the new covenant (with

---

[16]Pesharim 10:4-5, in I. Howard Marshall, *Last Supper and Lord's Supper* (Exeter: Paternoster, 1980), p. 22.

[17]*"anamnesis,"* in *Exegetical Dictionary of the New Testament* (Edinburgh: T & T Clark, 1990), 1:85.

its forgiveness) that Christ established. This remembering was constitutive of identity and community."[18]

Passover and longing. The Passover setting also helps us grasp the eschatological character of the Supper. By the time of Jesus, the Passover had become a feast of longing for the Messiah. How could it be otherwise? The remembrance of God's deliverance of his people from tyranny in Egypt could not help but remind them that they were under the power of Rome. Rebellions against Rome were common around Passover time, which also accounts for Pilate's nervousness.

This Passover longing can best be seen in the traditional rabbinical interpretation of Psalm 118, the culminating psalm of the Passover Seder that was current at Jesus' time. The psalm was a depiction of the final day of redemption. The Messiah is the one who "comes in the name of the Lord" while all the people shout "Hosanna." It was commonly believed that the Messiah would come at the Passover, which explains that when Jesus came into Jerusalem on Palm Sunday at the beginning of the Passover festival, he was greeted with the words of this psalm as the coming Messiah/King. Jesus himself interpreted the psalm messianically. He was the "stone the builders rejected" which has "become the chief cornerstone" (Ps 118:22; Mk 8:31; Lk 17:25). Jesus and his disciples sang this psalm as they went out from the supper to the Garden of Gethsemane in the dark of that night of betrayal. The Messiah will die, but it will be the opening act of the eschatological fulfillment.[19]

Both Matthew and Mark tell us that after the cup Jesus said, "I will never again drink of the fruit of the vine until that day when I drink it new with you in the kingdom of God" (Mk 14:25). This was a farewell meal, a "last supper," but it also pointed to a meal when they would be together again in the kingdom of God. In Luke's Gospel this sense of farewell is heightened even further, and is connected directly with the Passover. "He said to them, 'I have eagerly desired to eat this Passover with you before I suffer; for I tell you, I will not eat it until it is fulfilled in the kingdom of God'" (Lk 22:15-16). Then, when Jesus blesses and

---

[18]Allen Verhey, "Remember, Remembrance," in *The Anchor Bible Dictionary* (New York: Doubleday, 1992), 5:669.
[19]Jeremias, *Eucharistic Words*, pp. 256-62.

passes what was probably the second cup of wine, he says dramatically, "Take this and divide it among yourselves" (v. 17). Clearly, he was not participating in the meal with them. Why not? Why would he himself fast on this final Passover night? Because he is the Passover sacrifice who is given for them, and it would be inappropriate, therefore, for him to eat with them. Jesus saw that this was the last Passover he will have with them until the great feast of fulfillment, the "Wedding Feast of the Lamb" (Rev 19:9). Paul echoes this hope when he says that in the sharing the bread and cup "you proclaim the Lord's death until he comes" (1 Cor 11:26).

As we eat and drink, like the Jews who celebrated Passover in Jesus' day, we still await the coming of the Messiah. Yes, he has come to save his people. As the Passover lamb he was slaughtered. In his resurrection and ascension to the right hand of God, the great and final exodus from slavery to freedom has begun. But we are waiting for the kingdom to come in its fullness when the King returns. While the Lord's Supper is a meal of Christ's presence with us, in a strange way it is also a meal of his absence.[20] At every Lord's Supper we join with the church in crying, "Maranatha! Come, Lord." We pray that the One who is present with us by his Spirit will soon be present with us in his glorious kingdom.

Clearly, we cannot understand the Lord's Supper apart from the fact that it was a Passover meal. That is why so many eucharistic liturgies over the centuries have invited the congregation to participate with the words, "Our paschal lamb, Christ, has been sacrificed. Therefore, let us celebrate the festival" (1 Cor 5:7-8).

Eating his flesh and drinking his blood. At the Last Supper, Jesus spoke those startling and mysterious words: "This is my body. . . . This is my blood," which form the core of the Lord's Supper. What do these words mean? That question has been a source of unfortunate controversy and even division for centuries. Later we will look at some of the historical and contemporary development of the interpretation of these words. Here we will confine ourselves to investigating their biblical settings.

In Jesus' great "bread of life" discourse in John 6, he refers to his

---

[20]See chapter twelve for a fuller discussion of Christ's absence.

flesh as the bread, and his blood as the drink that he gives for the life of the world: "Very truly, I tell you, unless you eat the flesh of the Son of Man and drink his blood, you have no life in you. Those who eat my flesh and drink my blood have eternal life, and I will raise them up on the last day; for my flesh is true food and my blood is true drink" (Jn 6:53-55). This graphic passage, which is part of a much longer discourse, has long been a source of dispute. The dispute (which goes back to the church fathers) revolves around whether Jesus is speaking of his death in a purely metaphorical way, or whether John or Jesus intended to refer directly or indirectly to the Lord's Supper. It is hard to believe that John's Christian readers near the end of the first century could read this passage and make *no* connection with the sacramental meal they celebrated each Lord's Day. It is also hard to interpret this passage apart from our own theological and sacramental prejudices. The majority of scholars have come to the conclusion that this discourse moves progressively from a purely metaphorical understanding of Jesus as the bread of life to at least a veiled reference to the sacramental eating and drinking of Jesus' flesh and blood.[21] The focus is certainly not on the sacramental bread and wine, but on Jesus' own flesh and blood given up for the life of the world. Nevertheless, Jesus' own flesh and blood are sacramentally given to us in the Lord's Supper.

Interestingly, the concluding verse of this discourse became the exegetical fulcrum for the interpretation of the entire passage by some of the Reformers: "It is the Spirit that gives life, the flesh is useless. The words that I have spoken to you are Spirit and life" (Jn 6:63). Zwingli took this verse to support his purely spiritual understanding of the sacrament. Calvin took it to support his understanding of the spiritual presence of Christ in the sacrament. Neither one did justice to the text.

The context of this verse is that the disciples cannot understand

---

[21]Three solid commentaries on John that, while differing somewhat in approach, lead to essentially the conclusion that John 6 ultimately points to the sacrament are: Raymond Brown, *The Gospel According to John* (Garden City, N.Y.: Doubleday, 1966); G. R. Beasley-Murray, *John*, Word Biblical Commentary (Waco, Tex.: Word, 1987); and Rudolf Schnackenburg, *The Gospel According to John* (London: Burns and Oates, 1980). For a sharply drawn conclusion that John intends only to refer to the death of Jesus and not in any way to the Lord's Supper, see Herman Ridderbos, *The Gospel of John* (Grand Rapids: Eerdmans, 1997).

Jesus' words (a typical situation in John's Gospel). In response, Jesus tells them that the flesh is useless; even his flesh, his incarnation, is useless unless his exaltation and the sending of the Holy Spirit follow as its natural conclusion. Only the Spirit regenerates and provides life. Only the Spirit deepens our understanding of Christ. Only the Spirit makes that faith possible which enables us to eat and drink Christ's flesh and blood for the nourishment of our souls to everlasting life. So this verse does not deny the sacramental interpretation of John 6 but sets it within the context of the ministry of the Holy Spirit.

If, as I see it, John 6 points toward the Lord's Supper, we can better grasp how Jesus intends for us to understand it. Jesus wants us to receive the bread and wine, which are his body and blood, as powerful symbols that carry with them the redeeming power of his death and resurrection that bring us into eternal life, and as a personal confirmation of his presence with us.

Returning to the original question, what does Jesus mean by inviting his disciples to eat his body and blood in remembrance of him? Just as the sacrificial lamb was consumed at the Passover meal, so Jesus, the Lamb of God, is consumed in this meal of remembrance. Consuming the bread and wine, now designated as his body and blood, we *participate* in his sacrifice by eating and drinking its blessings and benefits. Paul refers to this participation in 1 Corinthians: "The cup of blessing that we bless, is it not a sharing in the blood of Christ? The bread that we break, is it not a sharing in the body of Christ? Because there is one bread, we who are many are one body, for we all partake of the one bread. Consider the people of Israel; are not those who eat the sacrifices partners in the altar?" (1 Cor 10:16-18). Eating Jesus' body and drinking his blood is the most vivid imaginable way of being both participants and beneficiaries of his death on the cross and the resurrection by which it won the victory over sin and death.

The blood of the covenant. The blood of Christ offered to us in the Lord's Supper is covenant blood. Both Mark and Matthew (whose accounts of the Last Supper are virtually identical) report that Jesus said over the cup of wine, "This is my blood of the covenant which is poured out for many." The blood of the covenant is not the blood of the Passover but points rather to that crucial event at the foot of Mt. Sinai where Moses ratified the covenant between God and Israel. Moses took half of the blood and splashed it against the altar. "Then he took the book of the covenant, and read it in the hearing of the people; and they said, 'All that the LORD has spoken we will do, and we will be obedient.'" Then Moses took the remaining blood and dashed it on the people, and said, "See the blood of the covenant that the LORD has made with you in accordance with all these words" (Ex 24:6-8). This solemn ceremony united God and his people in covenant blood.

Tragically, Israel did not keep their covenant responsibilities and constantly fell into disobedience. Still, God never went back on the promises he made and ratified in blood. So when Jesus refers to his blood as the blood of the covenant, he is telling his disciples and us that he will keep the blood covenant by the shedding of his own blood as the covenant representative, the one who comes to stand for all of Israel, the Christ, the anointed. William Lane says, "The saying over the cup directs attention to Jesus as the one who fulfills the divine will to enter covenant fellowship with his people on a new and enduring basis."[22]

Paul also mentions the covenant in his account of the institution of the Lord's Supper, but with a slight change: "This cup is the *new* covenant in my blood" (1 Cor 11:25). Here the reference seems to be not only the covenant ratified at Sinai but also the new covenant prophesied by Jeremiah:

> "The days are surely coming," says the LORD, "when I will make a new covenant with the house of Israel and the house of Judah. It will not be like the covenant that I made with their ancestors when I took them by the hand to bring them out of the land of Egypt—a covenant that they broke. . . . But this is the covenant that I will make with the house of Israel after those days," says the LORD: "I will put my law within them, and I will write it on their hearts; and I will be their God, and they shall be my people. . . . For I will forgive their iniquity, and remember their sin no more." (Jer 31:31-34)

This new covenant will not be written on tablets of stone, but on their hearts. It will involve a close and personal relationship between God and his people and a forgiveness of their sins. This new covenant

---

[22]William L. Lane, *The Gospel According to Mark* (Grand Rapids: Eerdmans, 1974), p. 507.

comes to its full expression and ratification through the blood of Jesus. His blood forgives sin, releases us from guilt and makes it possible for us to serve God in the freedom of the Spirit.

As a covenant meal, the Lord's Supper has the character of a pledge, an absolute commitment on God's part to forgive our sins through the cross of Jesus, and therefore it guarantees a right relationship with God. Every time we share in the Supper, we renew our covenant relationship with God through Jesus Christ. We receive the covenant blood that was shed for us in faith and by grace, and we pledge ourselves again to love and obedience in the name of our covenant representative, Jesus Christ. This covenant meaning of the Lord's Supper echoes through many eucharistic prayers. At some point, either before or after the reception of the bread and wine, the believing community dedicates itself anew to the service of God. The Lord's Supper, like the covenant that it commemorates, involves a gift of grace and a response of faith and commitment in and through Jesus Christ, the covenant-keeper.

Meals with the risen Lord. It is important not to focus all our attention on the accounts of Jesus' Last Supper with his disciples. It was not really the last supper, since after his resurrection Jesus again ate and drank with his disciples in meals of Easter joy.

Jesus' meal with the two disciples at Emmaus offers a good example. After his resurrection, Jesus joined two unnamed disciples who were on their way home to Emmaus in despair over Jesus' tragic death, and they did not recognize him. Jesus upbraided them for their lack of faith and their slowness of heart, and then began to expound the Scriptures to them, showing that they all point to him. When they arrived at home, they invited Jesus to join them for a meal, which was an expected act of Jewish hospitality. Suddenly Jesus, the guest, became the host. He *took* the bread, *blessed* it, *broke* it and *gave* it to them. These four verbs immediately recall Jesus' words in Luke 22:19 at the Passover. As Laurence Stookey points out, "Luke was much too careful a writer for this similarity of language to be mistaken for an accident. Instead it is a powerful affirmation: the pre- and post-resurrection meals cannot be separated."[23] Luke says, "Then their eyes were opened and they recog-

---

[23]Laurence Hull Stookey, *Eucharist, Christ's Feast Within the Church* (Nashville: Abingdon, 1993), p. 36.

nized him" (24:31). While this was not a formal repetition of the Last
Supper, Luke certainly means to recall that supper. As one commentator explains it, "Luke wants to make the point that the Christians of his
day were able to have the living Lord made known to them in their
'breaking of the bread' in a manner that was at least analogous to the
experience of the Emmaus disciples."[24]

So Jesus' fellowship around the breaking of the bread continues
with his disciples after his resurrection. It is, in fact, one of the most important ways in which he solidifies his post-resurrection fellowship
with them. Luke goes on in chapter 24 to describe Jesus' later meeting
with all the disciples. There he ate again, this time some fish (the bread
and fish together recalling the feeding of the five thousand in Luke 9).
John also tells of Jesus eating with the disciples on the beach after his
resurrection, but only Luke's account of the Emmaus disciples so directly recalls the Last Supper itself.

When Luke continues the story in Acts, he describes the vibrant fellowship of those first days after Pentecost, "They devoted themselves
to the apostle's teaching and fellowship, to the breaking of bread and
the prayers" (Lk 2:42). Almost every commentator, going back to
Calvin and beyond, agrees that this is Luke's way of saying that they
immediately followed Jesus' command from the Passover meal and
celebrated the Supper in remembrance of the Lord. Luke often refers to
the Lord's Supper by that simple phrase, "the breaking of bread," because this action of blessing the bread represented the whole meal.
Later, Luke says in Acts: "On the first day of the week, when we met to
break bread, Paul was holding a discussion with them" (Acts 20:7).
Again, this clearly is a celebration of the Lord's Supper, not only because of the reference to the breaking of bread, but because this happened on the first day of the week, the day of worship. It is almost certain that the Supper was celebrated then as part of a larger meal, later
called the *Agape*. We see this in Paul's description of the Lord's Supper
at Corinth as well (1 Cor 11:21).

Keeping in mind these references to the breaking of the bread after
Christ's resurrection ensures that we will not mistakenly assume that
the Lord's Supper merely carries the somber mood of the impending

---

[24]John Nolland, *Luke* (Dallas: Word, 1993), p. 1208.

crucifixion. Yes, we eat and drink to "proclaim the Lord's death," as Paul puts it (1 Cor 11: 26). But we also do so "until he comes [again]," which puts us in the mood of joyful anticipation. Above all, we need to remember that each celebration is not just a "Last Supper" remembrance with its overtones of grief and pain, but a meal with the risen Lord, who promises to be present with us by his Spirit and unites us with his ascended and glorious new humanity.

The meal that creates community. The Lord's Supper not only gathers a community, it creates a community.[25] We have already sensed the dynamics of that concept in the Jewish concept of the table blessing. The blessing and sharing of the bread and cup makes each person at the table a participant in them. And in a special way, since the Passover is, as we have seen, a sacrificial meal, the sharing of the bread and cup create a community that participates in the sacrifice. In fact, in every facet of the Lord's Supper that we have described so far, that communal aspect looms large.

It is in Paul's letters, however, that we discover the community-creating power of the Lord's Supper. In 1 Corinthians 11 Paul presents his most comprehensive discussion of the Supper, but the occasion is not a theological discourse on its meaning but a messy church fight. The church in Corinth is divided in several ways. One split separates people according to the leader to which they are loyal and who perhaps baptized them. Another fault line runs through the differing charisms and their relative importance. In chapter 11, however, Paul addresses another shocking division, between the haves and the have-nots.

As mentioned earlier, the likely setting of the Lord's Supper in the early church is an *agape* feast, a church potluck if you will, to which all were invited on a Sunday. At some point in the meal the bread and cup of the Lord's Supper were shared, eaten and drunk. The problem at Corinth evidently revolved around this larger meal. Here's how Laurence Stookey envisions it:

> The affluent members, because of their flexible schedules, could arrive early with the ample provisions. But those who had to work stated hours

---

[25]For a more in-depth and contemporary look at this theme, see chapter twelve.

could not arrive as soon, and those who were poor could contribute little or nothing to the community table. Rather than waiting for everyone to arrive, the wealthier members of the congregation began feasting early in the evening. By the time others arrived, most of the food and drinks were gone, and some people were indeed intoxicated.[26]

Paul's response to this situation is truly startling, not only for what it says about the sinful division in the church, but for what it says about the real power of the Lord's Supper. The groundwork for his response is already laid in the previous chapter. There he warns the Corinthians, using the lessons of Israel, that just because they have been baptized, and just because they participate in the Supper, does not mean they are saved. The Israelites were "baptized into Moses in the cloud and in the sea" (1 Cor 10:2), and they all "drank from the spiritual rock . . . , and the rock was Christ" (1 Cor 10:4). But they all died in the wilderness. They never made it to the Promised Land. Well, says Paul, the same thing will happen to you. Your baptism and your participation in the Supper does not guarantee your salvation (1 Cor 10:6-13).

Paul then addresses one of the most vexing problems at Corinth, the worship of idols in pagan ceremonies by some of the people. Without getting into the details of the historical background or Paul's response, for our purposes the important point Paul makes regards the power of the Lord's Supper to unite people into a community. "The cup of blessing that we bless, is it not a sharing in the blood of Christ? The bread that we break, is it not a sharing in the body of Christ?" (1 Cor 10:16). Those who gather around the table of the Lord and share in the body and blood of the Lord are bound together in a profound way.

But Paul is not finished with them. After a stern rebuke (1 Cor 11:17-22) and a solemn reminder of the central meaning of the Supper in the Lord's death, Paul makes the most startling claim of all:

> Whoever, therefore, eats the bread or drinks the cup of the Lord in an un-
> worthy manner will be answerable for the body and blood of the Lord.
>   Examine yourselves, and only then eat of the bread and drink of the
> cup. For all who eat and drink without discerning the body, eat and

---

[26]Stookey, *Eucharist*, p. 33.

drink judgment against themselves. For this reason many of you are weak and ill, and some have died. But if we judged ourselves, we would not be judged. But when we are judged by the Lord, we are disciplined so that we may not be condemned along with the world. (1 Cor 11:27-32)

The failure to "discern the body" refers, not to their failure to properly understand the presence of Christ's body in the bread and cup in some theological sense, but their failure to see that in their eating and drinking at this sacred meal they participate in the body of Christ. The two bodies, the body of Christ given for them on the cross and in the bread, and the body of Christ created by fellowship in him, cannot be separated. Their attempt to make such a separation was the real desecration of the meal. The community-making power of the Lord's Supper was so real for Paul that carelessly disregarding it brought illness and death into the fellowship.

For Paul, the Lord's Supper binds the participants together with Christ and with each other into a single body. This bond is not a mere symbol but actually points to the deepest reality of community. The one loaf which is Christ, and the one cup which is the sharing in his sacrifice binds us together so powerfully that breaking these bonds through carelessness or lovelessness has demonstrable physical effects. "It is the hidden depth of the church that the Eucharist discloses," says Alisdair Heron, "a hidden depth that lies in Christ, and only through him in the church itself."[27]

The Sunday feast. One final note on the New Testament's teaching about the Lord's Supper. The weekly Sunday gathering of the community always involved fellowship at the Lord's Table. As already noted, the very first description of the new community of disciples in Acts pictures "the breaking of bread" (Acts 2:42, 46). In Acts 20, in describing Paul's brief stay in Troas, Luke writes, "On the first day of the week, *when we met to break bread,* Paul was holding a discussion with them" (v. 7). Later it becomes clear that not even a young man falling from the window can keep them from the meal. In 1 Corinthians 11:20 we find the same expectation that each gathering includes the Lord's Supper. The Sunday gathering was from the beginning a combination

---

[27]Heron, *Table and Tradition*, p. 41.

of the synagogue and the upper room, the word and the meal. And the very earliest testimonies of the church's worship beyond the New Testament in Justin Martyr and Hippolytus likewise testify to the same unbreakable bond of word and sacrament.

It was also likely that Luke had this practice in mind in his story of the disciples on the road to Emmaus. In that journey on the "first day of the week," Luke also describes the well-worn path of the weekly liturgy: the word which burned within their hearts, and the breaking of the bread in which the living Christ was made known (Lk 24:13-35). How ironic that among many Protestants, who so honor the authoritative preaching of the Word, this practice has been neglected for so long.

SUMMARY

The sacrament that was instituted by the Lord at the Last Supper with his disciples has its roots in the Old Testament feast of the Passover. This Passover connection, in fact, informs much of the meaning and purpose of the meal. It is a sacrificial meal undertaken in a profound remembrance of God's saving acts, to which Jesus attached the commemoration of his own final and fulfilling sacrifice in the words over the bread and the wine. The Lord's Supper is also a meal of fellowship with the risen Christ, and the infant church immediately began to "break bread" together at their weekly Sunday celebrations. Paul further deepens our understanding of the meal by asserting its community-forming power and warning against any violation of that community as a violation of the body of Christ received in the Supper. The sacrament, finally, points us to its fulfillment in the great "wedding feast of the Lamb" and inspires the cry of expectation, "*maranatha!*" as we eat and drink "till he comes."

10

A BRIEF HISTORY OF THE THEOLOGY OF THE LORD'S SUPPER

Before I would have mere wine with the fanatics,

I would rather receive sheer blood with the Pope.

MARTIN LUTHER

Since many of the issues surrounding the understanding of the Lord's Supper today have their roots in specific historical developments, this brief survey is meant to help the reader grasp the main lines of these developments. I invite those readers who already have a good grasp of this historical development to skip this chapter and go on, with the option of returning here to answer specific questions. For those who want a deeper study, I recommend one of many other books that cover this development in much greater detail.[1]

More than with baptism, the Lord's Supper became the focus of strong theological differences through church history, and these differences still affect how we understand the sacrament today. My purpose here is to highlight as succinctly as I can the history of the development

---

[1]Brian Gerrish, *Grace and Gratitude* (Minneapolis: Fortress, 1993); Howard Hageman, *Pulpit and Table* (Richmond, Va.: John Knox Press, 1962); Alasdair I. C. Heron, *Table and Tradition* (Philadelphia: Westminster Press, 1983); Laurence H. Stookey, *Eucharist: Christ's Feast with the Church* (Nashville: Abingdon, 1993); Francis J. Maloney, *A Body Broken for a Broken People* (Peabody, Mass.: Hendrickson, 1993); T. F. Torrance, *Theology in Reconciliation* (London: G. Chapman, 1975), and *Conflict and Agreement in the Church* (London: Lutterworth, 1960).

of the theology and practice of the Supper. Perhaps this quick tour of the highlights will whet your appetite for more in-depth study.

Even a casual reader of the New Testament would have to agree that it constantly confronts us with a trinitarian God. But the New Testament does not offer a comprehensive theology of the Trinity. That remained for future generations to work out right up to the present day. The same can be said for the Lord's Supper. The New Testament tells us that the Supper was being celebrated regularly—weekly, in fact—in the church. It firmly anchors its institution in the narrative structure of the Passover, and it deals with some striking abuses that crept into its celebration. But the Bible does not give us a theology of the Lord's Supper. It does not answer some of the questions that have vexed and even divided the church in subsequent centuries over the meal that is the essence of its unity. For example, in what way are we to understand the word "is" when Christ says, "This is my body . . . this is my blood." Like so many other fascinating and knotty issues, such as the Trinity and the relationship of divine and human natures of Christ, that was left to be worked out by the Spirit-guided church over the centuries. As the church worked through these questions, it necessarily did so through the lenses of its own contemporary culture, philosophy and even politics.

The Early Church Fathers

The value of the early church fathers in our study of the Lord's Supper is that they offer us a viewpoint that is relatively close to the New Testament itself and not as yet caught up in the philosophical controversies that occupied the medieval church. For our purposes we will take Justin Martyr and Irenaeus as representative of this era.

Justin lived and wrote around A.D. 100 to 165, and is regarded as one of the finest apologists for the Christian faith in that era. We learn about his views on the Supper mainly from his brief accounts of the ways in which baptism and the Eucharist were celebrated at that time in order to ward of any misunderstandings of the practices. But while he is most concerned to let his readers know what was going on the Christian meetings, he also says something about what the Supper meant to the church.

For not as common bread and common drink do we receive these; but in like manner as Jesus Christ our Savior, having been made flesh by the Word of God, had both flesh and blood for our salvation, so likewise have we been taught that the food which is blessed by the prayer of His word, and from which our blood and flesh by transmutation are nourished, is the flesh and blood of that Jesus who was made flesh.[2]

In this brief passage we already find several developments that, while thoroughly based on the New Testament, move beyond it. First, Justin links the incarnation of Christ by the word of God with the food and drink of the Lord's Supper. Just as Christ became flesh by God's word, so by his word the bread and wine are "transmuted" to our flesh and blood to nourish us with himself. Already for Justin, the bread and wine were not common food; they had come to carry, somehow, "the very flesh and blood of that Jesus who was made flesh." Justin makes absolutely no attempt to explain this transaction, but almost casually affirms it. For Justin and his church, the bread and cup, in a very real way, carried with them the very life and presence of Jesus, his flesh and blood.

We find the same direct and simple explanation of the meaning of the Supper in Irenaeus (around A.D. 130-200). Irenaeus's great work was *Against the Heretics*. The heretics against whom he wrote were the Gnostic heretics who considered matter inherently evil and who therefore had no appreciation for sacraments, which convey spiritual reality through material things.

Arguing against Gnostic opponents by citing the sacraments as an essential element in Christian faith and worship, Irenaeus wrote,

> How can they say that the flesh which is nourished with the body of the Lord and with His blood, goes to corruption, and does not partake of life. . . . But our opinion is in accordance with the Eucharist, and the Eucharist in turn establishes our opinion. For we offer to Him His own, announcing consistently the fellowship and union of the flesh and the Spirit. For when the bread, which is produced from the earth, when it receives the invocation of God, is no longer common bread, but the Eucharist, consisting of two realities, earthly and heavenly, so also our bodies, when they receive the Eucharist, are no longer corruptible, having the hope of resurrection to eternity.

---

[2]Quoted in Heron, *Table and Tradition*, p. 60.

Whenever the mingled cup [water mixed with wine as was the cus-
tom] and the manufactured bread receives the word of God, and the Eucharist becomes the body of Christ, from which things the substance of
our flesh is increased and supported, how can they [Gnostics] affirm that
the flesh is incapable of receiving the gift of God which is eternal life,
which [flesh] is nourished from the body and blood of the Lord, and is a
member of him?[3]

Again we find the same almost naive (to ears trained by long years
of controversy) assertion as in Justin that by the word of God the common bread and wine become for believers the body and blood of the
Lord. Irenaeus offers no philosophical arguments or theological explanations. He takes as self-evident what must have been the common belief of the church at that time, that in the Communion bread and wine
Christians receive Christ's body and blood.

To this Irenaeus adds another idea that was broadly held in the church
at that time: that the eucharistic food was the food of eternal life. It was,
as another writer called it, "the medicine of immortality." The only New
Testament text that would clearly support this view is a eucharistic reading of John 6:54, "Those who eat my flesh and drink my blood have eternal life, and I will raise them up at the last day." We also know that Irenaeus was a student of Polycarp, who, in turn, was likely a student and
protégé of John. Indeed, as we can learn from other sources, John 6 was
widely interpreted eucharistically in the early church.

Irenaeus makes no attempt to get beyond the assertion that the consecrated bread and wine become the body and blood of Christ and the
food of immortality. He does not ask how this happens or at what exact
point it happens, except that it occurs in conjunction with Jesus' words.
For him and many of his contemporaries, the identity of the bread and
wine with Christ was a simple, universally acknowledged biblical fact.

As we move into the third century, however, some of this simple understanding of the Eucharist as the body and blood of the Lord falls under the more discerning eyes of Origen (c. 152-254).[4] In this era, especially under the influence of the Alexandrian school, a much more

---

[3]Irenaeus *Against the Heretics*, 5.2.3.
[4]For the following analysis of the early church fathers through Augustine, I am indebted to
the very fine work of Heron in *Table and Tradition*, pp. 69-79.

allegorical and figurative method of interpreting scripture came into vogue. Origin exemplifies this movement:

> Let the bread and cup be understood by the simpler people according to the general teaching about the Eucharist. But those who have learned a deeper comprehension ought also to observe what sacred proclamation teaches concerning the nourishing Word of truth. (Commentary on John 32.24)[5]

He explains this "deeper" understanding elsewhere:

> Even in respect of the bread, the benefit for the receiver depends on his sharing in the bread with a pure mind and a clear conscience. We are not deprived of any good merely by not eating of the bread sanctified by the word of God and prayer, nor do we [gain] any good by merely eating. ...In respect of the prayer which is added to it, it becomes profitable ... and is the cause of spiritual discernment in the mind which looks to its spiritual advantage. It is not the material bread that profits the person who eats the bread of the Lord, and does so worthily: rather it is the word which is spoken over it. (Commentary on Matthew 11.14)[6]

While there is nothing overtly objectionable in Origen's analysis, we do see the sharp end of a wedge between the spiritual and the physical that will grow increasingly broad as time goes by, so that they no longer hold together in the kind of seamless unity we find in Justin and Irenaeus.

THE PIVOTAL INFLUENCE OF AUGUSTINE

No other figure in the early church so towered over the next thousand years of church history through the Reformation as did Augustine of Hippo. Both the Roman church and the Reformers would call him their mentor in sacramental theology. It was Augustine who worked out some of the basic concepts of a sacrament which were to guide the church right up to the present. The word *sacrament* was already in common usage in Augustine's day. It was a standard translation of the Greek *mysterion*, a word which occurs a few times in the New Testament, and refers to the mystery, the unknown of God's will in Christ,

---

[5]Quoted in Heron, p. 68.
[6]Ibid., pp. 68-69.

which is being revealed in him through the church. The Latin word *sacramentum* was used in military life and denoted an oath administered upon enlistment in the army, or a pledge of money set aside in a legal dispute. It could either mean a solemn religious observance or a devoted object. Augustine's contribution was that he used the word to get at the ways in which things or actions could have the extra dimension of a sacred meaning.

In his observations of all religious people, pagan as well as Christian, Augustine noted that external, public and visible rituals are necessary for the practice of any religion, and these elements prevent it from receding into the purely private sphere. But, anticipating modern ritual theory, Augustine insisted that these public and visible rituals were more than mere externals. They had a deeper meaning, a broader impact. The two levels, the public and visible and the personal and spiritual, interacted with each other.

Augustine noted a twofold link between the visible and invisible aspects of the sacrament. The first is that the sacrament had to hold a likeness to what it signified. There had to be some kind of visible, sensible link between the inner and outer aspect. Second, the sign had to be identified as a sign by a word spoken about it. The link had to be made verbally. Hence, Augustine's famous dictum, "The word is added to the element and there results the sacrament."[7] Clearly, however, for Augustine the most important side of this linkage of invisible and visible, spiritual and physical, was the invisible and the spiritual. Commenting on Jesus' words in John 6, "He who eats of this bread will not die," Augustine writes, "But this is what belongs to the virtue of the sacrament, not the visible sacrament; he that eateth in his heart, not who presses with his teeth."[8]

This emphasis on the "spiritual" core of sacramental eating and drinking may certainly have corrected some possible misunderstandings of Justin's and Irenaeus's earlier simple association of the bread and wine with the body and blood of the Lord. It removes some magical possibilities from the outward signs and points to the importance

---

[7]Augustine "Tractates on the Gospel of John" *Tractate* 80.3, in *The Nicene and Post-Nicene Fathers* (Grand Rapids: Eerdmans, 1986), p. 344.
[8]Ibid., 26.12.

of faith. At the same time it opens the door to the inherently unbiblical dualism that will reverberate through the years to come. The danger Augustine raises is that the two sides of the sacramental equation, the invisible and the visible, the spiritual and the physical, may fall apart.

As Heron points out, Augustine himself did not escape this danger because his whole approach was deeply colored by his neo-Platonist thought and background.

> It was commonplace in that philosophical tradition that the world which we perceive is a copy of invisible realities which are discerned by the mind rather than by the eye. In a way, therefore, the whole universe could quite easily be understood as "sacramental" in Augustine's sense, and everything in it a reflection of invisible things. . . . The bond between the two sides could, as it were, be taken for granted; and so it has repeatedly through the centuries of the West, where Augustine's understanding of a sacrament as "the visible sign of invisible reality" has lodged itself deep into the foundations of Christian thinking, and come to serve as the almost unquestioned starting point for reflection upon "the sacraments." . . . What then is all too easily lost to sight is the fact that the bond between visible and invisible on which everything turns in Christian theology is not that supplied by a "sacramental universe," but is rather Jesus Christ himself. There is *the* link between God and man, heaven and earth, the divine and the creaturely, and, we must add, the spiritual and the material.[9]

Heron warns that we should not look to our ontological systems of philosophy to discover the inner dynamics of the sacraments,[10] but to Christ himself, who is the heart of the sacraments. His unique being, divine and human in two natures, indissolubly united yet unmixed, provides the framework of our understanding of the sacrament. So while there is a fruitful advance in Augustine's thought, we can also say that it placed the theology of the sacraments on the wrong track for centuries, and we are still struggling to find the way back.

---

[9]Heron, *Table and Tradition*, p. 73. Heron's correct assertion that Augustine kept the visible and invisible together in a "sacramental universe" may seem to collide with the title and content of my first chapter, but I believe that only the incarnation can hold together the visible and the spiritual, thus making possible a world which is sacramental.

[10]This is not to say that philosophical investigation does not contribute to our understanding of the sacraments.

A number of other embryonic theological and philosophical ideas
that would later come to birth began in these earliest days of the
church. Among them Heron especially emphasizes two: the increasing
focus on the divinity of Christ in response to the Arian heresy, which
denied Christ's divinity; and an increased conviction that the church is
the divinely instituted, hierarchically run, representative of Christ's
authority on earth. Both of these emphases, along with the split between physical and spiritual already seen in Augustine, would contribute to the situation we find by the time of the Reformation in which
the church is the controller and dispenser of grace through the sacrifice
of the Mass.[11]

THE MEDIEVAL EDIFICE

The development of medieval eucharistic thought can be traced along
the lines of two important philosophies, Augustinian neo-Platonism
and Aristotelian natural philosophy. These philosophies provide the
underpinning for the medieval church's understanding of the sacraments.[12] For those of you who have lost your notes from that one philosophy course you took way back in college or seminary, Laurence
Stookey offers a concise summary of these schools of thought, especially focusing on how they relate to the meaning of the Lord's Supper.[13] Augustinian dualism, as described above, was later given a more
rigorous philosophical underpinning in Aristotle's natural philosophy.
The question was this: If, according to Augustine, the sacrament is the
visible and material manifestation of spiritual reality, then how is the
bread and wine connected with the actual body and blood of Christ?
Or how is Christ present to us in the sacrament?

The first major influence was Plato as adapted by Plotinus in the
third century. It was Plotinus's brand of Platonism (or neo-Platonism)
that was particularly influential with Augustine. Within this mode of
thinking the church found an elegant and satisfying way of "solving"

---

[11]See ibid., pp. 74-87.

[12]Since there are a number of good summaries of the theology of the sacrament up to the
Reformation, I will not take the time to rehearse its development here. Two especially clear
and brief summaries are Torrance, *Theology in Reconciliation*, pp. 122ff., and Heron, *Table
and Tradition*, pp. 80-107.

[13]Much of what follows in the next few paragraphs are nicely distilled in Laurence H.
Stookey, *Eucharist: Christ's Feast with the Church* (Nashville: Abingdon, 1993), pp. 42-52.

the mystery of how the bread and wine "became" the body and blood of the Lord.

One of the central issues of Plato's thought was the question of the identity of things. Noting that the same things we all call trees may in fact be very different from each other in form and size, leaves and fruit, the Platonists' answer was that there is something shared by all trees that exists apart from any particular tree. You might say that there is such a thing as an ideal or universal tree, which contains all "treeness." Furthermore, the difference between that ideal or universal tree and the particular trees we see is to be found in their actual existence in space and time.

To use the terminology of this philosophical framework, the particular trees were called "things" (Latin, *res*). The ideal tree exists before the thing we call a tree, and that ideal tree contains the essence, the most basic identity of the thing we see. This whole approach is called *realism*, not because the thing itself is so real, but because its real essence, its core identity, exists beforehand in the ideal. Christians who were influenced by this kind of neo-Platonist thought clearly saw the Creator behind all that is seen in the world. In the Creator's mind the ideal exists long before it takes on the form of the thing in the world.

Stookey explains how this philosophical idea was applied to the meaning of the Lord's Supper:

> We come to church bearing bread from our ovens and wine from our vineyards. They are bread and wine because they are shadows or sketches of The Bread and The Wine in heaven, which call into being all loaves of bread and all jugs of wine in the world. The bread and wine we bring to church are the "particulars" of The Bread and The Wine just as oaks and pines are particulars of The Tree and in the mind of God.
>
> In the course of the liturgy, however, a transfer of identity occurs. As a result the earthly bread is made real not by The Bread in heaven which shapes the ordinary loaves, but by the True Bread of Heaven, Jesus Christ. . . . But . . . this has nothing to do with the chemical composition of the bread and wine. . . . What is changed is the external [nonphysical] identity of the thing, not the identifiable characteristics of the thing.[14]

Though this way of thinking may seem far removed from our scientific

---

[14]Ibid., p. 44.

age, the early church, under the influence of the Platonists, found in it a satisfying explanation for how the bread and wine were, at the same time, the body and blood of the Lord. Augustine, a follower of Plotinus, thus emphasized the relationship between the sign (the actual bread and wine) and that to which the sign points: the body and blood of Christ.

As time went on, however, the idealism of Plato came to be replaced more and more by the "moderate realism" of Aristotle. For Aristotle a thing did not have identity outside of, or prior to, a particular thing. This is moderate realism because the particular is less separated from its true identity. Yet what might be called a thing's core identity was still separate from the actual physical characteristics. Those theologians who followed Aristotle's ideas taught that all physical objects have two components. One is its substance, the core identity. Even though it does not exist in some "heavenly form" like Plato's ideal, it was still not visible or observable. It was simply asserted that all trees have a substance that one might call "treeness." The other component of physical objects was the set of characteristics that varied from tree to tree: the size, color, shape, etc. These are called the "accidents" in contrast to the "substance."

As Stookey describes it, "The crucial difference between the two ancient philosophical systems is that Christian Platonists believed the true identity of a thing to be in a perfect or divine pattern in the mind of God prior to the creation of the object. Christian Aristotelians located the true identity within the object itself—in the 'substance' of that object, put there by God as part of the creative act."[15] We can see the difference this causes as we apply it to the bread and wine of the Lord's Supper. Platonists had no particular problem. By the word of Christ the bread and wine become the true bread and wine, the body and blood of Christ, which is what it "really" was anyway. For the Aristotelians, the issue was more complex. For them substance inhered in the thing itself, not in some heavenly ideal. Bread of various kinds share one substance, it is bread. If the bread of the sacrament is to be the body of Christ, the actual substance adhering to the object itself has to change. The medieval Aristotelian solution was that the bread baked

---

[15]Ibid., p. 47.

in the bakery and brought to church was both in *accidents* and *substance*, or essence, "bread"; but in the course of the liturgy, by the consecrating word of the priest (*hoc est corpus meum*, "this is my body") the substance changes into the body and blood of Christ. The same is true of the wine. At the Lord's Table a miraculous transfer of substance occurs. It was with this in mind that the term "transubstantiation" came into use. The substance is transformed into the body and blood of Christ even though the *accidents* (the taste, color, texture and physical makeup) of the bread never changes. Because the substance is the basic but invisible core reality of the bread and wine, they could say that it is truly changed from bread and wine to the body and blood of Christ. Now this is a very simple description of a much more complex philosophical construct. Yet it at least helps us to grasp the basic thinking behind transubstantiation.

That this change takes place in the liturgy points to a very important factor in the medieval understanding and practice of the sacrament. The church, through its priests, had the "power" to make this change take place. Instead of receiving the gift of Christ from God through the promise of his Word, the grace of Christ's presence and sacrifice were given *through the consecrating power of the church as the dispenser of grace through the sacraments.*

It is important to bear in mind that while these concepts seem odd and artificial to our modern way of thinking, they were almost universally accepted and utilized by the philosophers and theologians of the Middle Ages. They conversed in those terms as easily as we talk in terms of megabytes, subatomic particles and virtual reality. Stookey reminds us that "had the church not sought to understand its faith in terms of the intellectual concepts of its day, it would have sacrificed integrity."[16] And, we might add, it would have lost the opportunity to speak to its generation.

Thomas Aquinas provided the fullest and most elegant statement of this doctrine of transubstantiation in his *Summa Theologica II, quaestiones 75-77*, which was affirmed later by the Council of Trent and summarized in the *Tridentine Confession of Faith* of 1564.

---

[16]Ibid., p. 50.

> I confess . . . that in the Mass there is offered to God a true, proper, and propitiatory sacrifice for the living and the dead; and that in the most holy sacrament of the Eucharist there is truly, really and substantially the body and blood of our Lord Jesus Christ, together with his soul and divinity; and that a conversion takes place of the whole substance of the bread into the body, and of the whole substance of the wine into the blood, which conversion the catholic church calls transubstantiation. I also vow that even under a single *species* the whole and complete Christ and the true sacrament is eaten.[17]

In this official summary statement, all the eucharistic battle lines of the Reformation come into full view: Mass as sacrifice, transubstantiation and receiving Communion in only one kind. In the monolithic culture of the late medieval age, this was much more than a theological dispute; it involved ecclesiastical power, money and politics. The whole edifice of Rome's power and influence was tied to its control of the Mass's spigot of grace in the lives of the people, high and low. The church, through the priesthood, controlled the words that made Christ's saving body and blood available to the people, and the sacrifice that offered propitiation for the sins of the living and the dead. Such power is not easily given up and demands the strongest theological support.

THE REFORMATION: DISUNITY AT THE TABLE

With all its benefits—a return to the authority of Scripture, the reform of ecclesiastical abuses, the rediscovery of the centrality of grace and faith—the Reformation had its tragic side. And one of its greatest tragedies was the split between the various leaders of the Reformation over the Lord's Supper, the sacrament of unity. While I do not intend to give complete analysis of the views of the various Reformers, it is important to understand the basic issues over which they disagreed since they still affect our understanding of the Lord's Supper today.[18]

In 1529 at Marburg, many of the leaders of the Reformation signed the "Fifteen Articles" representing their agreement on the fundamental

---

[17]Quoted in ibid., p. 107.
[18]For a fuller analysis of the divisions over the Lord's Supper among the Reformers, see Heron, *Tradition and Table,* and Gerrish, *Grace and Gratitude.*

principles of evangelical doctrine. One issue remained unsolved. They could not agree on "whether the true body and true blood of Christ were really present in bread and wine."[19] The Reformers roughly divided into three viewpoints.

Luther had "devoured" Augustine over the years, and was deeply suspicious of the ways in which the sacrament had been held captive in Aristotelian categories. Luther's emphasis was on the clarity of the promises of God's Word. He clung fiercely to Jesus' words, "This is my body. . . . This is my blood" as the only true and worthy objects of our faith, and considered a rational or philosophical explanation of their meaning to be unnecessary.

Even though Luther found the doctrine of transubstantiation both biblically and philosophically unsupportable, he was willing to allow it to stand as an "opinion." Luther did not object to the *intention* of the transubstantiation, which was to make Christ truly present at the Lord's Table, but he objected to it as an *explanation* of how Christ was present. As Heron explains, "[Luther's] chief resentment is against [the imposition of transubstantiation] as an article of faith binding the conscience of believers, not at all against the virtual identification of the eucharistic bread with the body of Christ and the wine with his blood."[20] That identification was the foundation of Luther's deepest conviction, and it was to be accepted in simple faith apart from any philosophical or theological explanations. Luther also held that the bond between the real presence of Christ and the bread and wine are the words of institution. Since they are the words of Christ himself, they carry the weight of his word of promise and are therefore to be trusted completely, rather than understood completely.

Though there was some room for agreement with Rome over transubstantiation, Luther shut the door when it came to the doctrine of the sacrifice of the Mass. He not only attacked the commercial abuse of the sacrifice of the Mass, "turn[ing] the holy sacrament into mere merchandise, a market, and a business run for profit," but also attacked its underlying assumption that the Mass is a sacrifice of Christ to God and

---

[19] Heiko Oberman, *Luther: The Man Between God and the Devil* (New York: Image Books, 1992), p. 241.
[20] Heron, *Table and Tradition*, p. 113.

priests are uniquely empowered to offer it. Luther "insists that the Mass can *only* be received from God, not offered to him, and is in no sense therefore a 'work.'"[21]

On the other side of the table at Marburg sat Ulrich Zwingli, a learned scholar and preacher from Zurich. He had never been a disciple of Luther, and his leanings were decidedly more toward Erasmian humanism than the medieval piety and scholastic theology that were more familiar to Luther. His approach to understanding the Lord's Supper was also much more radical than Luther's. If Luther's watchword was "This is my body . . . ," Zwingli's was "Do this in remembrance of me." For him, Christ was not present at all in the sacramental signs. They only pointed the believer to Christ, reminding him or her of Christ's redeeming work and calling forth faith in Christ. The Eucharist became a testimony of faith in Christ but not a way of receiving Christ. For Zwingli grace and forgiveness came solely through the Holy Spirit, and the Spirit neither needs nor uses any intermediary vehicle such as the Eucharist. The sacrament is a sign of a past grace, of pardon consummated on the cross. It is merely a picture of that grace upon which we may meditate.

All this may sound vaguely familiar because Zwingli's view of the sacrament has become the primary view of many modern evangelicals. It places such an emphasis on the spiritual reality of Christ that the physical aspect of the bread and wine are merely incidental. For Zwingli, as for most evangelicals today, the stuff of physical life simply cannot carry the freight of spiritual reality. The Lord's Supper is essentially an opportunity for Christians to meditate with faith on the gift of grace and salvation offered in the cross of Christ as it is remembered at the table.

Both Luther, and later Calvin (who was not a participant at Marburg and had not yet begun his life's work) and their followers saw a fatal flaw in Zwingli's approach. Nothing really happened in the Eucharist except in the mind and faith of the recipient. The sacramental sign was an empty sign denying the foundational Augustinian conviction that the sacramental sign and the spiritual reality could not be separated. For Zwingli, God was simply not involved in the transaction. Only hu-

---

[21]Ibid., p. 113.

man faith was at work in the sacrament in such a way that the sign only called forth faith in Christ's redeeming work.

Fredrick Dale Bruner describes how Luther and Calvin fit between Zwingli on the one side and Rome on the other. "Luther and Calvin believed that both the Roman church on the right and the Zwinglian and Anabaptist churches on the left made the Lord's Supper too much a place *where believers did things for God*—either by offering Christ to God (Rome) or by offering their deep devotion to God (the Radical Protestants). The main direction of the Supper, in both of these views, was up."[22]

Both Luther and Calvin, deeply influenced by the fathers of the early church, felt that there was far more going on. The sacramental signs had to carry the freight of what God promised in them, namely the saving power of Christ's body and blood, his sacrifice on the cross, and his living presence.

It is safe to say that many historians and theologians across a wide spectrum of opinion have recognized the unique contribution that Calvin made to the theology of the Lord's Supper.[23] His way was truly a *via media* between the dualist tendencies of Zwingli and the lingering scholasticism of Luther. But, as Brian Gerrish points out, Calvin suffered the fate of many well-intentioned mediators: he was rejected by both sides. Bullinger, Zwingli's successor, wrote to Calvin: "I do not see how your doctrine differs from the doctrine of the papists, who teach that the sacraments confer grace on all who take them."[24] On the other hand, the Lutherans gave up trying to find accommodation with

---

[22]Fredrick Dale Bruner, *The Churchbook, Matthew 13—28* (Dallas: Word, 1990), p. 958.

[23]The main thrust of Calvin's own thoughts on the Lord's Supper may be found in *Institutes of the Christian Religion* 4.17, trans. by Ford Lewis Battles (Atlanta: John Knox Press, 1975); and "Short Treatise on the Holy Supper of Our Lord Jesus Christ," in *John Calvin: Selections from His Writings,* ed. John Dillenberger (Garden City, N.Y.: American Academy of Religion, Anchor Books Edition, 1971), p. 507. Excellent recent summaries of Calvin's theology of the Lord's Supper are Brian Gerrish, *Grace and Gratitude* (Minneapolis: Fortress, 1993); and Alisdair Heron, *Table and Tradition: Toward an Ecumenical Understanding of the Eucharist* (Philadelphia: Westminster Press, 1985), pp. 122-45. An older work that is still one of the most insightful summaries of Calvin's sacramental theology ever written is John Nevin, *The Mystical Presence and Other Writings on the Eucharist,* ed. Bard Thompson and George Bricker, Lancaster Series on the Mercersberg Theology, vol. 4. (Philadelphia: United Church Press, 1966). Nevin's work is also nicely summarized in James Hastings Nichols, *The Mercersburg Theology* (New York: Oxford University Press, 1966).

[24]Quoted in Gerrish, *Grace and Gratitude,* p. 3.

Calvin over the sacraments because they saw no real difference between him and Zwingli.

Calvin's path was to consistently affirm that Christ was truly given to believers in the Lord's Supper while denying Christ's physical presence in the bread and wine. Here is his own summary of what he hoped, in vain as it turned out, to be an agreement that would bring all the parties together:

> We all confess, then, with one mouth, that, in receiving the sacrament in faith, according to the ordinance of the Lord, we are truly made partakers of the real substance of the body and blood of Christ. How this is done, some may deduce more clearly than others. But be this as it may, on the one hand we must, to shut out all carnal fancies, raise our hearts on high to heaven, not thinking that our Lord Jesus Christ is so abased as to be enclosed under any corruptible elements. On the other hand, not to diminish the efficacy of the sacred mystery, we must hold that it is accomplished by the secret and miraculous virtue of God and that the spirit of God is the bond of participation, for which reason it is called spiritual.[25]

As this summary shows, at the heart of Calvin's theology of the Lord's Supper stands his insistence on some form of "real" presence of Christ in the bread and wine by the operation of the Holy Spirit. Those who receive the sacrament genuinely participate in the body and blood of Christ and are united with this divine and human person through the signs of the Supper in a way in which the sign and the reality are distinguished but not separated. He writes, "We will confess, without doubt, that to deny that a true communication of Jesus Christ is presented to us in the Supper, is to render this holy sacrament frivolous and useless—an execrable blasphemy unfit to be listened to."[26] The sign and the reality cannot be separated, as Zwingli does. The words of Christ at the table, "This is my body . . . this is my blood," affirm a solemn promise to us, and Calvin very clearly believes that what God promises, he does.

Promise is the important word. One of the main distinctions between the Roman doctrine of the Eucharist and the Calvinist doctrine is that for Calvin the focus is on God and not on the signs of bread and wine.

---

[25]Calvin, "Short Treatise on the Holy Supper," p. 540.
[26]Ibid., p. 513.

As Nicholas Wolterstorff describes it, "A sacrament, says Thomas, is a sign that both signifies a sacred reality and effects sanctification in human beings." For Thomas the focus is on the signs and what they effect. For Calvin, however, "A sacrament is a sign whereby God effects in us the promise that God signs and seals to us with that sign." The difference is that for Thomas, the sign is the agent, and for Calvin, God is the agent. If God is the sacramental agent, then issues of the nature of the change in the substance become less important.[27]

However, there is a distinction to be made between the signs and the reality. Calvin had no sympathy at all for the idea that Christ is somehow physically present, in such a way that he is "enclosed under any corruptible elements." But underlying this unthinkable debasement of Christ is the theological issue of Christ's locality. The ascended Lord is at God's right hand in his humanity and divinity. In order for him to be fully and physically present in the Supper, his humanity as well as his divinity would need to be ubiquitous. "We must neither destroy the reality of the nature [of the Lord's humanity], nor derogate in any respect from his state of glory. To do so we must always raise our thoughts on high, and there seek our Redeemer. For if we would place him under the corruptible elements of this world, besides subverting his human nature, we annihilate the glory of his ascension."[28] One might think that a neat solution to the problem would be to think of Christ's presence in the Supper in his divinity alone. This solution was rejected by one and all, since it would separate the natures of Christ, which cannot be separated, and it would deny what the real presence of Christ demands, that we commune with his whole person, including his human nature in which he won our redemption.

Calvin's solution to the dilemma of affirming the real presence of Christ without making it crassly physical was to turn eastward. "Calvin took up again the insight of the Eastern tradition and the Greek fathers, pointing to the need for a proper place for the *epiclesis* [calling forth] of the Spirit in the eucharistic celebration."[29] The Holy Spirit unites us to the ascended Lord, as the Lord himself promised.

---

[27]Nicholas Wolterstorff, "Not Presence, but Action: Calvin on Sacraments," *Perspectives* 16 (March 1994): 16-22.
[28]Calvin, "Short Treatise on the Holy Supper," p. 530.
[29]Heron, *Table and Tradition*, p. 128.

But in a special way the Spirit enables us to share in our union with Christ sacramentally. This means much more than something as vague as Zwingli's assertion that Christ is "spiritually" present in the Supper. Calvin asserted that the Holy Spirit is the agent that links us to Christ in the sacrament in such a way that the fullness of Christ's body and blood are communicated to us. This sacramental presence is not accomplished by our faith, as Zwingli would have it, but by the Holy Spirit himself, through whom we actually receive Christ in the bread and wine. "Even though it seems unbelievable to us that Christ's flesh, separated from us by such a great distance, penetrates to us, so that it becomes our food, let us remember how far the secret power of the Holy Spirit towers above all our senses."[30] For Calvin, the *sursum corda*, "lift up your hearts," was a favorite liturgical phrase, because at the Lord's Table we lift up our hearts to Christ in heaven by the Spirit who has united us with him in his glorified humanity. By the same Spirit and through the sharing of the bread and wine, we now partake in a unique way of that union with Christ.

The word *spiritual* has been so debased in modern usage, that it is inaccurate to classify Calvin's view of Christ's presence by means of the Holy Spirit as merely "spiritual." It does not mean that Christ is present only in "spirit," or only through the believer's exercise of imagination or faith. The Holy Spirit is the bond of union between the worshipper and Christ, binding her to the life-giving flesh and blood of Christ and his whole divine/human person. The sacraments are the Spirit's means of grace in the same way as the Spirit uses the Word to bind believers to Christ. But in the case of the Supper, the Spirit binds us with Christ's own flesh and blood.

John Nevin, an insightful nineteenth-century interpreter, clarifies Calvin's view:

> The communion in question is not simply with Christ in his *divine nature* separately taken, or with the *Holy Ghost* as the representative of his presence in the world. . . . [I]t is a real communion with the Word made flesh, not simply with the divinity of Christ but with his humanity also, since both are inseparably joined together in his person, and a living union with him in the one view implies necessarily a living union with him in

---

[30]John Calvin *Institutes* 4.17.10.

the other view likewise. In the Lord's Supper, accordingly, the believer communicates not only with the Spirit of Christ, or with his divine nature, but with Christ himself in his whole living person, so that he may be said to be fed and nourished by his very flesh and blood. The communion is truly and fully with the *man* Christ Jesus, and not simply with Jesus as the Son of God.[31]

Calvin never claimed to explain or even understand this sacramental mystery:

> Now if anyone should ask me how this takes place, I shall not be ashamed to confess that it is a secret too lofty for either my mind to comprehend or my words to declare. And, to speak more plainly, I rather experience than understand it. Therefore I here embrace without controversy the truth of God in which I may safely rest. He declares his flesh the food of my soul, his blood its drink. I offer my soul to him to be fed with such food. In his sacred supper he bids me take, eat, and drink his body and blood under the symbols of bread and wine. I do not doubt that he himself truly presents them, and that I receive them.[32]

In this statement of faith we can also see the importance Calvin places, with Luther, on the plain and simple meaning of Christ's words. He takes them as a promise which Christ himself fulfills through the operation of the Holy Spirit in our hearts. The proper stance of the believer in partaking of the Supper is not therefore to meditate on Christ's presence and sacrifice, but to receive it in faith as a child receives its mother's milk. Partakers of the sacrament "may be understood not to receive it solely by imagination or understanding of the mind, but to enjoy the thing itself as nourishment to eternal life."[33]

My favorite expression of Calvin's theology of the Eucharist comes from the Scots Catechism of 1560:

> We assuredly believe . . . that in the Supper rightly used, Christ Jesus is so joined with us, that he become very nourishment and food of our souls. Not that we imagine any transubstantiation of bread into Christ's body, and of wine into his natural blood . . . but this union and conjunc-

---

[31]Quoted in James Hastings Nichol, ed., *The Mercersburg Theology* (New York: Oxford University Press, 1966), p. 203.
[32]Calvin *Institutes* 4.17.32.
[33]Calvin *Institutes* 4.17.19.

tion, which we have with the body and blood of Christ Jesus in the right use of the sacraments, is wrought by operation of the Holy Ghost, who by true faith carries us above all things that are visible, carnal and earthly, and makes us to feed upon the body and blood of Christ Jesus, which was once broken and shed for us, which is now in heaven and appears in the presence of his Father for us. . . . So that we confess, and undoubtedly believe, that the faithful, in the right use of the Lord's Table, do eat the body and drink the blood of the Lord Jesus, that he remains in them and them in him . . . And therefore, whosoever slanders us, as that we affirm or believe sacraments to be naked and bare signs, sows injury unto us, and speaks against the manifest truth.

With the close of the age of the Reformation, the various views, Roman Catholic, Zwinglian (Anabaptist), Lutheran and Calvinist, remained fairly constant into the twentieth century. One important exception on the Calvinist side was the general tendency of the Reformed churches toward a Zwinglian view of the sacraments.[34] I discovered an interesting example of this gradual shift in a conservative twentieth-century Reformed theologian, Louis Berkhof. In his *Systematic Theology*, Berkhof quotes Charles Hodge approvingly: "A very common interpretation of the *dubious* points in Calvin's doctrine [Calvin's too literal idea of the communicant partaking of the body and blood of Christ] is that the body and blood of Christ are present only virtually, that is, in the words of Dr. Hodge, 'that the *virtues and effects* of the sacrifice of the body of the Redeemer on the cross are made present and are actually conveyed in the sacrament to the worthy receiver by the power of the Holy Ghost, who uses the sacrament as His instrument according to His sovereign will.'"[35] This interpretation, sometimes called "virtualism," became the orthodox Calvinist interpretation of the Lord's Supper in the late nineteenth and early twentieth centuries. Its basic idea is that we do not really receive Christ's body and blood, but only its virtues or benefits. Contrast this with Calvin's own words:

Hence we conclude that *two* things are presented to us in the Supper, viz., *Jesus Christ* as the source and substance of all good; and, *secondly, the*

---

[34]This is thoroughly discussed in Howard Hageman, *Pulpit and Table* (Richmond, Va.: John Knox Press, 1962).
[35]Louis Berkhof, *Systematic Theology* (Grand Rapids: Eerdmans, 1965), p. 654 (italics mine).

fruit and efficacy of his death and passion. This is implied in the words which were used. . . . Hereby he intimates, first, that we ought not simply to communicate in his body and blood, without any other consideration, but in order to receive the fruit derived to us from his death and passion; secondly, that we can attain the enjoyment of such fruit only by participating in his body and blood, from which it is derived.[36]

Calvin always affirmed that in the sacrament the "sum and substance" is Christ himself, and *through* him we also receive the benefits of his sacrifice. Later Calvinists, like Hodge, truncated this to understand that we receive *only* the benefits of his death and resurrection in the Supper.

TWENTIETH-CENTURY ECUMENICAL DISCUSSIONS

While the various approaches laid down at the time of the Reformation remained fairly static for centuries, more recently a fresh discussion of these issues has taken place across the ecumenical spectrum. On the Roman Catholic side, realizing that the Aristotelian philosophical underpinnings of the doctrine of transubstantiation no longer worked in the atmosphere of the twentieth century, theologians have creatively sought to bring some nuance to the tradition. In the heady days leading up to Vatican II, Roman Catholic theologians began to experiment with different ways of expressing classical Catholic doctrine of the Eucharist. Karl Rahner spoke of the presence of Christ in the Eucharist as a "real symbol," and Dutch theologian Edward Schillebeeckx introduced the idea of "transignification" as a refinement of transubstantiation, while German theologian Hans Küng virtually adopted Calvin's eucharistic doctrine.

Schillebeeckx offers the most interesting example of a Roman Catholic rethinking the formulas from the Council of Trent by seeking to speak in the philosophical and theological language of the twentieth century.[37] He, along with a number of other contemporary Roman Catholic theologians, struggled with the language of Trent, particularly its Aristotelian thought patterns, because they realize that the Ar-

---

[36]Calvin, "Short Treatise on the Holy Supper," p. 513 (italics mine)

[37]Edward Schillebeeckx, *The Eucharist* (New York: Sheed and Ward, 1968). Joseph M. Powers offers a very concise explanation of Schillebeeckx in "*Mysterium Fidei* and the Theology of the Eucharist," *Worship* 40, no. 1 (1968): 17-35.

istotelian framework has been largely discarded by twentieth-century philosophers. He wanted to move away "from a purely physical level to the specifically sacramental level, the level on which the inner meaning of ritual and liturgical language is the content of the power of the sacrament: the sacraments of the new law contain the grace *which they signify.*"[38] By a "sacramental level of understanding" Schillebeeckx seems to mean that the very language of ritual and liturgy convey meaning and reality to us in ways that go beyond the purely physical. It is not merely the sacramental food, but the setting in which they are given that feed us on a sacramental level. For example, "a colored piece of cloth may be purely decorative, but if the government declares that this is the national flag, its meaning has radically changed since it is the organ through which patriotism is expressed."[39] Within the context of liturgical life, Christ gives himself personally to his people. Christ does not merely make a "visit" in the physical transformation of the bread and wine, but he truly gives himself. "In this *commemorative* meal, bread and wine become the subject of a new *establishment of meaning*, not by men, but by the living Lord of the church, through which they become the *sign* of the real presence of Christ giving himself to us."[40]

Schillebeeckx was self-consciously using a new language to describe the eucharistic presence of Christ. He used the term "transignification" to bypass the implications of transubstantiation. Transignification involves the personal and real presence of Christ communicated through the signs of bread and wine. "This is what is effected, in an infinitely, ontologically deeper way, in the intimate presence of Christ in our hearts by means of this real presence offered to us in bread and wine become sacramental food." Over and over Schillebeeckx emphasizes the personal presence of Christ in the hearts of believers through the bread and wine, a thought so dear to Calvin as well. He opposes what he calls "eucharistic materialism" with

> an interpersonal relationship in which Christ gives himself to man by means of bread and wine which, by this very gift, have undergone . . . an ontological and therefore radical transignification. . . . The chemical,

---

[38]Powers, "*Mysterium Fidei*," p. 31.
[39]Horton Davies, *Bread of Life, Cup of Joy* (Grand Rapids: Eerdmans, 1993), p. 223.
[40]Quoted in Powers, "*Mysterium Fidei*," p. 223 (italics mine).

physical, or botanical reality of bread and wine is not changed; otherwise, Christ would not be present under the sign of eatable bread and drinkable wine. Eucharistic sacramentality demands precisely that the physical reality does not change, otherwise there would no longer be a eucharistic sign. But in its ontological reality, to the question "What *is* this bread ultimately, what *is* this wine ultimately?" one can no longer answer, "bread and wine," but instead, "The real presence of Christ offered under the sacramental sign of bread and wine."[41]

It seemed for a time that a fruitful dialogue between Catholics and Protestants on the Eucharist had emerged, and much good work took place. If Catholics like Schillebeeckx were backing away from a more crassly physical understanding of Christ's presence in the sacrament, Protestants began to be flexible about their favorite formulas, and genuine ecumenical concord around the Eucharist appeared possible. As time went on, however, concord became elusive. Pope Paul's encyclical *Mysterium Fidei* began to rein in some of these efforts on the part of Catholics; ecumenical dialogue began to falter along the old fault lines.

Interestingly, Schillebeeckx, whether out of deep conviction or because of the political realities of the Roman Catholic Church, struggled with the differences between his concept of transignification and the more traditional transubstantiation. He warned that just as a gardener must treat plants gently that have been transplanted, theologians have to be careful in the language they use when reworking the formulas of Trent. He acknowledged that he, along with other theologians, may sometimes upset the faithful. But he also charges that the clumsy reactions of the more conservative theologians, who identify the dogma of transubstantiation "with an almost chemical theology," not only overreact but misrepresent the true intent of Trent.[42] Schillebeeckx and his colleagues were trying to carry out the delicate task of remaining loyal to an older formulation of Christ's real presence while restating it in very different terms.

According to a *New York Times* survey in 1994, more than half the Catholics who attend weekly Mass believed that the bread and wine are "strictly the symbolic presence of Christ." Perhaps because of this, the

---

[41]Ibid., p. 189.
[42]Ibid., p. 184.

pendulum seems to be swinging back in present-day Catholicism, as we see more retrenchment than dialogue. In 2001 the U.S. Catholic Bishops released a Pastoral Letter on "The Real Presence of Jesus Christ in the Sacrament of the Eucharist." This document reflects an obvious concern that many Catholics are adopting a more "symbolic" view of the sacrament (as in Rahner and Schillebeeckx and their popularizers) rather than the traditional doctrine of transubstantiation. The bishops move decisively back toward Trent. They ask, for example, "Does the bread cease to be bread and the wine cease to be wine?" The answer: "Yes. In order for the whole Christ to be present—body, blood, soul, and divinity—the bread and wine cannot remain, but must give way so that the glorified Body and Blood may be present."[43] While the bishops seem to want to reintroduce the terminology of Aristotle and Trent, one can only wonder what the laity must be making of these terms. In my opinion, while this may lead to a sense of deeper mystery for some, it will lead many to conclude that the sacrament has little or no meaning for their lives. And it will certainly set back ecumenical discussions for some time. We can only hope that Protestant-Roman Catholic dialogue will continue, since it is critically important for the church's health and its witness to the world that we can gather at one table.

Meanwhile, on the Protestant side, much fruitful dialogue and some substantial agreement has come about in the past twenty-five years. The Evangelical Lutherans and the Episcopalians have recently come together in common table fellowship, having come to agreement on such thorny issues as Christ's real presence and the sacrificial nature of the Eucharist.[44] The Lima liturgy of 1982 provides the broad outline of an ecumenical agreement on the issues that have separated Christians at the table. While the liturgy slides over some of the thornier issues such as transubstantiation by offering alternate *epicleses*, it stands as a monument to how far we have come in a common understanding of the Eucharist and opens the possibility that we can more and more sit at the table together.

On the other hand, much of evangelical Protestantism seems uninter-

---

[43]Issued by the National Conference of Catholic Bishops, June 15, 2001. Available at <www.usccb.org/dpp/realpresence.htm>.

[44] See the "Concordat of Agreement" at <www.elca.org/ea/archives/concordat.html>.

ested in the sacrament, content to bring out the table from time to time as a kind of visual aid of redemption. In characterizing the theology and practice of the Lord's Supper among Reformed churches, Nicholas Wolterstorff succinctly covers much of the history I have described, and captures the situation among Protestant evangelicals generally:

> And so it is that, in spite of the sacramental theology of the Reformed churches and in spite of Calvin's strong preference regarding practice, the Reformed liturgy became a liturgy in which the sermon assumed looming prominence. The Reformed service became a preaching service—except for those four times a year when it was a Lord's Supper service. Whereas the medievals tilted Justin's [Martyr's] nicely balanced bifocal service way over toward the Eucharist, the Reformed now tilted it almost all the way toward the sermon. Calvin's theological victory was overwhelmed by Zwingli's liturgical victory.[45]

---

[45]In Donald McKim, ed., *Major Themes in the Reformed Tradition* (Grand Rapids: Eerdmans, 1992), p. 295.

11

A Theology of the Lord's Supper for Today

Love bade me welcome, yet my soul drew back,
  Guilty of dust and sin.
But quick-ey'd Love, observing me grow slack
  From my first entrance in,
Drew nearer to me, sweetly questioning
  If I lack'd anything.

"A guest," I answer'd, "worthy to be here";
  Love said, "You shall be he."
"I, the unkind, the ungrateful? ah my dear,
  I cannot look on thee."
Love took my hand and smiling did reply,
  "Who made the eyes but I?"

"Truth, Lord, but I have marr'd them; let my shame
  Go where it doth deserve."
"And know you not," says Love, "who bore the blame?"
  "My dear, then I will serve."
"You must sit down," says Love, "and taste my meat."
  So I did sit and eat.

GEORGE HERBERT, *LOVE III*

Each generation has the task of seeking to reframe theological tradition handed down to it in terms of its own intellectual and cultural setting. While we stand within the apostolic authority of the Bible and on the shoulders of our forebears, we need to say what it means to share in Christ at the table for us today. In some ways we will not be saying anything new but only retelling the tradition in a fresh way. In other cases, we may be given a new insight into the Lord's Supper because of the context in which we participate in it. In this chapter I will try to look at some of the historical issues in fresh ways, and in the next chapter to look at some of the practical and liturgical questions surrounding the sacrament that come from reframing it in the context of the contemporary church and culture.

For centuries the main questions asked of the Lord's Supper have been what? and how? Today, especially among evangelicals, the real question is why? Why celebrate the Lord's Supper at all? What good is it? What spiritual benefits does it bring? As we have seen in various ways over the course of this book, a particular kind of dualism has become dominant in American evangelicalism. It is less surely anchored in Christ's true humanity and much more comfortable with his divinity, and therefore it has a greater tendency toward losing that crucial bond between the physical and the spiritual, the earthly and the heavenly, the sign of the sacrament and the reality of Christ's presence it conveys. In terms of the Reformation split, Zwingli's understanding of the sacrament as a testament of our faith and reminder of Christ's loving sacrifice to our believing hearts typifies the understanding that most evangelicals have of the Lord's Supper, even among churches that are historically more open to sacramental understanding. Already in the mid-nineteenth century, John Williamson Nevin and Philip Schaff, the remarkably intuitive Mercersburg theologians, challenged the abandonment of Calvin's rich sacramental heritage by historically Calvinist churches.[1]

In practice, this means that the preaching of the Word (and now in many cases the singing of "praise and worship" songs) dominates our

---

[1]See James H. Nichols, *The Mercersburg Theology* (New York: Oxford University Press, 1966).

worship, while the sacrament has been sidelined.[2] Most evangelicals feel comfortable with this situation, mainly because they do not understand how the sacraments, and specifically the Lord's Supper, operate within the life of faith. They would contend that they receive Christ through faith in God's Word that comes in the preaching of the gospel. In the Word we encounter Christ through the work of the Holy Spirit. Few would argue with that contention. But where does the sacrament fit in? What do I receive in the sacrament except for an occasional vivid reminder of Christ's sacrifice for me? And, in this day of PowerPoint and other media, the sacrament doesn't even do a very good job of that. We might better watch some scenes from the movie *The Passion of the Christ*. Calvin and Luther and their successors clearly taught that the Word and the sacraments are both means of grace, ways in which we appropriate God's grace in Christ. We have lost an understanding of what the role of the sacrament is in relation to the preaching of the Word. Or, in other words, what do I get in the sacrament that I do not get in the Word alone? Why the sacrament?

Philosopher Nicholas Wolterstorff, who is committed to a rejuvenation of sacramental life in the church, has examined this question, looking at it through the prism of modern communication theory (just as Aquinas and the medieval scholastics looked at the sacrament through the lens of Aristotelian philosophy).[3] Wolterstorff uses J. L. Austin's pioneering way of thinking about communication called "speech-action theory." He defines speech-action in three categories: locutionary actions, illocutionary actions and perlocutionary actions. Wolterstorff helps explain these distinctions with an example: "Suppose I relieve your anxiety by promising that I will buy new tires for your car and I do so by leaving a note for you on which I have inscribed the words, 'I'll buy new tires for your car this afternoon.' In that case, my **locutionary** act is the act of *inscribing* the words; 'I'll buy new tires for the car this afternoon.' My **illocutionary** act is the act of *promising* you that I will buy new tires for the car this afternoon; my act of inscribing those words *counts* as my act of making the promise. And my **perlocutionary**

---

[2]For an informative summary of this historical process, see Howard Hageman, *Pulpit and Table* (Richmond, Va.: John Knox Press, 1962).
[3]Nicholas Wolterstorff, "Not Presence, but Action: Calvin on Sacraments," *Perspectives* 16 (March 1994): 18-22. (The following paragraphs summarize Wolterstorff's fine article.)

act is my act of *relieving your anxiety* by making that promise to you; my performance of this act adheres in the causal *effect* of my illocutionary action."[4] The point of all this is that speech/action operates on different levels and for different purposes.

Wolterstorff applies this to the relationship of Word and sacrament with particular attention to Calvin. The nexus of the relationship of Word and sacrament roughly fits the relationship between locutionary and illocutionary speech/action. The locutionary act is making a promise. The illocutionary act is writing a note, the writing of which stands for the promise itself. But we can immediately sense that there might be a number of other ways in which locutions become illocutions. Pictures, gestures and signals of various kinds can be substituted for written words on a note but convey the promise in a new way.

Sacraments do the same thing; they present Christ to us. In that sense "the content of the sacraments is the same as the content of the preached Word; both of them present to us the promise of our redemption in Jesus Christ." Yet while Word and sacrament both present Christ to us, they do so in distinct and complementary ways. Their illocutionary stance (as Austin calls it) is different. Calvin's favorite metaphor for the sacrament is a seal. In the sacrament God seals, ratifies, guarantees and confirms his promises in Christ to us. "The seals which are attached to government documents and other public acts are nothing taken by themselves, for they would be attached in vain if the parchment had nothing written on it. Yet when added to the writing, they do not on that account fail to confirm and seal what is written."[5]

One problem with the metaphor of a seal is that the content of an official document does not count until the seal is attached. Calvin did not mean to say that the preached Word does not count until the seal of the sacrament is attached to it. God's promise of redemption has been made in Christ and it is proclaimed in Scripture and preaching. Wolterstorff offers a clarification of Calvin's metaphor. While the official seal validates the document and its contents when it is attached "then and there," the sacrament offers God's assurance "here and now" that what God promises remains in effect. "In the sermon God tells us, by way of

---

[4]Ibid., p. 18 (italics his, bold mine).
[5]John Calvin *Institutes* 4.14.5.

the words of the preacher, of the promise already made in Jesus Christ. In the sacrament God doesn't so much *tell* us of that promise as *here and now assure us* that it remains in effect."[6] Preaching the gospel tells us about a promise once made, and in which we are called to believe; while receiving the sacrament here and now assures us that it remains in effect. To use Austin's terminology, the sermon is locutionary, the sacrament is illocutionary. Preaching declares God's promises; the Supper offers the concrete and physical here-and-now assurance of that promise.

Getting back to the original question—Why do we need to celebrate the Supper when we have the preaching of the Word?—we begin to see that preaching and sacrament are different mediums of communication of the same Word, both of which are essential. What the sacrament offers is a more personally reassuring medium of God's promise than what comes through Scripture and preaching. While the sacrament without Scripture and preaching would be an empty sign, Scripture and preaching without the sacrament do not offer us the here-and-now assurance we need. For Calvin, "the sacraments, therefore, are exercises which make us *more certain* of the trustworthiness of God's Word" because God "attests his good will and love toward us more expressly than by word."[7] That is not a point most of us would have expected Calvin to make! Calvin, who so honors Scripture and preaching, says that the sacrament presents the promises of the gospel to us more clearly. "The Lord here not only recalls to our memory . . . the abundance of his bounty. But, so to speak, gives it into our hands and arouses us to recognize it."[8]

We need the sacrament alongside the Word simply because we are human. It's not merely that the sacrament aids our human *understanding* of God's promises. That is Zwingli's approach. It's rather more that the sacrament aids our *appropriation* of God's promises. First, we need physical and material confirmation of our new relationship with God in Jesus Christ because we are physical and material beings. Second, we need assurance because of our human weakness, and especially the

---

[6]Wolterstorff, "Not Presence," p. 19.
[7]Calvin *Institutes* 4.14.6 (italics mine).
[8]Calvin *Institutes* 4.17.37.

weakness of our faith. The Reformed confessions play these two themes whenever they speak of the sacraments, as in this portion of the Belgic Confession of 1561:

> We believe that our good God, mindful of our *crudeness and weakness,* had ordained sacraments for us to seal his promises in us, to pledge his good will and grace toward us, and also to nourish and sustain our faith. He has *added* these to the Word of the gospel to represent better to our *external senses* both what he enables us to understand by his Word and what he does inwardly in our hearts, *confirming* in us the salvation he imparts to us.[9]

In the sacrament, then, God communicates to us in a way that is particularly suited to our creatureliness. As humbling as that may be, we need more than talk, more than words on a page; we need a touch, a smell, a taste—just as lovers need more than the words "I love you" but also a kiss or an embrace. But the sacrament is more than a medium of communication; it is a medium of action, God's action. The sacrament, to use Austin's terms, is speech/action. This "speech" accomplishes what it says. It assures us of the promises of God in Christ. In Austin's terms, it has a perlocutionary effect.

Remember that in the analogy of the note about fixing the tire, the "**perlocutionary** act is my act of *relieving your anxiety* by making that promise to you; my performance of this act adheres in the causal *effect* of my illocutionary action."[10] In other words, the sacrament must have the effect of offering assurance by its action. For Calvin the agent of that perlocutionary act is the Holy Spirit. The Holy Spirit operates in our hearts so that they open up to what the Word and sacraments convey. "The sacraments properly fulfill their office only when the Spirit, that inward teacher, comes to them, by whose power alone our hearts are penetrated and affections moved and our souls opened for the sacraments to enter in. If the Spirit be lacking, the sacraments can accomplish nothing more in our minds than the splendor of the sun shining upon blind eyes, or a voice sounding on deaf ears."[11] In this way the Holy Spirit acts in the sacraments in exactly the same way as in the

---

[9]Belgic Confession, Article 33 (italics mine).
[10]Wolterstorff, "Not Presence," p. 18 (bold mine).
[11]Calvin *Institutes* 4.14.9.

reading and preaching of the Word. The Holy Spirit teaches, authenticates and applies the promises of God in Christ in both Word and sacrament. And in both cases, the Holy Spirit acts to stimulate faith in the truth of God's promises by the Word, and in the assurance that they are ours by the sacraments.

Why do we need the sacrament of Holy Communion alongside the Word? The sacrament offers us something the Word alone cannot: deep assurance that is exactly fitted by God to our human need and receptivity. The Lord's Supper is a physical handle faith grabs hold of, allowing us to grasp God's promises with our bodies as well as our minds. We dare not neglect this handle that God has so graciously and wisely provided. The sacrament "incarnates" the Word, in a way that is analogous to how Christ was the original incarnate Word. Just as we needed his incarnation to reach us in our lostness and save us, so we need this liturgical and sacramental incarnation of the Word at the table to reach our hearts and awaken them to true faith in Christ.

I am familiar with a congregation that moved, a number of years ago, from a monthly celebration of Communion to a weekly celebration. There was a great deal of discussion about the fear that this might lead to over-familiarity, therefore reducing the effectiveness of the sacrament. (Try the same argument for sermons or even prayer.) Some people simply felt they didn't need the sacrament that often. After some time, the reaction of the vast majority of the congregation was that they could never return to a more sporadic celebration of the sacrament. The more they experienced the Lord's Supper, the more they realized their human need for this particular medium of God's promise, and the assurance it provides.

THE PRESENCE OF CHRIST

The age-old issue of the way in which Christ is present in the sacrament is more than just an exercise in philosophical gymnastics. It lies at the core of the sacrament's meaning and efficacy. The Heidelberg Catechism asks, "What does it mean to eat the crucified body of Christ and to drink his poured-out blood?" The answer is: "It means to accept with a believing heart the entire suffering and death of Christ and by believing to receive forgiveness of sins and eternal life." This is a fair representation of what many evangelicals mean by "asking Jesus into your heart." However, the Catechism, sensitive to the particular medium of the sacraments, goes further: "But it means more. Through the Holy Spirit, who lives both in Christ and in us, we are united more and more to Christ's blessed body. And so, although he is in heaven and we are on earth, we are flesh of his flesh and bone of his bone."[12]

Of course, Christ has promised his presence, and he is present with his people in a variety of ways. He is with us by his Spirit, the promised Paraclete, who unites us with him and teaches us with Christ's own words (Jn 14:15-18). He is with us in his church, "wherever two or three are gathered together in my name" (Mt 18:20). His culminating promise in Matthew speaks of his abiding presence, "And remember, I am with you always, to the end of the age" (Mt 28:20).

However, the fullest sign of his presence and union with his people is in the Supper which he established on the "night in which he was betrayed." The Eucharist bears the presence of Christ in a unique way that cannot be compared with any other mode of his presence. When he gathered in the upper room and said, "This is my body . . . this is my blood," the church has always believed that what Jesus there promised must be true, even though we may not be able to explain exactly how. So when the church still gathers around the table, it is with and in Christ, who again and again offers his living and saving presence in the bread and the wine.

In the New Testament, salvation is spoken of as much more than faith in Christ, or even faith in Christ's death and resurrection. Salvation is union with Christ. We become members of his body, united to him and identified with him by the Holy Spirit. "In Christ" is Paul's consistent way of describing a believer's union with Christ.[13] "So if anyone is *in Christ*, there is a new creation: everything old has passed away; see, everything has become new!" (2 Cor 5:17). His frequent use of that phrase tells us that the particular way in which we experience salvation is to be united with Christ who is the new human.

Both sacraments are means by which God effects and makes real to us our union with Christ. Baptism marks our identification with

---

[12]Heidelberg Catechism, Q and A 76 (1975 translation approved by the Synod of the Christian Reformed Church).

[13]For a full discussion of the theology of union with Christ, including its relationship to the Lord's Supper, see Lewis B. Smedes, *All Things Made New* (Grand Rapids: Eerdmans, 1970).

Christ, and the Lord's Supper continues to unite us with Christ and assure us of his grace as we eat his flesh and drink his blood. Jesus said, "Very truly, I tell you, unless you eat the flesh of the Son of Man and drink his blood, you have no life in you. Those who eat my flesh and drink my blood have eternal life, and I will raise them up on the last day; for my flesh is true food and my blood is true drink. Those who eat my flesh and drink my blood abide in me, and I in them" (Jn 6:53-56). As problematic as this passage may be, even if Jesus is not directly speaking of the Eucharist, John's first-century readers could hardly read it without applying Jesus' words to their experience of the Eucharist.[14] This is particularly true of the way in which Jesus moves from eating and drinking his flesh and blood to union with him. "Those who eat my flesh and drink my blood abide in me and I in them" (Jn 6:56). Very early, in reflecting on these verses, the church believed that the sacrament effected our union with Christ in a special way. It is no wonder, then, that the "real" presence of Christ in the Lord's Supper became and remains an important issue.

When Paul addresses the issues surrounding the Lord's Supper in 1 Corinthians 10—11, he also clearly indicates that union with Christ lies at the heart of the meaning of the sacrament. "The cup of blessing that we bless, is it not a sharing in the blood of Christ? The bread that we break, is it not a sharing in the body of Christ? Because there is one bread, we who are many are one body, for we all partake of the one bread" (1 Cor 10:16-17). The cup of blessing and the bread are both a "sharing" in the body and blood of Christ. Sharing here means participation, fellowship, union and, by implication, presence. As the church partakes of the Supper, Christ and his church come into what earlier theologians called "mystical union" with each other, pointing to the fact that it is a mystery beyond human understanding. Paul does not explain it, but he assumes it. What is true for Christ and his church is also true for Christians themselves. They become one body because

---

[14]Interestingly, While Calvin denies that in this portion of John 6 Jesus is discussing the Eucharist, he has no problem with applying these words to our eucharistic understanding: "And yet, at the same time, I acknowledge that there is nothing said here that is not figuratively represented, and actually bestowed on believers, in the Lord's Supper; and Christ even intended that the holy Supper should be, as it were, a seal and confirmation" (*Commentary on John*, p. 234).

they all partake of the one loaf, which is Christ. The Lord's Supper is a
sacrament of unity and presence, bringing into one body Christ and his
church. The sacrament does not merely picture this unity; it effects it
by the Holy Spirit. As I have mentioned before, when Paul comes to the
conclusion of his teaching on the Supper, he tells the Corinthians in the
plainest terms that their violation of body life through their disunity
brings dire spiritual and physical consequences to the church. Something is happening here that is far more than a picture or a mere symbol; their disunity violates the mystical unifying presence of Christ that
is effected in the bread and the cup.

For Calvin, this sacramental means of union with Christ becomes
one of the pillars on which he builds his theology of the sacrament.
One feels the excitement in his words:

> Godly souls can gather great assurance and delight from this Sacrament;
> in it they have a witness of our growth into one body with Christ such
> that whatever is his may be called ours. . . . This is the *wonderful exchange*
> which, out of his measureless benevolence, he has made with us; that,
> becoming Son of man with us, he has made us sons of God with him;
> that, by his descent to earth, he has prepared an ascent to heaven for us;
> that, by taking on our mortality, he has conferred his immortality upon
> us; that, accepting our weakness, he has strengthened us by his power;
> that, receiving our poverty unto himself, he has transferred his wealth to
> us; that, taking the weight of our iniquity upon himself (which op-
> pressed us), he has clothed us with his righteousness.[15]

> Through the sacrament we have access to all the blessings of our union
> with Christ because by the Spirit we are lifted up and brought into his
> presence. In this Sacrament we have such full witness of all these things
> that we must certainly consider them as if *Christ here present were himself
> set before our eyes and touched by our hands.* For his word cannot lie or de-
> ceive us: "Take, eat, drink: this is my body, which is given for you; this is
> my blood, which is shed for forgiveness of sins." . . . By bidding us take,
> he indicates that it is ours; by bidding us eat, that it is made one sub-
> stance with us; by declaring that his body is given for us and his blood
> shed for us, he teaches that both are not so much his as ours.[16]

Calvin goes on to distinguish his understanding of Christ's presence in

---

[15]Calvin *Institutes* 4.17.2 (italics mine).
[16]Calvin *Institutes* 4.17.3 (italics mine).

the Supper from Zwingli and others who "define the eating of Christ's flesh and the drinking of his blood as, in one word, nothing but to believe in Christ."[17] (Here Calvin might just as well be describing the views of many evangelical Christians today.) He admits that there is no other eating than the eating of faith: "But here is the difference between my words and theirs: for them to eat is to believe; I say that we eat Christ's flesh in believing."[18]

Calvin's distinction may seem too fine a point, but it makes all the difference. He maintains that the eating of Christ's flesh and blood in the sacrament is a way of believing in Christ that actually brings us into a nourishing communion with him. "In this way the Lord intended, by calling himself the 'bread of life' [Jn 6:51], to teach not only that salvation for us rests in faith in his death and resurrection, but also that, by partaking of him, *his life passes into us and is made ours*—just as bread when taken as food imparts vigor to the body."[19]

What do we really mean when we say that in the sacrament we receive the benefits of our union with Christ? What Christ is this? Calvin emphasized that by the Holy Spirit we are united with the Son of God in his glorified humanity now at God's right hand. This is one of the reasons he had problems with the approach of both Luther and the Roman church. In one way or another they would have Christ's physical, human presence on the altar so that Christ descends in the sacrament. For Calvin this violates the once-for-all ascension of Christ with his humanity to God's right hand:

> But greatly mistaken are those who conceive no presence of flesh in the Supper unless it lies in the bread. For thus they leave nothing to the secret working of the Spirit, which unites Christ himself to us. To them Christ does not seem present unless he comes down to us. As though, if he should lift us to himself, we should not just as much enjoy his presence! The question is therefore only of the manner, for they place Christ in the bread, while we do not think it lawful for us to drag him from heaven. Let our readers decide which one is more correct. Only away with that calumny that Christ is removed from his Supper unless he lies hidden under the covering of bread! For since this mystery is heavenly,

---

[17]Calvin *Institutes* 4.17.5.
[18]Ibid.
[19]Ibid. (italics mine).

there is no need to draw Christ to earth that he may be joined to us.[20]

Our union is with the crucified, risen and ascended Lord, our Savior and brother in heaven. In the Lord's Supper, Christ does not descend, we ascend through the power of the Holy Spirit to participate in the life and worship of our ascended Lord.[21] That is why the words "Lift up your hearts" were so central to Calvin's Communion liturgy. "[I]n his humanity there also dwells fullness of life, so that whoever has partaken of his flesh and blood may at the same time enjoy participation in life."[22] It is his glorified human life, a life that conquers sin and death, which nourishes us when we eat and drink his flesh and blood. Commenting on John 6 where Jesus calls himself the "bread of life" who now "gives life to the world," Calvin ties this life-giving power of Christ to the sacrament: "It is therefore a special comfort for the godly that they now find life in their own flesh. For thus not only do they reach it by an easy approach, but have it spontaneously presented and laid out before them. Let them but open the bosom of their heart to embrace its presence, and they will obtain it."[23]

One of the more helpful advances in the often thorny discussion of Christ's presence in the sacrament is the more recent movement away from talking about what Christ's "real" presence means to talk about it as Christ's personal presence. Max Thurian describes Christ's presence in the Eucharist as a "personal presence which enters into personal relationship with those who believe and receive." The emphasis falls on the person-to-person relationship. "A piece of furniture is not *present* in a room; it is *simply there*. People can be very near to one another, even crowded together in one place, in a bus, for instance, without being present to one another." Real presence assumes a personal relationship, mind to mind, heart to heart. Still, presence assumes not only a "spiritual" relationship, but also a physical one: "This personal relationship between people, this being present . . . cannot occur without the mediation of our bodies by which we give each other personal signs of being present."[24]

---

[20]Calvin, *Institutes* 4.17.31.
[21]See more on the role of the Holy Spirit below, pp. 200-204.
[22]Calvin *Institutes* 4.17.9.
[23]Calvin *Institutes* 4.17.8.
[24]Max Thurian, *The Mystery of the Eucharist* (Grand Rapids: Eerdmans, 1984), p. 52.

Commenting on the fact that his father died when he was four, philosopher Kevin Corcoran tells of keeping a sweater of his father's tucked away in a closet. Recently he moved, found the sweater and, before he even thought about it, buried his nose in it, trying "perhaps foolishly, to discover still in its fibers residual traces of what my father must have smelled like. My father's sweaters are not merely articles of clothing; they are sacred things, fraught with meaning. I choose the word *sacred* carefully. . . . My father's sweaters are sacred. But in them I do not find my father. As important to me as they are, I do not find in them what I want most to find. But here in the bread and the wine, I am not only reminded of Jesus, I am presented with him. For clothed in these common elements, like ordinary flesh in which God once came to us, God comes to us again and again. God comes to nourish, to heal, and to dress our deep wounds."[25]

The Lord's Supper is more than a faded memory of a long-gone person, it brings us his life-giving presence. Communion is not just another name for the sacrament of the Lord's Supper; it describes the very essence of what takes place in that sacrament. Christ brings us into a special communion with himself and with each other so that his life and saving power nourishes our bodies and souls. We become, as the Heidelberg Catechism says, "flesh of his flesh and bone of his bone."[26] And this communion with Christ is not merely some spiritual presence, but a Spirit-wrought communion with his actual person, his glorified humanity, and his life-giving flesh and blood. This is the testimony of Paul and John in the Bible, of the church fathers and of the Reformed tradition—and increasingly, of the ecumenical church.

The presence of Christ in the Lord's Supper involves this kind of personal presence which assumes a relationship of mutual love and is mediated through the physical means as any human relationship must. The presence of Christ in the sacrament may be called a "spiritual" presence in the sense that the Holy Spirit mediates it, but that term may mislead us into thinking that Christ's presence is purely symbolic and not, therefore, a "real" presence. Christ's presence must also be physical; that is, it must be a Communion of the body and blood

---

[25]Kevin Corcoran, "Taste and See," *Perspectives* (January 1997): 3.
[26]Heidelberg Catechism, Q and A 76.

of Christ. So we must insist that through the sacrament we are actually united with the very Son of God in his glorified humanity. All this is accomplished through the Holy Spirit, who is the bond between us and our ascended Lord.

To close this section I need to add that I believe that the fundamental truth around which we can arrive at an understanding of the Supper that has biblical and theological integrity is simply this: In the bread and wine of the sacrament we receive and share in the living Christ. However that may be explained or unexplained is secondary to the gracious gift we receive in it.

MEDIATED THROUGH THE HOLY SPIRIT

One of Calvin's most important contributions to the theology of the Eucharist is his emphasis on the Holy Spirit's work in personally bringing us into Christ presence through the sacrament.[27]

> Even though it seems unbelievable that Christ's flesh, separated from us by such great distance, penetrates to us, so that it becomes our food, let us remember how far the secret power of the Holy Spirit towers above all our senses, and how foolish it is to wish to measure his immeasurableness by our measure. What, then, our mind does not comprehend, let faith conceive: that the Spirit truly unites things separated in space.[28]

Here Calvin was drawing on his deep acquaintance with the Eastern Fathers. Their doctrine of *perichoresis,* or the co-inherence of the trinitarian persons emphasizes that the Holy Spirit links them to each other and to us. Jürgen Moltmann describes *perichoresis* as a "concept that grasps the circulatory character of the eternal divine life. An eternal life process takes place in the triune God through the exchange of energies. The Father exists in the Son, the Son in the Father, and both of them in the Spirit, just as the Spirit exists both in the Father and the Son. By vir-

---

[27]Some have criticized it, however, alleging that it is too simple, too contrived a solution. Kilian McDonnell, for example, while he supports Calvin's reliance on the Holy Spirit's work in the Supper also remarks, "It is not at all clear, not even tolerably unclear, as to how the Spirit makes present the body of Christ. There is much one could praise in Calvin's pneumatology but one has the impression that the Holy Spirit, to put it bluntly, is used" (*John Calvin, the Church, and the Eucharist* [Princeton, N.J.: Princeton University Press, 1967], p. 376).

[28]Calvin *Institutes* 4.17.10.

tue of their eternal love they live in one another to such an extent, that they are one. It is a process of the most perfect and intense empathy."[29] In this same *perichoretic* dynamic, the Holy Spirit who binds the Father and the Son in love and purpose, also binds us to Christ. Christ's real presence to us in the Lord's Supper is part of our whole relationship to Christ and to the Father through the Holy Spirit.

In order to understand this dynamic relationship it is necessary to recall that the Holy Spirit was deeply involved in everything the Lord is and does. The Holy Spirit caused his incarnation. The Holy Spirit empowered Jesus' ministry, as evidenced by the Spirit's descent at Jesus' baptism. The Spirit created a new humanity through Jesus' life, death, resurrection and ascension. So when we say that through the Spirit we have actual communion with Christ in the Lord's Supper, it is the very same activity that began in Jesus' redemptive and vicarious human life. The Son and the Spirit together are the agents of God's re-creation. Their intimate union, their dance of love and salvation, cannot be explained, for it belongs to the very nature of the most intimate relations of the Holy Trinity. The same Spirit whose life is entwined with Christ, he has now given to us. He is the *Paraclete* promised by Jesus in chapters 14 and 16 of John's Gospel, the same Spirit who powerfully filled the church at Pentecost. Our relationship to Christ, our union with him as the new human being through his vicarious life, death, resurrection and ascension, is really the opening up of the *perichoretic* embrace of the Father, Son and Holy Spirit to include us in that trinitarian fellowship.

Our fellowship with Christ in the Lord's Supper, what has classically been called his "real presence," is all part of this one great trinitarian fellowship effected through the Holy Spirit. As I noted in the previous section, Calvin consistently speaks of our participation in Christ in the sacrament as our ascent, rather than Christ's descent, for Christ has ascended in our glorious new humanity once and for all. While the "up" and "down" language may seem outdated, the idea is clear. Our communion with Christ in the sacrament takes place in heaven by means of the Spirit's lifting up our hearts to the ascended Lord. This way of thinking seemed somehow distant and unsatisfying

---

[29]Jürgen Moltmann, *The Trinity and the Kingdom* (Minneapolis: Fortress, 1993), p. 174.

until I recalled that Calvin was drawing on the insights of the Eastern Fathers for whom all of worship, and not just Holy Communion, centered on our involvement in the heavenly worship through the Holy Spirit. For them, and to a certain extent for Calvin too, worship is always joining heaven's ceaseless praise.

Let one eloquent theologian, Alexander Schmemann, elaborate this principle of worship through Eastern Orthodox eyes:

> The early Christians realized that in order to become the temple of the Holy Spirit they must *ascend to heaven* where Christ has ascended. They realized also that this ascension was the very condition of their mission in the world, of their ministry in the world. For there—in heaven—they were immersed in the new life of the Kingdom; and when, after this "liturgy of ascension," they returned to the world, their faces reflected the light, the "joy and peace" of that Kingdom and they were truly its witnesses. . . . In the church today, we so often find we meet the same old world, not Christ and His Kingdom. We do not realize that we never get anywhere because we never leave any place behind us.[30]

When we understand that all our worship involves joining the heavenly worship, every aspect of it becomes transformed. For one thing, it's not our worship, our work; it is part of the finished work of Christ. Worship is always in the name of the Son through the Holy Spirit. It is in the name of the Son because he is the mediator of the new covenant in whom God has joined human life, and the one in whom we draw near to God through the Spirit. "And thus in the Eucharist it is [the Holy Spirit] who *seals* and *confirms* our ascension into heaven, who transforms the church into the body of Christ—and therefore *manifests* the elements of our offering as *communion in the Holy Spirit*."[31]

James B. Torrance speaks of the God-humanward movement and the human-Godward movement of worship that culminates in Christ. The God-humanward movement is the movement of incarnation, of Christ's total identification with our fallen human nature. The human-Godward movement does not refer to our attempts to please or even worship God, but rather to our sharing in Christ's response of obedient

---

[30]Alexander Schmemann, *For the Life of the World: Sacraments and Orthodoxy* (Crestwood, N.Y.: St. Vladimir's Press, 1973), p. 28.
[31]Ibid., p. 44.

love and worship as our faithful high priest. "In worship we offer ourselves to the Father 'in the name of Christ' because he has already in our name made the one true offering to the Father, the offering by which he has sanctified for all time those who come to God by him (Heb. 10:10, 14) and because he ever lives to intercede for us in our name [as human]."[32]

In Christ, through the Holy Spirit, the whole relationship between God and humanity is concentrated. He not only reconciles us to God, but he is also the one in whom and through whom we worship God, which is our true destiny. That is what the book of Hebrews, so dear to Calvin, means by calling Jesus our only true high priest. Torrance uses the analogy of an embrace. When we hug someone, there is a double movement. We open our arms and in so doing give ourselves to the beloved. But in the embrace we also draw that person close to us. "That is a parable of the double movement of grace, the God-humanward and the human-Godward movement of the priesthood of Christ and the ministry of the Holy Spirit. In Christ, the Word made flesh, and in the Holy Spirit—his two hands—God our Father in grace gives himself to us as God."[33] One hand, Christ, opens the relationship, the other hand, the Holy Spirit draws us into that relationship with the Father.

If all of worship is ascent, that is, if all of worship is our participation in the one offering of our redeemed humanity to God, then the Lord's Supper also moves in this direction. When Calvin speaks of the Holy Spirit as the one who brings us into the presence of the ascended Christ and feeds us on his new and glorified humanity, it is one aspect of the total reality of the worship of Christ and in Christ. To understand the relationship between ourselves and Christ in the Lord's Supper, we need to look beyond a direct causal relationship between Christ and the Supper and between the Supper and ourselves. Rather, we must see it though our participation in the whole of Christ's redeeming life, death, resurrection and ascension through the Holy Spirit. Christ is the center and the content of the Supper, for it is the remembrance of his saving life. Christ gives meaning and efficacy to the celebration of the

---

[32]James B. Torrance, *Worship, Community and the Triune God of Grace* (Downers Grove, Ill.: InterVarsity Press, 1996), p. 50.
[33]Ibid., p. 66.

Supper "by being savingly and creatively present in his mediatorial
agency as often as we *'do this in anamnesis'* of him, blessing what we do
on earth at his command and accepting it as his own act done in
heaven."[34] All this takes place, as Calvin asserts, through the agency of
the Holy Spirit, who is always the bond between us and our Lord. That
is why the *epiclesis*, the prayer by which we invoke the Holy Spirit to
unite us to Christ in the bread and the wine is the true focal point of the
celebration of the Supper. While most epicletic prayers call upon the
Holy Spirit to sanctify the bread and wine so that they may be for us
the body and blood of Christ, few express the full mystery of our ascent
to Christ. The best example of this goes all the way back to Basil the
Great in the fourth century, a great example of the Eastern tradition
that was so deeply trinitarian and so aware of the work of the Spirit:

> Most holy Master, we sinners and your unworthy servants have been
> considered worthy to serve at your holy altar . . . because of your com-
> passion and your mercies, which you shed abundantly upon us; in con-
> fidence we approach your holy altar, and having laid before you the 'an-
> titypes' of the sacred body and blood of your Christ, we pray. . . . Holiest
> of the holy . . . let your Holy Spirit come upon us and upon these gifts
> before you, that he may bless them and sanctify them.[35]

It is clear in this prayer that Basil sees the "holy altar" on earth, like the
bread and wine themselves, as an antitype of the heavenly altar which
is the one eternal offering of Christ himself before the Father in heaven
in which we participate. And the bond between the type and antitype,
earth and heaven, the church and her Lord, is the Holy Spirit.

SUPPER AND SACRIFICE

One of the deepest grievances the Reformers brought against the Roman Catholic Church was the sacrifice of the Mass as it was understood at that time. The language of the Tridentine Mass made it clear
that Christ was being sacrificed for sin at the altar and that the eucharistic sacrifice effected propitiation and forgiveness.[36] As mentioned

---

[34]Torrance, *Theology in Reconciliation*, p. 109.
[35]Quoted in Thurian, *The Mystery of the Eucharist*, p. 69.
[36]See the previous discussion of the sacrificial character of the Lord's Supper as Passover
meal in chapter nine.

earlier, there was great sacerdotal power in this scheme, not to mention possibilities for the enrichment of the church by those who were willing to pay for the liturgical sacrifice. All this disgusted the Reformers. They proclaimed the biblical truth that there was only one sacrifice for sin, made once and for all on the cross of Calvary. A somewhat later version of the Heidelberg Catechism condemns the Mass as a "condemnable idolatry" that explicitly teaches that the "the living and the dead do not have their sins forgiven through the sufferings of Christ unless Christ is still offered for them daily by the priests."[37] This is not language designed to promote dialogue.[38]

One result of this horror over the sacrifice of the Mass was that for the most part the Reformers tended to abandon any sacrificial meaning or language associated with the sacrament. The only sacrificial language that can be found almost universally among the Reformers and their successors is that in the Eucharist we bring to God a sacrifice of praise and thanksgiving (Heb 13:15). This is in spite of the fact that 1 Corinthians 10:16-21 alludes to the Lord's Supper as a sacrificial meal.

Remembering that Jesus instituted the sacrament in the context of the Passover, with the sacrifice of lambs so central to its celebration, Protestants need to grapple more deeply with its obvious sacrificial elements. While Calvin, like his fellow Reformers, reacted forcefully to the Roman Catholic abuse of the Mass as a sacrifice, there is a passage in which he brings together, ever so carefully, the idea of the Eucharist as a sacrifice of praise and the way in which that sacrifice rests in Christ's sacrifice on the cross:

> The Lord's Supper cannot be without a sacrifice of [praise], in which, while we proclaim his death 1 Cor 11:26] and give thanks, we do nothing but offer a sacrifice of praise. From this office of sacrificing, all Christians are called a royal priesthood [1 Pet 2:9], because through Christ we offer that sacrifice of praise to God of which the apostle speaks: "the fruit of lips confessing his name" [Heb 13:15]. And we do not appear with our gifts before God without an intercessor. *The Mediator interceding for us is Christ, by whom we offer ourselves and what is ours to the Father. He is our*

---

[37]Heidelberg Catechism, Q and A 80.

[38]While this crassly sacrificial understanding of the Mass was true in practice, there is ample evidence that the medieval theologians were much more nuanced in distinguishing the one sacrifice of Christ from the sacrifice of the Mass.

Pontiff, who has entered the heavenly sanctuary [Heb 9:24] and opens a way for us to enter [cf. Heb 10:20]. He is the altar [Heb 13:10] upon which we lay our gifts, that whatever we venture to do, we may undertake in him. He it is, I say, that has made us a kingdom and priests unto the Father [Rev 1:6].[39]

Calvin recognizes here that the only way we offer our sacrifice of praise is to do it in and through the one sacrifice of Christ.

With this in mind we can move into a fuller appreciation of the sacrificial nature of the sacrament. Clearly, the Supper was instituted by Christ to "proclaim the Lord's death until he comes" (1 Cor 11:26). The sacrament can therefore properly be said to represent the sacrifice of the Lord's death to us. But the Lord's Supper is also a form of prayer in which, again and again, we claim Christ's one sacrifice on our behalf. The key to a biblical understanding of the sacrificial character of the Lord's Supper is its connection with the continuing ministry of Christ in his intercession before God, which is grounded in his once-for-all sacrifice on the cross. So in our eucharistic prayers we lift up and remember the sufficiency of Christ's atoning death with gratitude and faith before our gracious God. We join our prayers with his intercession for us which is grounded in his perfect and complete sacrifice. It is not that we doubt the efficacy of Christ's sacrifice and need to make sure of it again, or that God somehow forgets it, but that the sacrament assures us of the present blessing and power of Christ's sacrifice though his continuing intercession for us.

Luther, who so stubbornly resisted the idea of sacrifice in the Eucharist, also recognized its link with Christ's work of intercession:

We do not offer Christ as a sacrifice, but . . . Christ offers us. And in this way it is permissible, yes profitable, to call the mass a sacrifice; not on its own account, but because we offer ourselves as a sacrifice along with Christ. That is, we lay ourselves on Christ by a firm faith in his testament and do not otherwise appear before God with our praise, prayer, and sacrifice except through Christ and His mediation. Nor do we doubt that Christ is our priest or minister in heaven before God. *Such faith truly brings it to pass that Christ takes up our cause, presents us and our prayers and praise, and also offers himself for us in heaven.*[40]

---

[39]Calvin *Institutes* 4.18.17 (italics mine).

[40]Quoted in Charles J. Evanson, "Worship and Sacrifice," *Concordia Theological Quarterly* 42 (October 1978): 353 (italics mine). Note that by "the mass" here Luther does not mean the Roman Catholic rite.

At first Luther seems to think of the eucharistic sacrifice only in terms of the offering of ourselves in Christ's sacrifice. But the closing sentence clinches the full sacrificial intent in a way that removes any sense in which the sacrifice takes place on the altar in the church. Christ, in his heavenly intercession, to which we are united in the Eucharist, continually offers himself to God on our behalf. Christ's sacrifice is remembered at the table and in heaven all at once.

Reformed liturgical theologian J.-J. von Allmen also sought to bring a proper sacrificial understanding back into the Lord's Supper. In the institution at the Last Supper, Jesus intended to interpret his death as a sacrifice for the whole world. This was the "new covenant in his blood." Von Allmen says that Christ's desire was "that what he did might remain fresh, so that those who enact the *anemnesis* [remembrance] might benefit from the reconciliation accomplished by Christ through the very *anemnesis* which they re-enact. In this way the Crucified might remain present among His followers to give Himself to them in the gift of what he has done for them."[41] Christ's sacrifice is thus not merely an historical act whose effects forever remain locked in the past. The Lord's Supper recalls it, renews it and re-presents it. Christ makes his historical sacrifice present now as we sacramentally eat and drink his sacrificed flesh and blood. The sacrifice is not repeated, but the effects of it are received by, and applied afresh to, believers in the sacrament.

Interestingly, it was Wesley, among all the Protestants, who most fully integrated the idea of sacrifice into his understanding of the Eucharist. As James F. White points out, Charles Wesley was a patristics scholar familiar with the ways in which the Fathers saw the Eucharist in sacrificial terms. This surfaces especially in Charles Wesley's splendid eucharistic hymnody, in which, White says, they were influenced by the seventeenth-century Anglican Dr. Daniel Brevint. Brevint's 1673 treatise *The Christian Sacrament and Sacrifice* speaks of the Eucharist as a memorial which "becomes a kind of *Sacrifice*, whereby we present before God the Father that precious oblation of His Son once offered." Thus the Wesleys can sing, "Victim Divine, Thy grace we claim / While thus Thy precious death we show" or again, "Memorial of Thy sacrifice, /

---

[41]J.-J. von Allmen, *The Lord's Supper* (London: Lutterworth, 1969), p. 90.

This Eucharistic Mystery."[42] Newer Protestant eucharistic prayers of thanksgiving reveal a growing awareness of the importance of the sacrificial dimension to the sacrament. The *Book of Common Worship* of the United Presbyterian Church USA, for example, has this prayer, based on an earlier prayer of the Church of Scotland:

> Therefore, remembering his incarnation and holy life, his death and glorious resurrection, his ascension and continual intercession for us, and awaiting his coming again in power and great glory, *we claim his eternal sacrifice* and celebrate with these your holy gifts the memorial your Son commanded us to make.[43]

"We claim his eternal sacrifice" wonderfully expresses the way in which by our participation in the sacrament we are recalling and receiving the assured benefits of Christ's sacrifice.

We should not forget, however, the sacrificial meaning of the sacrament most widely recognized by the Reformers, the sacrifice of ourselves in praise and thanksgiving. In the sacrament, we offer ourselves in and through the offering of Christ. When we receive the bread and cup of Christ's sacrifice, we are drawn into his sacrificial love for God and for the world. "The body on which we feed," writes James Torrance, "is the body which [Christ] assumed for our sakes, that in our worship we might be sanctified by the once and for all self-offering of Christ. In the communion of the Spirit, in the virtue of this exchange, we know that his humanity is our humanity, so graciously assumed, his death our death, which we show forth, his life our life, till he comes, his self-offering our offering."[44] This is why many liturgies of Communion end with a thanksgiving in which the worshipers pray: "Send us now into the world in peace, and grant us strength and courage to love and serve you with gladness and singleness of heart; through Christ our Lord."[45] As the sacrament concludes, we realize that we are now participants in the offering of Christ, not just because we have received its benefits, but because our lives are now

---

[42]Quoted in James F. White, *The Sacraments in Protestant Practice and Faith* (Nashville: Abingdon, 1999), p. 113.

[43]*Book of Common Worship* (Louisville, Ky.: Westminster John Knox, 1993), p. 140 (italics mine).

[44]James Torrance, *Worship, Community and the Triune God*, p. 90.

[45]*Book of Common Prayer* (New York: Church Publishing, 1979), p. 365.

renewed and redirected in his sacrificial self-giving.

Another aspect of the sacrificial nature of the Lord's Supper found in the Roman Catholic and Orthodox traditions is now being freshly appropriated by some Protestants as well. In the Eucharist we offer the fruit of creation to God so that it may be given back to us as the body and blood of Christ. This is best exemplified by the preparatory part of the eucharistic prayer in the Lima Liturgy, a consensus ecumenical liturgy produced by the Faith and Order Committee of the World Council of Churches in 1982:

> Blessed are you, God of the universe, you are the giver of this bread, fruit of the earth and of human labor, let it become the bread of Life. Blessed are you, God of the universe, you are the giver of this wine, fruit of the vine and of human labour, let it become the wine of the eternal Kingdom.[46]

This prayer highlights the attractive idea that we are offering the bread and wine to God to be given back to us as the Communion of Christ's body and blood. It goes as far back as Hippolytus of Rome in the beginning of the third century, linking the wonderful acts of God in creation and redemption. Max Thurian makes clear that this self-offering can only be valid when it is linked with Christ's self-offering:

> The church's offertory, in which it brings to the altar the material and spiritual possessions of the faithful, is, as it were, an impulse to make offering which involves a crisis. When the church has gathered everything together to present it to God, it realizes its utter poverty; all it can do is to put this utter poverty into the hands of Christ who, taking it up into his own sacrifice presented in intercession, makes it a true praise, an efficacious prayer, a valid sacrifice.[47]

T. F. Torrance also places the emphasis of the sacrificial meaning of the Lord's Supper on Christ's own eternal offering. "This eucharistic sacrifice means that we *through the Spirit* are so intimately united to Christ, by communion in his body and blood, that we participate in his self-offering to the Father and thus appear with him and in him and through him before the majesty of God in worship, praise, and adora-

---

[46]Max Thurian, ed., *Ecumenical Perspectives on Baptism, Eucharist, and Ministry* (Geneva: World Council of Churches, Faith and Order Paper No. 116, 1983), p. 241.
[47]Thurian, *Mystery of the Eucharist*, p. 102.

tion with no other sacrifice than the sacrifice of Jesus Christ our Mediator and High Priest."[48] The Supper is a sacrifice of our intercession combined with the living and perfectly effective intercession of the ascended Lord at the right hand of God, praying for the forgiveness of our sins and for our final glory in him at the coming of God's kingdom.

When Torrance says that we "participate in his self-offering," he also affirms that we bring the offering of ourselves in and through Christ in response to God's grace. "I appeal to you therefore, brothers and sisters, by the mercies of God, to present your bodies as a living sacrifice, holy and acceptable to God, which is your spiritual worship" (Rom 12:1).

IN REMEMBRANCE OF ME

The most potent form of teaching the meaning of the sacrament of the Lord's Supper is etched on thousands of Communion tables in Protestant churches: "Do this in remembrance of me." Ask most any Protestant about the meaning of the Supper, and you will hear the word *remembrance*. The problem is that a too-simplistic understanding of the Lord's command has limited the meaning of the sacrament in the minds of many to the recollection of a long-ago historical event. It tends to place the weight of the sacramental meaning in the minds, heart and faith of the participant, as he or she struggles to remember, with faith and gratitude, what the Lord did for them on the cross. Rather than coming as a gift, it comes as a mental exercise, an act of pious, prayerful reflection. In that sense, the Supper offers the believer, not a gift of grace, but a mere reminder of grace; not an assuring seal of God's forgiveness, but a distant memory of its basis; not union with the risen and living Christ, but a memory of him. This represents a fundamental diminution of the sacraments meaning and intent.

As I have commented earlier, the remembrance, or *anamnesis*, to which Christ calls us comes from the richness of the Passover feast (see chapter nine). It is a not just a call to historical memory, but a call to a present participation in the saving events of history. Remembrance in the Passover meant the identification by the participant of these past events with their present involvement in those events that happened long before.

---

[48]Torrance, *Theology in Reconciliation,* p. 134.

We can begin to understand the memorial of the Lord's Supper through the sacramental liturgy itself. The *anamnesis* comes to expression within the great prayer of thanksgiving, which includes the whole recitation of the events of God's saving works from creation through new creation. By telling God's story week after week in the great prayer, worshipers find their identity and destiny in it. That story's focal point is, of course, the paschal mystery, the death and resurrection of Christ. It is there that the whole of God's saving work reaches its climax. We recite this great story as our story, just as the Jews recited the story of that night of redemption from slavery in Egypt as their story.

It's interesting that almost every Jew, even the more "secular" variety celebrates Passover, rehearsing each year its deep remembrances even though they practice little else of what the Torah teaches. The reason for this adherence, it seems to me, is that this ritual remembering speaks to their identity. In the Seder, Jews remember who they are. Through the rituals of the Seder they become a part of that community going back to the slaves who left Egypt. The Lord's Supper too is an identity-making meal of remembrance. Joseph Jetter suggests that the opposite of remembering is not just forgetting but dismembering.[49] If you fail to re-member, you dis-member.

When my wife Jeanne came into our family after my first wife's death, she obviously didn't share in the stories that a family of two parents and four children had carried through the years. To that extent she was not part of this stream of shared memory; she was not a member of the family yet. At first she sometimes felt dis-membered, or un-membered. But it did not take long for us to share the stories with her, the family memories that gave us our identity. Through these shared memories and the little rituals of Christmas and birthdays that accompanied them, she was re-membered. She became a part of the family. And through this sharing we were all re-membering each other in the formation of a somewhat new ongoing family unit.

One of the most powerful aspects of this meal that we celebrate in memory of Jesus is that it re-members us. We are lost in our sins, separated from God our Creator. Our lives may be broken and troubled, our

---

[49]Joseph R. Jetter Jr., *Re/Membering* (St. Louis: Chalice, 1996), p. 147.

relationships sometimes full of tension or bitterness. When we do this in remembrance of Jesus, when we take the bread and wine that are his body and blood and share them with each other, we are re-membering. We find our identity again in that stream of shared memory that is the Christian story, anchored in Jesus' cross and resurrection. We are being put back together, reunited through Jesus with our Father in heaven, and united with each other as brothers and sisters in Christ.

"Do this in remembrance of me" is more than an act of imaginative recollection. It's our Seder. It's the Christian Passover. In it we are called to participate in a meal that not only pulls us into the story of Jesus but also actually unites us with Jesus and his disciples that dark night, and with all his people here and through all times and places.

Michael Welker emphasizes that here too, our participation by re-membrance is through the Holy Spirit: "The Holy Spirit is the power which continually renews the act of bringing human beings together for the solidification, renewal, revitalization, and enrichment of the memory of Christ."[50] Since the Holy Spirit is the Spirit of Christ, Christ himself is present among believers, bringing us a share in his saving work.

Alexander Schmemann, the great Orthodox theologian, summarizes all that this remembrance means:

> The whole liturgy is a *remembrance* of Christ. It is all a sacrament and experience of his presence: of the Son of God, who came down from heaven and was incarnate that he might in himself lead us up to heaven. He "gathers us as his church," he transforms our gathering into an entrance and ascent, he "opens our mind" to the hearing of his word, he, as "the offerer and the offered," makes his offering ours and ours his, he fulfills our unity as unity in his love, and, finally, through his thanksgiving, which has been granted to us, he leads us to heaven, he opens to us access to his Father. . . . [T]he remembrance is the very reality of the Kingdom . . . comprehended as *real*, as present "in our midst," because Christ manifested it and appointed it then, on that night, at that table.[51]

THE ABSENCE OF CHRIST AND THE MEAL OF HOPE

In our earlier discussion of the sacramental presence of Christ, we

---

[50]Michael Welker, *What Happens at Holy Communion?* (Grand Rapids: Eerdmans, 2000), p. 132.
[51]Alexander Schmemann, *Eucharist* (Crestwood, N.Y.: St. Vladimir's Seminary Press, 1988), pp. 199-200.

passed over an equally important aspect of the sacrament of Holy Communion. At its core, the Eucharist confronts us with the mystery of absence as well as presence. Christ's presence in the Eucharist becomes necessary because he is absent in the flesh from this space/time world. Our whole understanding of the Eucharist, and by extension, of the church, revolves around this tension of presence and absence.

Calvin's fundamental objection to Rome's insistence on transubstantiation and Luther's compromise of consubstantiation was that both of them assume a ubiquitous Christ. Calvin firmly believed that the real humanity of Christ could only be truly believed when the church affirms the ascension of his glorified body to God's right hand in heaven. His concern was that if Christ is understood to be universally present as a kind of spiritual vapor in the world, his distinct human body, "localized" in heaven becomes lost. And that loss is pivotal, for with it the church loses its identity as the body of Christ in the world, and its members lose their destiny of sharing Christ's glorious humanity.

In his groundbreaking study of the ascension, Eucharist and the church, Douglas Farrow quotes a theological dictionary on the subject of Christ's ascension. This quotation and Farrow's commentary on it pinpoint the issues that revolve around Christ's ascension:

> Thus, even if it Jesus appears to be absent from his church, in one sense, he is, in fact, more profoundly and intimately present to the church, in another sense. For he is now in "heaven" with God—in the heaven which, according to the biblical tradition is a symbol not only of God's transcendence and inaccessibility but also of God's omnipresence. Paradoxically, being in heaven with God, Jesus is also present in the world in the way that God is present.[52]

Farrow points out that there is some truth in this statement, and it represents a very common way of explaining away Christ's ascended absence. He's really not gone after all; he's just present in a different way. But this way of thinking about the ascension also raises enormous questions:

> In what way *is* God present, and how can Jesus be present in that way? How does his presence in the church differ from his presence in the

---

[52]Douglas Farrow, *Ascension and Ecclesia* (Grand Rapids: Eerdmans, 1999), p. 12.

world, or does it? If not, what is the church? How is he to return from such a heaven, and what can heaven possibly mean for the rest of us? Above all, what does the ascension, so interpreted, do to his humanity? Is there not a marked tendency toward the de-humanization of Jesus?[53]

This was precisely Calvin's point. When the ascension becomes a kind of universalization of a divine Christ, a ubiquitous presence, then Christ's essential humanity is lost. "Christ everywhere really means Jesus of Nazareth nowhere."[54] In this process, the church is in danger of losing not only the real humanity of Christ, but also its eschatological future. What does Christ's return in glory mean if he is universally present now? What happens to our hope as John's first epistle expresses it: "Beloved we are God's children now; what we will be has not yet been revealed. What we do know is this: when he is revealed, we will be like him, for we will see him as he is" (1 Jn 3:2). The universal hope of the New Testament is that when Christ returns we will come to share in his glorified humanity. "This same Jesus . . ." (Acts 1:11) is the New Testament's common testimony concerning the ascension and the parousia.

Now, what does all this have to do with our present subject of the Lord's Supper? As hinted at above, Calvin, more than any of the Reformers, was a theologian of the ascension. He understood it as the crucial foundation of Christ's continued humanity and our future glory. And, for him, the issue was joined in the Lord's Supper.

But if we are lifted up to heaven with our eyes and minds, to seek Christ there in the glory of his Kingdom, as the symbols invite us to him in his wholeness, so under the symbol of bread we shall be fed by his body, under the symbol of wine we shall separately drink his blood, to enjoy him at last in his wholeness. For though he has taken his flesh away from us, and in the body has ascended into heaven, yet he sits at the right hand of the Father—that is, he reigns in the Father's power and majesty and glory. This Kingdom is neither bounded by location in space nor circumscribed by any limits. Thus Christ is not prevented from exerting his power wherever he pleases, in heaven and on earth. He shows his presence in power and strength, is always among his own people, and breathes his life upon them, and lives in them, sustaining them, strength-

---

[53]Ibid.
[54]Ibid.

ening, quickening, keeping them unharmed, as if he were present in the body. In short, he feeds his people with his own body, the communion of which he bestows upon them by the power of his Spirit. In this manner, the body and blood of Christ are shown to us in the Sacrament.[55]

For Calvin, Christ is absent in his humanity, localized, for want of a better term, in heaven. His place, however, is at God's right hand, assuring us of his kingly reign over the church and the world. This is the sense in which he assures his disciples that he "will be with you always, even to the close of the age" (Mt 28:20). While absent in his human body, he watches over and defends them from every enemy and preserves them to eventually share fully in his reign. However, Calvin makes it clear that Christ's real body and blood presence in the church is his eucharistic presence, bridged by the Holy Spirit who is the bond of union between the ascended Lord and his church.

Calvin asserts that the presence of Christ in the Supper must always avoid enclosing him in the elements or making him present in many places at once by a kind of vague spiritual presence of "boundless magnitude":

> Let us never allow these two limitations to be taken away from us: (1) Let nothing be withdrawn from Christ's heavenly glory—as happens when he is brought under the corruptible elements of this world, or bound to any earthly creatures. (2) Let nothing inappropriate to human nature be ascribed to his body, as happens when it is said either to be infinite or to be put in a number of places at once.[56]

In this way, Christ's bodily ascension and session at God's right hand become the anchor of his true humanity, and the Supper unites us to him by feeding us by his Spirit with the glorified humanity of the ascended Lord. The Lord's Supper is a sign of both absence and presence, both of which must be carefully balanced and deeply appreciated. Too much emphasis on Christ's presence dehumanizes and universalizes him. Too much emphasis on his absence calls into question the work of the Spirit as the Paraclete.

---

[55]Calvin *Institutes* 4.17.18.
[56]Calvin *Institutes* 4.17.19.

T. F. Torrance summarizes the relationship of Christ's absence, his presence and the work of the Holy Spirit:

> Jesus Christ who rose again from the dead in his full Humanity has withdrawn his body from us, out of the visible succession of history, and he waits the day when he will come again in Body, to judge and to renew the world. And yet, after his ascension the Lord poured out His Spirit on the Church . . . to participate in the power of his resurrection. On the one hand, then, the Church through the Spirit is joined to the Body of the risen Christ and is One Body with him; but on the other hand, Christ has removed his Body from us so that we have to think of the relation of the Church to the risen Body of Christ in terms of the distance of the ascension and the nearness of the *parousia* in Glory. There is an *eschatological reserve* in the relation of our union with Christ, an eschatological lag waiting for the last Word or the final Act of God.[57]

Christ is both present and absent; this "eschatological reserve" must inform all our thinking about the church and the sacrament. We can rightly grasp the sacrament eschatologically. The presence of Christ that the sacrament offers is not his full presence, as transubstantiation would offer, nor is it some ubiquitous presence throughout the universe as Luther and his many followers would seem to have it. We are united to his ascended, glorified and *absent* humanity by the Holy Spirit in a way that provides a foretaste of our union with him in glory when we will fully share in his glorified humanity. But it's only a taste, not the full reality. That is why in the earliest liturgies we have, the cry *"maranatha"* climaxes the meal. After sharing in the body and blood of Christ through his Spirit, the church longs for the fullness of what the Supper anticipates, the "wedding feast of the Lamb."

Douglas Farrow delves into the mystery of how Jesus' "incomprehensible absence" confronts us with the "anomalous character of our alienated time and place." We live between the two great acts of the divine drama, Christ's death/resurrection/ascension, and his final advent. Christ says to us, like he said to Mary. "Do not hold on to me, because . . . I am ascending to my Father and your Father" (Jn 20:17).

But who understands the divine irony? Who is really aware of this ab-

---

[57]T. F. Torrance, *Royal Priesthood*, 2nd ed. (Edinburgh: T & T Clark, 1993), p. 45 (italics mine).

sence? As an absence without parallel it is little noticed, much less identified for what it is, even where talk of absence (in the abstract) may be
all the rage. Indeed it would not be noticed or identified at all but for the
work of the Holy Spirit who here and there tantalizes us with a real presence [in the Eucharist] so that we may discover what real absence is, this
learning to love and long for Jesus' appearing.[58]

Paul says that in the Supper we "proclaim the Lord's death until he
comes" (1 Cor 11:26). I think this simple phrase may go farther in
plumbing the eschatological depths of the sacrament than we often
recognize. When Paul says "we proclaim the Lord's death," he means
that in the absence of the historical Christ, the sacrament binds us to
him through the remembrance of what he said and did surrounding
his death. In particular, it recalls the words he spoke, and which Paul
has just quoted, at the Last Supper. When we gather at the Lord's Table,
it proclaims his death, which includes his resurrection and ascension,
that whole historical memory of Christ's great paschal mystery. "We
proclaim the Lord's death" also reminds us that this meal is not one of
unmitigated joy and gladness. We live, and we eat and drink this meal
under the shadow of the cross. It enables us to remember the cross that
is borne in our own lives as well as in the lives of countless others now
and throughout history. It brings us into fellowship with the "lamb
that was slain."

But Paul continues, "We proclaim his death *until he comes.*" Just as
the Supper unites us with the historical Jesus in his death, resurrection and ascension, it also unites us with Jesus, who dwells at the Father's right hand in glory. Just as it thrusts us back in time, it pushes
us forward to the end of time. The sacrament unites us with the body
of the ascended and glorified Christ in a way that anticipates our future union with him. Christ's absence, to which the sacrament witnesses, exposes its very nature as a sacrament. We commune with
Christ sacramentally because of our historical condition. "The Christian times . . . are the times 'between,' when Christ is present to the
Church in the mode of absence, but for all that really; in his body, but
not as it was when Jesus was among us as the historical individual
2000 years ago—more present than that—not yet as it will be after our

---

[58]Farrow, *Ascension and Ecclesia*, p. 45.

own resurrection—less present than that."[59]

Without a real ascension and the eschatological absence it leaves in its place, we have no distinction between Christ's eucharistic presence and a kind of cosmic presence that plays havoc with the necessary distinction between the church and the world, the present and the future, the incarnation/ascension and the *parousia*.

Whatever we make of this "absence" or "eschatological reserve," it must not dim the eschatological joy that this banquet anticipates and celebrates. As Jeremy Taylor, the eighteenth-century Anglican priest put it, each Eucharist is an "antepast of heaven." Indeed, in nearly every eucharistic prayer of thanksgiving, we find ourselves joining in the very worship of heaven, singing, "Holy, Holy, Holy Lord, the whole earth is full of your glory. " Absence, as the old saying goes, makes the heart grow fonder. And in the case of Christ's eschatological absence, it makes the heart beat faster in anticipating the joy of reunion.

We are pilgrims on our way to the heavenly city, the new Jerusalem. The way is often hard, and the cross looms large. But when we gather for the meal, the feast of the new creation beckons us again. Constance H. Cooke's fine Communion hymn catches the presence in the absence and its cry of hope:

In the quiet consecration
of this glad communion hour,
Here we rest in you, Lord Jesus,
taste your love and touch your power.

By your death for sin atoning,
by your resurrection life,
hold us fast in joyful union;
strengthen us to face the strife.

While in joyful holy radiance
shines the feast that is to come
After conflict, toil, and testing—
your great feast of love and home![60]

[59]Denys Turner, "The Darkness of God and the Light of Christ: Negative Theology and Eucharistic Presence," *Modern Theology* 15, no. 2 (April 1999): 153.
[60]Constance H. Cooke, "In the Quiet Consecration," *Psalter Hymnal* (Grand Rapids: CRC Publications, 1987), 302.

SUMMARY

We can only understand and experience the Lord's Supper if we grasp its crucial importance for the life of faith. It confirms our faith in Christ and conveys all the benefits of his finished work at a depth of human need that the Word alone cannot touch. God gives us this Supper also as a sacrificial feast where we may claim over and over the grace and victory of Christ's life, death and resurrection. Finally, it is a feast that offers us Christ's real presence through the bond of the Holy Spirit, while at the same time it also aches with Christ's real absence, calling us to hope for the final advent and the wedding feast of the Lamb and to join in the ancient cry, *Maranatha!*

Alexander Schmemann best sums up how in the Eucharist we make a sacrifice of ourselves and of the whole creation in and through the sacrifice of Christ:

> We come again and again with our lives to offer; we bring and "sacrifice"—that is, give to God—what he has given us; and each time we come to the *End* of all sacrifices, of all offerings, of all eucharist, because each time it is revealed to us that Christ has *offered* all that exists, and that He and all that exists has been offered in His offering of himself. We are included in the Eucharist of Christ and Christ is our Eucharist.[61]

---

[61]Schmemann, *For the Life of the World*, p. 35 (italics in the original).

12

WHAT HAPPENS AT
THE TABLE?

A Wider-Angle View

Man is what he eats.

FEUERBACH

Kathleen Norris describes a weekend when she and her fiancé attended a Roman Catholic wedding on Long Island. The night before the wedding she was invited to the obligatory family potluck. "The marvelous abundance and seemingly bottomless hospitality were overwhelming to my timid Protestant soul—the feasting! The drinking! The toddlers, dogs and cats contending for scraps under the picnic tables. . . . Enough for everyone; more than enough."

The wedding Mass the following day was her first as an adult. She had put aside any Christian faith just a few years before, only attending church once in a while when she visited her grandparents in South Dakota, where she enjoyed going to church with her grandmother and singing the hymns, but found that the worship itself held little meaning. Yet here she was, sitting toward the back of a Roman Catholic church, watching the Mass with mild interest until something that happened startled and amazed her:

> I gasped. "Look," I said, tugging on David's sleeve. "Look at that! The priest is cleaning up! He's doing the dishes!" My husband-to-be shrugged; others in the pew looked at me and then at him, as if to say—

Dave, your girlfriend has gone soft in the head.

But I found it remarkable—and still find it all remarkable—that in that big fancy church, after all of the dress-up and the formalities of the wedding mass, homage was being paid to the lowly truth that we human beings must wash the dishes after we eat and drink. The chalice, which had held the very blood of Christ, was no exception. And I found it enormously comforting to see the priest as a kind of daft housewife, overdressed for the kitchen, in bulky robes, puttering about the altar, washing up after having served so great a meal to so many people. It brought the mass home to me and gave it meaning. It welcomed me, a stranger, someone who did not know the responses of the mass, or even the words of the sanctus. After the experience of a liturgy that had left me feeling disorientated, eating and drinking were something I could understand. That and the housework. This was my first image of the mass, my door in, as it were, and it has served me well for years.[1]

Norris's humorous angle reminds us that the sacrament operates at various levels of meaning in ways we do not expect. I previously told the story of how my brother and I, who weren't allowed to take communion at the time, would sit in the balcony of our large church and watch when the Lord's Supper was celebrated. We found lots of things quite funny, but I now realize that on a deeper level we were being formed by what we watched, in ways both good and bad. The solemnity of the observance certainly formed our realization that this was a very important matter. The smell of the bread and wine as they were uncovered formed the awareness that this was a feast for the senses. The stiff formalities of the servers and private pieties of the people led us to think of this meal as something completely unconnected with the meals of our everyday lives. Yet the overall impression was one that finally hushed our giggles and stifled our mockery. This was Holy Communion, and with all the mysterious and humorous aspects, it was, I knew deep inside, a matter of life and death, of mercy and judgment, of forgiveness and repentance. We learned as we watched.

These very different experiences both point to something important about the sacrament that we easily overlook: the ordinary meanings within the extraordinary meaning of the sacrament; the "quotidian

---

[1]Kathleen Norris, *The Quotidian Mysteries* (New York/Mahwah, N.J.: Paulist Press, 1998), pp. 1-3.

mysteries," as Kathleen Norris calls them.

Peter Leithart offers a helpful analogy in suggesting that our usual way of looking at the sacraments is analogous to focusing on them with a "zoom lens." We zoom in on the bread and wine on the table and ask all sorts of questions about what they mean and how that meaning is conveyed in the sacrament. He suggests that although these questions are important, they represent only one view, one focus. Why not take off the zoom and put on a wide-angle lens.

> Instead of attending only to bread and wine on a table, we see people and they are doing things. They are not simply observing the elements but passing them from hand to hand, sharing them, eating and drinking them. Words are being spoken. . . . Through the zoom lens, the eucharist is presented as a miraculous puzzle of physics and metaphysics; through a wide-angle lens, the eucharist becomes a focal point for more theologically central issues: the relationships of the church's members to one another, creation, and God.[2]

This approach suggests that we may actually gain a fuller grasp on the sacraments, and they may shape us more deeply, if we pay less attention to the metaphysical/theological questions of how the baptismal water cleanses and incorporates us into Christ, or how Christ's real presence is conveyed in the bread and wine, and pay more attention to how the whole sacramental event—the water, bread and wine—comes embedded in the communal worship of the body of Christ. This approach notices the clean-up as well as the consecration, the meal as well as the mystery. When we do this, something quite paradoxical occurs. While it appears that we are looking merely at the surface of the eucharistic rite, we are actually led into new depths of understanding and meaning.

THE MEAL

The first thing we observe is that this is a meal. It's not a mere ceremony or liturgical act, but it is a *ritual meal*. When we call it a meal, all sorts of associations and memories come to our minds just as they

---

[2]Peter Leithart, "The Way Things Really Ought to Be: Eucharist, Eschatology, and Culture," *Westminster Theological Journal* 59 (1997): 161. I am indebted to Liethart's incisive work for some of the basic ideas of this chapter.

must have come to mind for the disciples as they gathered with Jesus for that last Passover.

A meal is one of the most common yet significant acts of human life. Nearly every important occasion centers in a meal: a wedding, a birthday, a holiday, a state occasion. But meals also lend significance to ordinary life. Alongside the platitude "The family that prays together stays together" can be added, "The family that sits down for a meal together stays together." Meals celebrate our communal life and form us in into community, even though a visit to a typical fast food restaurant may not bear out this truth. The sharing of our food ritualizes the sharing of our lives. It is the quintessential action and emblem of our being bound together. At this moment in 2003, the Syrians and Israelis are negotiating peace at Shepherdstown, Maryland. A news commentator thought it a significant breakthrough that for the first time they, as he put it in almost biblical terms, "broke bread together."

Alexander Schmemann highlights the continuing ritual significance of the meal. "A meal is still a rite—the last 'natural sacrament' of family and friendship, of life that is more than 'eating' and 'drinking.' To eat is still something more than to maintain bodily functions. People may not understand what that 'something more' is, but they nonetheless desire to celebrate it." In Schmemann's thinking "they are still hungry and thirsty for sacramental life."[3]

That the Lord's Supper is a meal was also the main reason why Paul pointed out the failures in the Corinthian church's conduct. "When you come together, it is not really to eat the Lord's supper. For when the time comes to eat, each of you goes ahead with your own supper, and one goes hungry and another becomes drunk" (1 Cor 11:20-21). The problem, of course, was that the church at Corinth was plagued with factionalism and elitism. It was because of these problems that Paul goes on to give his solemn instructions from the Lord as to the proper conduct of the Lord's Supper. He closes the argument with the stunning observation that whenever they eat and drink without discerning the body, that is, the communion of the saints in the body of Christ, they "eat and drink judgment against themselves" (1 Cor 11:29).

---

[3]Alexander Schmemann, *For the Life of the World: Sacraments and Orthodoxy* (Crestwood, N.Y.: St. Vladimir's Press, 1973), p. 16.

What we too often miss in our "zoom lens" approach is that Paul does not instruct the Corinthians on the precise meanings of the words of institution or the nature of Christ's presence. He faults them for their failure to honor the basic rituals of hospitality and courtesy. The Corinthian's failure to recognize the depth of the meaning of the Lord's Supper *as a meal* leads to dire physical consequences for the church and its members. "For this reason many of you are weak and ill, and some have died" (11:30). Whether he means that this is a direct judgment of God or a natural result of the stress of conflict is not clear, but the meal character of the Lord's Supper looms so large that failing to honor it brings dire physical consequences. As Leithart observes, "The difference between the Lord's supper and its perversion does not consist in any difference in the ritual actions, the elements used, or the words spoken [and I might add any intellectual understanding of the transaction of the bread and wine], but rather lies in the way people behave toward one another. The Lord's death is proclaimed only when the church celebrates rightly, that is, when Christian peace, love, and unity are manifested in the meal."[4]

When we pay attention to the Supper as a meal, we will understand it and participate in it with fresh meaning. In this sacred ritual meal we identify ourselves as the body of Christ with all that that means. Calvin loves to talk about the Lord's Supper as the Father's family meal:

> God has received us, once for all, into his family, to hold us not only as servants but as sons. Thereafter, to fulfill the duties of a most excellent Father concerned with his offspring, he undertakes also to nourish us throughout the course of our life. And not content with this alone, he has willed by giving his pledge, to assure us of this continuing liberality. To this end, therefore, he has, through the hand of his only begotten son, given to his church another sacrament, that is, a spiritual banquet, wherein Christ attests himself to be the life-giving bread, upon which our souls feed unto true and blessed immortality. (John 6:51)[5]

But it is more than a matter of identification; the Supper actually forms us into the body of Christ. Sacraments not only inform us, they form us. They not only affirm our personal relationship with Jesus in

---

[4] Leithart, "The Way Things Really Ought to Be," p. 173.
[5] John Calvin *Institutes* 4.17.1.

his sacrifice and victory, but they affirm the character of our *koinonia* together as the body of Christ.

Because we are so used to looking at the Lord's Supper through the zoom lens, we sometimes only pay attention to the way in which the presence of Christ becomes real in the breaking of the bread. When we look at the Supper through the wide-angle lens, viewing the community at the meal, we pay attention to the way Christ's body is being formed by it. Because we are not used to thinking of it in this way, fresh insights and important meanings can result.

THE SOCIOLOGY OF THE MEAL

Sociologist Robert Bellah, who has given years of thought to the quest for community in an individualistic society, has recently noted the importance of the Lord's Supper in bridging the gap between our individuality and the formation of true community.

In a seminal article building on his work in *Habits of the Heart* and *The Good Society*, Bellah compares the Protestant and the Catholic vision of the individual and society. He begins with Andrew Greely's stark contrast of the Catholic and Protestant approach:

> The Catholic tends to see society as a "sacrament" of God, a set of ordered relationships, governed by both justice and love, that reveal, however imperfectly, the presence of God. Society is "natural" and "good", therefore, for humans and their "natural" response to God is social. The Protestant tends to see society as "God-forsaken" and therefore unnatural and oppressive. The individual stands over against society and is not integrated into it. The human becomes fully human only when he is able to break away from social oppression and relate to the absent God as a completely free individual.[6]

Bellah thinks that this contrast is too radical and ignores notable Protestant social contributions, but he largely agrees that a Protestant "cultural code" has deeply injured our social cohesion.

He points to two distinct Protestant beliefs that contribute most to the Protestant ethos: predestination and the "divinization of the self." Predestination so radically emphasizes divine transcendence that it

---

[6]Robert N. Bellah, "Religion and the Shape of National Culture," *America* 181 (July 31-August 7, 1999): 9.

opened up the way to atheistic naturalism. "Even more ominously, into the empty space left by the absence of God came an understanding of the self as absolutely autonomous that borrows an essential attribute of God to apply to the self."[7] Calvinist that I am, I'm not sure about his assertions concerning predestination, but the second factor, the "divinization of the self," seems very much alive and well today. He describes it as "The near exclusive focus on the relationship between Jesus and the individual, where accepting Jesus as one's personal Lord and Savior becomes almost the whole of piety."[8] Bellah sees this as a form of gnosticism as described in Harold Bloom's *The American Religion*. "The doctrine of the of the God-Man easily slips into the doctrine of the Man-God."[9] Bloom sees evangelical Protestantism's focus on the personal relation of the individual believer to Jesus as one of the major sources of American gnosticism.

The loose connection between individuals means that while people feel that voluntary associations are important, they are less and less willing to affiliate with them. "What has been happening to us can be summed up in the title of Robert Wuthnow's book, *Loose Connections*. People are not plugged in very tightly to groups and associations."[10] The accompanying metaphor is "porous institutions" that do not hold individuals together. Institutions like the family and the lodge and the church, or even the bowling league, are becoming less and less able to bind people in community. Bellah summarizes the situation:

> Just when we are in many ways moving to an ever greater validation of the sacredness of the individual person, our capacity to imagine a social fabric that would hold individuals together is vanishing. This is in part because of the fact that our ethical individualism, deriving, as I have argued, from the Protestant religious tradition in America, is linked to an economic individualism that, ironically, knows nothing of the sacredness of the individual.[11]

The main hope Bellah has of overcoming this dangerous flaw in the body politic of American society is a new religious imagination that

---

[7] Ibid., p. 10.
[8] Ibid., p. 11.
[9] Quoted in ibid., p. 13.
[10] Ibid., p. 14.
[11] Ibid.

can fuse the individual and the society, which he locates in a profoundly earthy and social understanding of the sacrament. The sacraments, especially the Eucharist, when rightly understood and celebrated, are one of the few places in which the fusion of the individual and society are deeply experienced, and the regular celebration of them strengthen the bonds.

In a very different context, the horrors of Latin American oppressive regimes, William T. Cavanaugh also helps us to see how the Eucharist forms and reforms community. His provocatively titled book *Torture and Eucharist* charts the relationship between the Roman Catholic Church and the Pinochet regime in Chile.[12] In the first half of the book he shows how the church unwittingly ceded its authority to the brutality of the Pinochet regime and hid behind the concept of the church as the "mystical body," a spiritualized concept that essentially divorced it from political reality. In Cavanaugh's view, the Pinochet regime, in its wide practice of torture, co-opted the body for the state. The antidote to that takeover of the "body" came late but decisively in a renewed practice of the Eucharist as a supreme community-creating act. The church came to see that in sharing the Eucharist, it reclaims itself as Christ's own body over which the state has no final authority or power.

I wonder what a renewed sense of the body-forming power of the Lord's Supper might mean in the North American consumer society. We too are co-opted—not by a torturing state, but by our market-driven, consumerist corporate economy that claims our bodies as advertising billboards and pleasure machines. I wonder whether the body-forming celebration of the Eucharist might stiffen us to new ways of resisting the spiritually coercive aspects of our culture. Only a clear and uncompromising teaching and practice of the Eucharist can restore Protestantism, at least, to a renewed sense of belonging to the body of Christ. I believe that a renewed practice of the Lord's Supper is vital to a renewed Christian social and political identity.

Archbishop Oscar Romero of El Salvador was also deeply aware of the community-shaping power of the Eucharist. Commenting on 1 Corinthians 10 and 11, where Paul struggles with unity and disunity in relation to the Lord's Supper, he focuses on the idolatry of Corinth and today:

---

[12]William T. Cavanaugh, *Torture and Eucharist* (Oxford: Blackwell, 1998).

Today the idols of the Corinthians no longer exist: idols of gold, figures of animals, of goddesses, of stars and suns. Today other idols exist, which we have often spoken of. If Christians are nourished in the eucharistic communion, where their faith tells them they are united to Christ's life, how can they live as idolaters of money, idolaters of power, selfish idolaters of themselves? How can a Christian who receives holy communion be an idolater?[13]

Romero believed that the Eucharist formed the body of Christ and anticipated the kingdom of God, when rich and poor would feast together. The eucharistic celebration was of a piece with his whole life and purpose.

A few weeks after Romero became archbishop of El Salvador, a death squad killed his friend and fellow priest Rutilio Grande. The oligarchy that ruled the land actually had high hopes for Romero, seeing him as someone who would dampen the rising tide of opposition to the government. Romero, however, made an extraordinary decision after Grande was killed. He decreed that the following Sunday there would be only one Mass for the entire diocese. That meant that in order to receive the Eucharist, every person would have to come to the cathedral in San Salvador:

The oligarchy reacted with alarm. The day after Romero announced the single mass, representatives of . . . a national businessmen's association met with Romero and demanded that the idea be dropped. The church, they said, was stirring up trouble and conflict. Besides, the wealthy Catholics of the plantations were complaining that they would be deprived of the opportunity to receive the eucharist and fulfill their Sunday obligation. They seem never to have considered the fact that the wealthy could easily drive into San Salvador for the mass, even if it did mean standing in the sun for three hours with a bunch of unwashed poor people.

But that, of course, was the whole point. Romero intended the one eucharist to be an anticipation of the kingdom, of the day when rich and poor would feast together, of the day when the body of Christ would not be wounded by division.[14]

---

[13]Quoted in William T. Cavanaugh, "Dying for the Eucharist?" *Theology Today* (July 2001): 182.

[14]Ibid., 185.

It's this sort of theological and sacramental integrity that eventually led to Romero's martyrdom while celebrating another Mass. He was killed at just the point when the Mass turns from the offertory to the Mass proper. We can't celebrate the death of Christ without the risk of martyrdom because participation in the death and resurrection of Christ, sharing in his crucified body and shed blood, changes who we are and how we act in the world.

But in order to discover this communal depth in the sacrament, Protestants have to recognize and affirm the formative nature of the sacrament as meal. Careful attention to the Pauline teaching concerning the Lord's Supper, as presented above will, I believe, create a growing awareness of this aspect of the sacraments. While Calvin effectively used the zoom lens to give us a rather new and helpful way of understanding the presence of Christ at the Supper through the Holy Spirit, he was not entirely oblivious to the body-forming aspect of the Supper as a meal. He wrote that the Supper acts to "exhort us all to sanctity and innocence, seeing that we are members of Jesus Christ, and particularly in unity and brotherly charity, as is especially recommended to us."[15]

Peter Leithart believes it is important that the church see itself as a culture, indeed a counter-culture: "To say that the church is a culture in respect to 'sacraments' suggests that the church's rites express her understanding of reality and her place in it, and challenge the world's conceptions of her and itself."[16] It can be hoped that a renewed emphasis on the Lord's Supper as a sacred meal that forms community will also restrain the tendency among Protestants toward continued splintering, the bitter fruit of our spiritual individualism. How can we continue our fractious ways as we share the same loaf and drink the same cup? Certainly, no less than at Corinth, continuing in our schismatic ways we risk "eating and drinking judgment to ourselves."

HOW OFTEN DO WE GATHER FOR THE MEAL?

Understanding the meal character of the Lord's Supper also invites us

---

[15]John Calvin, *Short Treatise on the Holy Supper*, ed. and trans. J. K. S. Reid (Philadelphia: Westminster Press, 1954), p. 144.

[16]Leithart, "The Way Things Really Ought to Be," p. 164. See also a provocative analysis of the church as counter-culture in Stanley Hauerwas and William Willimon, *Resident Aliens* (Nashville: Abingdon, 1989).

to look at the ways in which it is practiced in most churches. We will first look at the frequency of celebration. It's clear that in the New Testament and well into the succeeding centuries, the Supper formed a regular part of Sunday worship (see chapter two). I believe that just as our home meals are not once-in-a-while events, but regular parts of our day, the Lord's Supper ought to be a regular part of every Sunday worship.

Calvin advocated weekly Communion as biblically correct and spiritually healthy, but he was thwarted in instituting it to the end if his life by the Geneva Council. Part of the reason was the rather rigorous spiritual preparation called for in the Geneva church as well as the fact that former Roman Catholics were likely to have communed only once a year, and thus weekly Communion seemed far too much. A pattern of quarterly Communion took root very early and continued for centuries. It was the practice in my own youth. More recently, many churches in the Reformed tradition have moved to a much more frequent celebration, though weekly Communion is still unusual.

Why this reticence? In my experience people offer many different reasons, from the fear that it will become routine to the assertion that it's simply not necessary for spiritual growth. It should be noted that historically some of the churches that held Communion services less frequently did so because of a *high* regard for the sacrament. They were concerned that in view of its importance, too frequent celebration might make it seem too ordinary. On reflection, this concern may say more about the spiritual condition of the worshippers than the frequency of the sacrament itself.[17] In many Protestant churches the preaching of the Word is still the main, indeed the only event, and weekly Communion appears to threaten that hegemony. My hunch is that behind the sacramental reticence there remains the old gnostic tendency that all this "stuff" is really not necessary when we have the pure spiritual Word of God—not to mention that the service might last too long.

Is infrequent celebration of the Lord's Supper merely a matter of taste or habit, or are there fundamental issues that move us toward weekly celebration? Nicholas Wolterstorff believes there are:

---

[17]There is a sensitive discussion of this whole issue from the Lutheran perspective in Frank C. Senn, *A Stewardship of the Mysteries* (Mahwah, N.J.: Paulist, 1999), p. 117.

There is, in my judgment, no more fundamental liturgical issue facing the Reformed churches today than this ancient dispute within the tradition over the place in the liturgy of the eucharist: ought the liturgy of the Reformed churches to exhibit the enduring structure of word and sacrament, and ought the people of God eat the Supper weekly? Or is it appropriate to keep word and sacrament in separate services and to celebrate the Lord's Supper only infrequently? Like all liturgical issues, this dispute raises a pastoral issue: does it serve the health of the church to celebrate the Lord's Supper infrequently? And like all liturgical issues, this dispute raises a theological issue: Was Calvin right in teaching that, by way of the celebration of the Lord's Supper, God acts toward us in love and we respond to God in faith, or was Zwingli right in teaching that the Lord's supper is no more than an expression of our response to God's action?[18]

For me, the fundamental issue is the same one we have met over and over in this study. If God feeds and confirms our faith in the sacrament, then we deprive ourselves of the fullness of his grace when we sit around the table only once in a while. We need every nourishment that God provides, and to miss the meal not only snubs his gracious hospitality but creates spiritual anorexics.

It also raises liturgical questions. Is a Sunday liturgy really complete without the celebration of the sacrament of Holy Communion? The early church didn't think so. Most of the Reformers didn't think so. Nor did Karl Barth. He seriously questioned whether his fellow Protestants had given sufficient consideration to the question of whether a service without sacraments is complete:

> As a rule we hold such outwardly incomplete services as if it were perfectly natural to do so. What right have we to do that? We may ask the Roman Catholic church why she celebrates mass without proper preaching, but we are asked ourselves what right we have to do what we do. Is there not a pressing danger that by omitting the natural beginning and ending of a true service the services we hold are incomplete inwardly and in essence as well? Would not the sermon not be delivered and listened to quite differently and would we not offer thanks during the service quite differently, if everything outwardly and visi-

---

[18]Nicholas P. Wolterstorff, "The Reformed Liturgy," in *Major Themes in the Reformed Tradition*, ed. Donald McKim (Grand Rapids: Eerdmans, 1992), p. 295.

bly began with baptism and moved towards the Lord's Supper?[19]

J.-J. von Allmen evokes a striking image to characterize the usual type of Protestant worship service: "It ends, not with a full stop but with a colon, the function of which is to introduce what is to follow. And after this pause 48 Sundays out of 52, we are left hungry and thirsty."[20]

Hungry and thirsty for what? Most importantly, weekly Communion guarantees that Christ and his redemption will be centrally featured each and every Sunday. Whether the sermon centers on the Ten Commandments or some Old Testament narrative, the Lord's Supper brings us back to that central drama around which everything else revolves. I believe this is even more important among evangelical churches today, where a "ten ways to improve your marriage" kind of preaching can easily turn worship into a self-help workshop. But no matter how far the sermon may range from the "gospel's joyful sound," when the service concludes at the Lord's table, the refreshment and grace of Christ's redeeming love brings the congregation back to the center of our faith.

Weekly Communion does not mean weekly participation. Frank Senn wisely counsels against creating an atmosphere at the Lord's table in which participation is expected by all the baptized. Participation in the sacrament is always a matter of individual conscience, and room too must be made for proper discipline exercised around the table. There may be times when, for example, a husband and wife, or friends in the congregation are locked in an unresolved conflict, one which may even be evident to the rest of the congregation. In that case, not communing shows a proper self-restraint, even while observing the sacrament might hopefully pull the irreconciled parties closer together.[21]

HOSPITALITY AT THE MEAL

Some have expressed a concern that the weekly celebration of the Supper might inhibit evangelism. They wonder how this might be viewed by "seekers" or visitors. It's interesting to note that in the early church

---

[19]Quoted in ibid.

[20]J.-J von Allmen, *Worship: Its Theology and Practice* (Eugene, Ore.: Wipf and Stock, 2002), p. 156.

[21]Senn, *Stewardship of the Mysteries*, p. 119.

the "catechumens," those who were in the process of instruction leading to baptism, were excused from the service before the sacrament. The first part of the worship, which focused on the Word, was also called the service of the catechumens, since they were welcome there. The "seeker service" pattern associated with Willow Creek Community Church, which encourages "seekers" to attend specifically evangelistic or pre-evangelistic services, while members attend "regular" worship, might be seen as a modern version of that separation. While some have advocated a renewal of the ancient practice, it does not seem likely to become widespread in North American culture.[22]

Since most churches hope and pray to have many seekers present at regular worship, what impact weekly or a more regular celebration of the Lord's Supper has on them is a valid question. How can we be hospitable at a table around which most of us have some fences, baptism at the very least? Kathleen Norris's story at the beginning of the chapter testifies to how much people take in just by observation, and how transforming that can be. While I offer no empirical evidence, it seems to me that because the Supper always moves the worship service toward its culmination in the paschal mystery of Christ, the seeker will at least observe that this meal is close to the center of Christian faith and practice. It all has to do with Christ, a cross, a sacrificial death and a symbolic meal by which we somehow participate in it all. Of course, seekers do not fully understand this truth, and for them the rituals might seem a mystery at best, and confusing or even offensive at worst.

T. F. Torrance, following John Wesley's example, calls the sacraments not only a "confirming ordinance" but a "converting ordinance," for in and through them the gospel strikes home to us in such a way as to draw us within the vicarious response to God which Jesus Christ constitutes in his own humanity.[23] Where else is the gospel more vividly displayed than in the Communion of Christ's body and blood? For those who have been baptized but have lost touch with a living faith, participation may be a very good way to begin their return to

---

[22]Reformed scholar J.-J. von Allmen argues for a return to excusing the catechumens from the service of the table. See von Allmen, *Worship*, p. 203. There is a renewal of a method of evangelism around the ancient idea of the catechumenate, especially among some Lutherans. See Senn, *Stewardship of the Mysteries*, pp. 29-39.

[23]T. F. Torrance, *The Mediation of Christ* (Grand Rapids: Eerdmans, 1983), p. 107.

faith, understanding the Supper as a "converting ordinance."

But what about those who cannot participate in the meal because they have not yet been baptized?[24] What kind of hospitality is it to invite a person to your church home and not invite them to eat and drink with you? These are serious considerations and need to be answered. Of course, no matter how often we have Communion there may very well be visitors whose status in faith or baptism we do not know. Most churches clearly invite all those who have been baptized to join at the table. But perhaps we should also say some reassuring and inviting words to those who are not baptized. We should certainly make it clear that we do not expect everyone to participate, since it is a sign of full faith and commitment to Christ and we know that not everyone gathered is at that point yet. We could further invite those who do not participate to listen and observe, since in this sacrament they will come to understand a great deal about the Christ we worship and the church he has called. I also know of some churches that make a point of inviting the unbaptized to come to the front (or some other place in the church) for a blessing or a prayer on their behalf, and many respond.

I believe that when we are aware of our responsibility of hospitality toward strangers, we can make them quite comfortable with the requirements and rituals of the table. While we may assume that visitors will be put off by our strange rituals, the truth is that many are fascinated by them. Any time we visit someone's home as a stranger, especially in a foreign culture, we know there are rituals and activities that will be strange to us. We often find them captivating, and through them we learn a great deal about that particular culture. Good hosts will explain them to us either at the time or later. The church is a foreign culture to many North Americans. Our churches and our members who invite seekers to join in our worship need to be prepared not only to welcome them but to help them to understand the words, rituals and values of this culture and perhaps stimulate a desire to become a part of it. Some assert that "seekers" will just not put up with this process of learning. That fails to recognize how in modern culture we are

---

[24]I have attended a few churches in which the unbaptized are specifically invited to Communion. I believe that this only works with an anemic view of the sacrament as an experience or simple remembrance. Baptism is the sacrament of entrance into Christ's body, while the Lord's Supper sustains us in our fellowship with Christ and each other.

always, often eagerly, learning new "languages," whether on our computers or our cameras, or in our brushes with the various subcultures that we view through the media. I wonder whether it may be precisely the "strangeness" of the Christian community displayed at the Lord's table that people might find attractive in our homogenous culture.

A WELL-SET TABLE

Finally, we should notice that the meal as celebrated in the New Testament was, in fact, a meal. What Paul describes in 1 Corinthians 11 is closer to a potluck supper than the formalized sacrament seen in most churches today. Again, the zoom lens of theological precision enabled the church to divorce the sacrament from any sort of real meal setting, abstracting the bread and cup into tiny portions that have little relationship to anything like a normal meal. The focus came to rest, not on the communal character of the meal, but on its exact theological meaning.

Anything we can do to restore that meal character will enhance the meaning and fruitfulness of the Supper in the life of the church. In one church I served, we had a practice of celebrating the sacrament on Christmas Eve at a festive meal in the church fellowship hall. (This was a small university church, and the Christmas Eve worshippers were relatively few.) Many spoke fondly of this setting as the most meaningful time in which they celebrated the Lord's Supper.

It is possible for most churches to celebrate the sacrament in a more truly meal-like setting, at least from time to time. But even when they cannot, there are various ways in which the meal character of the Supper can be emphasized. For example, real bread should be used, like the bread we might find on our own dinner tables, rather than cardboard-like wafers or precision-cut cubes of Wonder bread.[25] The problem of falling crumbs is certainly outweighed by the benefits of seeing bread that looks like bread.

---

[25]William Willimon writes: "[The Reformers] changed the medieval altars into real tables with real bread and wine. Today many of us are in the embarrassing position of saying to people, 'This wafer is a symbol of bread which is a symbol of the presence of grace which is a symbol of. . . .' No wonder so many lose the point along the way. Our church gives bread recipes to families in the congregation. When a family bakes a loaf of bread and then presents that loaf on the table on Sunday, everyone knows what communion means" ("The Lord's Supper: Making It happen in Your Church," *Reformed Liturgy and Music* 19, no. 1 ([1985]: 12).

I'm aware of one congregation in which the participants gather in a complete circle around the table and share the bread and cup by passing it to each other with appropriate words. This simple action powerfully creates the sense of a true meal, a true sharing in Christ at the table. It also subtly suggests that we *receive* the bread and wine rather than *take* Communion. Many churches have also found that with the modern fear of contagion, we can still avoid the little individual cups by passing goblets of wine in which to dip the bread ("intinction").

The presider should always have in mind that he or she is acting as host of a meal. The focus of concentration should not be so much on the right words as on the right gestures, tone of voice and eye contact with the worshipers.[26] Simple and appropriate gestures of welcome, a tone of warmth and invitation, and the use of beautiful but practical earthenware utensils instead of the stainless steel towers or gilded chalices, not to mention the individually sealed plastic cups now used in some mega-churches, can do much to enhance the experience of the congregation gathering around a meal.

EATING AND DRINKING TOGETHER WITH THANKSGIVING

At the meal called the Lord's Supper we *eat and drink*. Eating and drinking is a most creaturely act. When we eat and drink, we express our dependence on something outside ourselves like every other creature. We must eat and drink to sustain life. And in order to eat and drink we are dependent on our Creator.

In the Bible, God is always feeding his creatures. It is quite enlightening to read through the Bible with only this aspect in view. It all begins in the Garden. When God gives humanity dominion (stewardship) over the earth, he also begins to tell them of his provision for their food. "See, I have given you every plant . . . and every tree bearing seed in its fruit" (Gen 1:29). Interestingly, after the flood, God's provision for human nourishment is extended to animal life (Gen 9:3), with the ex-

---

[26]Willimon again: "Mechanics are everything. The main difference between a meal at a fast-food restaurant and a gourmet dinner is a difference of how the food is prepared and served. One system makes you feel like a cow being herded through a feed trough; another makes you feel like a human being. No one should serve communion who does not know how to hand someone a piece of bread in a gracious manner. The moment should be intimate and personal. Look in their eyes. Touch their hands. Call their names, if you know them" (ibid.).

ception of the blood, which we soon find out has the special significance of life, life taken and life restored. Noah, who saved the animals
from the flood, also receives the animals for food from God. Many of
the adventures of the patriarchs also center on God's provision of food,
and it is famine that finally leads the whole clan to Egypt. After God
delivered them, they were hungry and thirsty, and God provided water from the rock and manna in the morning. God finally led them into
a land "flowing with milk and honey." The psalmists praise God for his
gracious provision of food for both humans and animals. "You visit the
earth and water it, you greatly enrich it. . . . You crown the year with
your bounty; your wagon tracks overflow with richness. The pastures
of the wilderness overflow, the hills gird themselves with joy . . . the
valleys deck themselves with grain, they shout and sing together for
joy" (Ps 65:9-13). In Psalm 81:10, Israel is directed to simply "open your
mouth wide and I will fill it." God feeds his people, and all the people
of the world.

Not surprisingly, then, we find Jesus providing people with food
and drink as the embodiment of the Father's loving provision. Every
Gospel records at least one miraculous feeding of a multitude of people by Jesus. In John 2, much to the embarrassment of some Christians,
Jesus attends a wedding at which the wine runs out but saves the party
by miraculously producing perfectly aged vintage wine out of some
jugs full of water for washing feet. The most telling of these episodes is
in John 6. After Jesus feeds the multitude they want to make him king.
There's nothing like a monarch who can supply bread at the snap of a
finger. As usual in John's Gospel, the misunderstanding of the crowd
evokes Jesus' deepest teaching. The bread they truly seek is the bread
from heaven, reminiscent of the manna in the wilderness: "I am the
bread of life. Whoever comes to me will never be hungry, and whoever
believes in me will never be thirsty" (Jn 6:35). And from this point, John
has Jesus move directly into his profound eucharistic meditation:
"Very truly I tell you, unless you eat the flesh of the Son of Man and
drink his blood, you have no life in you" (Jn 6:53). Humans are creatures who need God's constant feeding in order to go on living, but on
a deeper level they need the very bread of Christ's flesh and his blood
to have true and eternal life. God's provision of food and drink address

humanity's most basic needs, the sustenance of their life for this life and for the life eternal. God is not only the *giver* of food; he *is* the food we most deeply need. Alexander Schmemann insists that "man is a hungry being. But he is hungry for God. Behind all the hunger of our life is God. All desire is finally a desire for Him."[27]

The food and drink of the Lord's Supper is bread and wine. Theologians have been so consumed by the properties of the Communion bread, its physics and especially its metaphysics, that they have forgotten the simple fact that it is bread. "Jesus could have instituted a ritual meal using roasted grain and red meat, which were used in Old Testament feasts, but he chose to signify the kingdom with a feast of bread."[28] It is interesting to compare bread with the manna with which God fed the Israelites in the wilderness. Bread is not a raw material; it is the product of human dominion and ingenuity. The production of bread needs a whole spectrum of activities and relationships from plowing, sowing and reaping, to milling, mixing, kneading and baking. It implies the rise of agriculture, economics, communities and organized human labor.

The Roman Mass points to this quality of the bread when in the prayer of consecration it is describes as bread "made by human hands." As Peter Leithart comments, "When bread is set on the table, an agricultural and culinary science and technology lies in the background."[29] All the ingenuity and complexities of human life are taken up into the bread, which is offered to God with thanksgiving. God then gives it back to us as the body of Christ in a sacred meal. All this implies that what we eat at the sacred meal is not only what God gives us but also that which we have labored to produce. In the bread we bring the fullness of human life and labor, offering it to God through Christ. "What we have offered—our food, ourselves, and the whole world—we offered in Christ and as Christ because he himself has assumed our life and is our life. And now all this is given back to us as the gift of new life, and therefore—necessarily—as *food.*"[30]

At the meal we also drink wine. Just as we have seen with the bread,

---

[27]Schmemann, *For the Life of the World,* p. 15.
[28]Leithart, "The Way Things Really Ought to Be," p. 168.
[29]Ibid., p. 169.
[30]Schmemann, *For the Life of the World,* p. 41.

the production of wine takes a certain amount of human involvement and creativity. It's not just the juice of the grape (though in many Protestant churches, for some good reasons to be sure, that's exactly what it is). But wine also points to the meal as celebration. We don't drink wine merely for its nutritional value; we drink it to enhance our joy in celebration. Again, to some Christians this is embarrassing, if not sinful. But we cannot read the story of the miracle of the wine at the wedding feast without realizing that Jesus was pointing to the kingdom feast of joy and gladness. Calvin realized the symbolic importance of wine. "When we see wine set forth as a symbol of blood, we must reflect on the benefits which wine imparts to the body, and so realize that the same are spiritually imparted to us by Christ's blood. These benefits are to nourish, refresh, strengthen, and *gladden*."[31] Tony Campolo titled a book *The Kingdom Is a Party*. Jesus himself understood this enough as to be falsely accused by his enemies as being a glutton and a drunkard (Mt 11:19).

When the worshipping community shares the cup of wine, it affirms what it already is and will become in God's kingdom, a community of joy and gladness, the feasting people of God. It enjoys the goodness and joy God built into creation, and it anticipates the wedding feast of the Lamb. "The Eucharistic wine proclaims the New Testament gospel of the kingdom: 'the time is fulfilled, the kingdom of heaven is at hand.'"[32]

At the Lord's table we eat and drink *together*. It is a shared meal, and, as Paul warns, when it is not properly shared, it is not the Lord's Supper. God is in the business of creating a new community in which he wants to include all people, from the east and west and north and south. The vision of the kingdom is for a time when "people will bring into it the glory and honor of the nations" (Rev 21:26). But already now we are together the body of Christ and individually members of it. We are one body because we share the same loaf.

I remember as a child that my parents and many other adults in the congregation would close their eyes in private meditation during the distribution of the communion bread and wine. The message was clear: "This is really a private matter between myself and the Lord."

---

[31]*Institutes* 4.17.3.
[32]Leithart, "The Way Things Really Ought to Be," p. 171.

There is certainly something to be said for personal meditation at the Lord's table, but it's the togetherness of our community at the table that the Supper highlights. We might spend some of our time meditating with eyes wide open, looking around at all our brothers and sisters. At my own church we often come forward for Communion. One of its spiritually enriching joys is that we can see the whole congregation on parade. Young and old, short and tall, ugly and beautiful, crippled and whole, rich and poor, men and women—fantastically diverse, yet one body in the one loaf, we are feasting together. "The cup of blessing that we bless, is it not a sharing in the blood of Christ? The bread that we break, is it not a sharing in the body of Christ? Because there is one bread, we who are many are one body, for we all partake of the one bread" (1 Cor 10:16-17).

Finally, we eat and drink together *with thanksgiving*. That's what Eucharist means (from the Greek *eucharistia*). Central to this feast from the beginning was not just a recitation of the events of the last supper of Jesus with his disciples (which too often happens among Protestant evangelicals today, making it what someone called "a meal at the tomb"), but a recitation of all the acts of God in creation, redemption and new creation. The great prayer of thanksgiving isn't just a segue into the real heart of the Lord's Supper, like a *pro forma* prayer before a meal signals that we can pick up our forks; it grounds the sacrament in the remembrance and celebration of the goodness of God in creation and redemption. The Lord's death and resurrection, which the Supper commemorates and communicates, are the central acts of God's drama of salvation. It's a kingdom feast, for it remembers, enacts and anticipates everything the kingdom stands for—a celebration of our dignity and wholeness as creatures of God, redeemed by the Son, called into a new community of love and sharing. So we sit down at a meal, eat and drink together with hearts full of thanksgiving for God's goodness and mercy.

Strangely, as the church practices it most often, this "feast" seems far removed from what we would normally call a feast. A feast implies abundance, an overflow of food and drink. We are more likely to get a morsel and a sip. I have commented before that it may be wise for us to set the Lord's table in the setting of a real meal, a church potluck supper, for example. Yet it's interesting that the church seems to have moved away from that, substituting the *agape* meal for the more liturgical setting of the Supper. There may be many reasons for the change, some good, some bad, but perhaps there is a certain wisdom that comes with the morsel and the sip.

Practically, the paucity of bread and wine says that this is not the "real" feast. These are only the hors d'oeuvres. And, of course, that's exactly right. David Powers points out that "the meal imagery with all the sense of replenishment belongs more to the eschatological hope than to present satisfaction. The present grace, which is certainly given, is not attached to the satisfaction of bodily delights but to the union with him who gives the Spirit, in which he himself has been transformed." The very skimpiness of the meal carries a prophetic warning. "Humanity may indeed supply the bodily food and drink, and by sharing these express its hope for the world's need, but it is only through the gift of the Spirit given in the morsel and the sip that true human hopes may be met and the banquet of God's kingdom laid out."[33]

After a meal, as Kathleen Norris reminded us, there's the cleanup. There are pots and pans to be washed and dishes to be put away. Again, looked at through the wide-angle lens, there are some interesting differences among various Christian traditions in how the meal ends. In some traditions, notably the Roman Catholic, Episcopal/Anglican and Lutheran, while the congregation prays, sings or meditates, some cleaning up is going on. Usually the priest or minister will gather the remainder of the bread and wine and consume it, or dispose of it in some other way, careful to clean the cup and paten.

Brother Max Thurian of Taize, whose background is French Reformed, has been deeply involved in ecumenical dialogue concerning the Lord's Supper. I was interested to find several references in his little book *The Mystery of the Eucharist* to this issue. Speaking of what happens to the bread and wine after the meal, he rather indignantly asks, "By what right would [the church] determine the time when the species of the bread and wine [he does not mean this in the Aristotelian sense, but merely to denote the outward elements] would no

---

[33]David Powers, in *Living Bread, Saving Cup*, ed. R. Kevin Seasoltz (Collegeville, Minn.: Liturgical Press, 1987), p. 169.

longer be the signs of the body and blood of Christ?"[34]

Protestants generally give much less thought as to what happens to the elements after the Communion, apart from collecting the little plastic cups. I remember being at an ecumenical gathering sitting next to an Orthodox priest while the Communion was being shared with loaves of bread. He looked horrified as the crumbs fell to the floor, and commented on the sloppiness (meaning disgracefulness and perhaps blasphemy) of Protestant practice.

Soon after I came, my present parish established the practice of using large round loaves of bread for communion. After the service, unknown to me, some kids would regularly come up to the table and finish off the bread. An older member came up to me quite troubled by this. Since we do not consider the bread to have been changed into the actual body and blood of Christ, he felt a little embarrassed that this bothered him. At first I dismissed it, believing that it mattered little whether the remainder of the bread was consumed by kids, or packed off to someone's home for sandwiches. But thinking about it more, I realized that the brother had a point. Apart from what we might specifically believe about the "real presence," this bread and wine had been set aside by holy words for a sacred purpose, to feed the congregation with the body and blood of Christ. If the congregation then sees their children playfully eat the leftovers, isn't the reaction likely to be that the Lord's Supper has less real meaning and importance?

My point here is not to lay down rules about how to dispose of leftover bread and wine, and certainly not to suggest that they be somehow venerated as holy, but to ask some questions about what our practice says about what we believe. If we believe that this is special food and drink, set aside for the sacramental purpose of sharing in our union with Christ and his sacrifice, such a belief might demand that we do something more fitting with the leftovers. The reason is not that we superstitiously believe that we are handling the actual body and blood of Christ, but that we are aware enough of the depth of meaning in the sacramental rite that its closing actions fit that meaning. Perhaps, for example, something could be said of the fact that what is left will be

---

[34]Max Thurian, *The Mystery of the Eucharist* (Grand Rapids: Eerdmans, 1984), p. 63.

taken to the shut-ins for Communion, and even placed in an appropriate receptacle for this purpose. I witnessed a moving ritual at an Episcopal church in which the priest blessed and prayed for the "parish visitors" who would bring the Communion to the many shut-ins. At the very least, we might carefully gather together the elements, cover them, and appropriately dispose of them.[35]

SUMMARY

Looking at the Lord's Supper from this wide-angle lens helps us to understand its meaning and power in new ways. When we see ourselves as creatures in God's good creation, the seemingly banal elements of the Lord's Supper take on a whole new significance. At the Supper we eat bread and drink wine together with thanksgiving not merely to *show* the way things ought to be but to *practice* the way things really ought to be. As a meal where we eat bread and drink wine together, we show forth the redemption that Christ won for us in the cross and the resurrection, and we experience it in powerful and life-shaping ways. The Lord's Supper shows us how to live the life of the kingdom of God and intensifies our longing for its fullness.

Leithart masterfully summarizes his insights in a way that touches close to the nerve of the sacrament:

> Frequent eating and drinking at the Lord's table will inoculate the church against the Gnosticism of modern Christianity (not to mention trendy spiritualisms) that would reduce religion to private, inner, purely "spiritual" experience; a church whose central rite includes baked goods is being trained in proper dominion over creation and will refuse resurgent nature worship in both its religious and its political guises; a church that celebrates a feast of wine is being formed into a joyful community that contests the equation of Christian seriousness with prudishness; a church that celebrates a common meal is bound into one body and will resist the corrosive individualism of modern culture that has too often invaded the church; a church that shares bread at the Lord's table is learning the virtues of generosity and humility; a church that proclaims the Lord's sacrificial death in the supper is exercising itself in self-sacrifice and becoming immune to the lure of self-fulfillment. Not automati-

---

[35]For an interesting discussion of this issue in relation to the care of the earth, see Senn, *Stewardship of the Mysteries*, pp. 171-75.

cally, but in the context of biblical teaching and a robust community life, the skills and virtues practiced at the Lord's table will spill over to fill the whole church with a eucharistic ethos.[36]

---

[36]Leithart, "The Way Things Really Ought to Be," p. 176.

Names Index

Scripture Index